True West

WILLIAM
HOLDEN · TR
GEORGE BANCROFT
Story by Michael Blankfort and Lewis Meltzer
Michael Blankfort · Directed by GEORGE
A COLUM

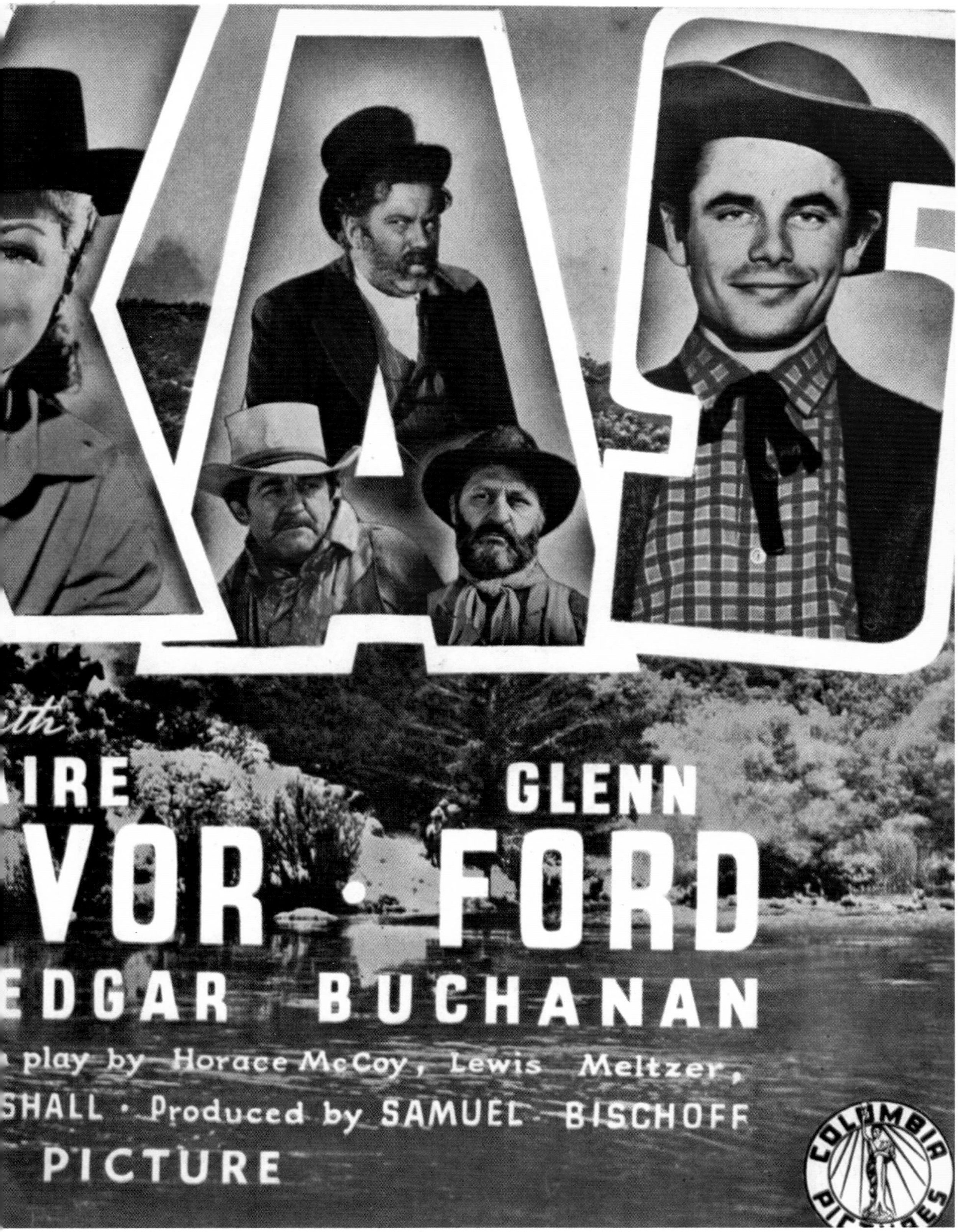

ith

IRE GLENN

VOR · FORD

EDGAR BUCHANAN

play by Horace McCoy, Lewis Meltzer,

SHALL · Produced by SAMUEL BISCHOFF

PICTURE

PUBLISHED BY THE STANDARD OIL COMPANY OF CALIFORNIA
JANUARY 1934

True West

An Illustrated Guide to the Heyday of the Western

Michael Barson

FOREWORD BY Robert B. Parker

TCU Press
Fort Worth, Texas

Library of Congress Cataloging-in-Publication Data

Barson, Michael.
True West: an illustrated guide to the heyday of the western / by Michael Barson; foreword by Robert B. Parker.
p. cm.
ISBN 978-0-87565-379-2 (paper : alk. paper)
1. West (U.S.)--In popular culture. 2. West (U.S.)--In popular culture--Pictorial works. 3. Popular culture--West (U.S.) 4. Popular culture--United States. 5. Americana--West (U.S.) 6. Western films--Miscellanea. 7. Western stories--Miscellanea. 8. Western television programs--Miscellanea. I. Title.
F591.B278 2008
978--dc22
2008014773

TCU Press
P. O. Box 298300
Fort Worth, Texas 76129
817.257.7822
http://www.prs.tcu.edu

To order books: 800.826.8911

Design and Production by Barbara Mathews Whitehead

To Mom and Dad,

who lovingly allowed me to watch

as many hours of Rawhide *and* Wagon Train

as pediatricians of 1960 recommended

to build strong bones.

"Okay, pardner... reach for Karo!

It's a rich, quick-energy food for growing youngsters . . . and all us cowboys love it!"

Actually, Mother, you're "boss" of the ranch.

And so—you should know this: all youngsters burn up gobs of energy . . . which must be replaced with food . . . the right kind. Now—let's reason this out.

Energy comes chiefly from car-bo-hy-drate foods. Delicious Karo® Syrup is a pure carbohydrate . . . which quickly provides abundant food energy.

As a blend of sugars, Karo does not irritate sensitive little stomachs . . . and being mildly sweet, Karo never encourages children's appetites for excessively sweet foods.

You can serve Karo Syrup in many, many ways . . . it makes other foods more enticing. All youngsters love this great American Syrup . . . and it's mighty good for them.

All children need a balanced diet, including proteins, minerals, vitamins and especially carbohydrates (the energy foods).

A good treat...bread and delicious Karo

Add nutritious Karo Syrup to milk and juices

Sweeten cereals, fruits and puddings with Karo

NOTE: *Both light and dark Karo Syrup are delicious . . . equally nutritious, and rich in dextrose, food-energy sugar.*

CONTENTS

PUBLISHED BY THE STANDARD OIL COMPANY OF CALIFORNIA

JUNE 1935

FOREWORD

The peculiarity of American institutions is the fact that they have been compelled to adapt themselves to the changes of an expanding people – to the changes involved in crossing a continent, in winning a wilderness, and in developing at each area of this progress out of the primitive economic and political conditions of the frontier, the complexity of city life.

Frederick Jackson Turner

Four centuries ago the frontier was Plymouth, or Jamestown, settled by people who had moved west from Europe looking for a better chance. And year-by-year the frontier moved west, across the Mississippi, over the fruited plain, through the purple mountains majesty, until it was gone and the nation stretched from sea to shining sea.

We have come to call the arena where this three-century trek took place the West. And we mean by that, probably, a place largely beyond civilization, where of necessity decisions were individual and interior. It became the myth of the West, and it is a myth that compels us. The real West was far more likely to be exhausted homesteaders standing in an empty landscape outside a sod hut. The real West had much to do with agribusiness and mining, railroads and land, in service of which, the real West destroyed indigenous cultures and killed indigenous people. But that is not the West we still celebrate a century after it disappeared. Though it is derived from the real West, our "True" West is mythic, centered on the man with a gun. The man is heroic, isolated, compelled by interior motives he cannot always articulate (Gary Cooper, *High Noon*). He is, I think, the American hero. And when the frontier ended, he endured. "The cowboy," in Leslie Fiedler's words, "adapted to life on the city streets, the embodiment of innocence moving untouched through universal guilt." Many of us who write detective stories, also write westerns (I have written three). And we are not straying far afield.

It is why the title of this book is so accurate. It is about not the "real" West, but rather the "true" West—the mythic West. The one that matters now. And that West was created and is perpetuated by all of the diverse matter which Michael Barson gives us here: film posters, paperback novels, comic books, pulp magazines, and a good deal more.

It is not simply nostalgia. Our vision of the West and the westerner informs our every condition: foreign policy, free trade, civil rights, welfare, gun legislation, and—probably—gender relationships as well. You might call it a national state of mind.

True West is not only a good book but an important one. We are all of us, willy-nilly, westerners of a kind, regardless of the zip codes where we actually reside. And *True West* endeavors to show us how that came to be.

—Robert B. Parker

True West

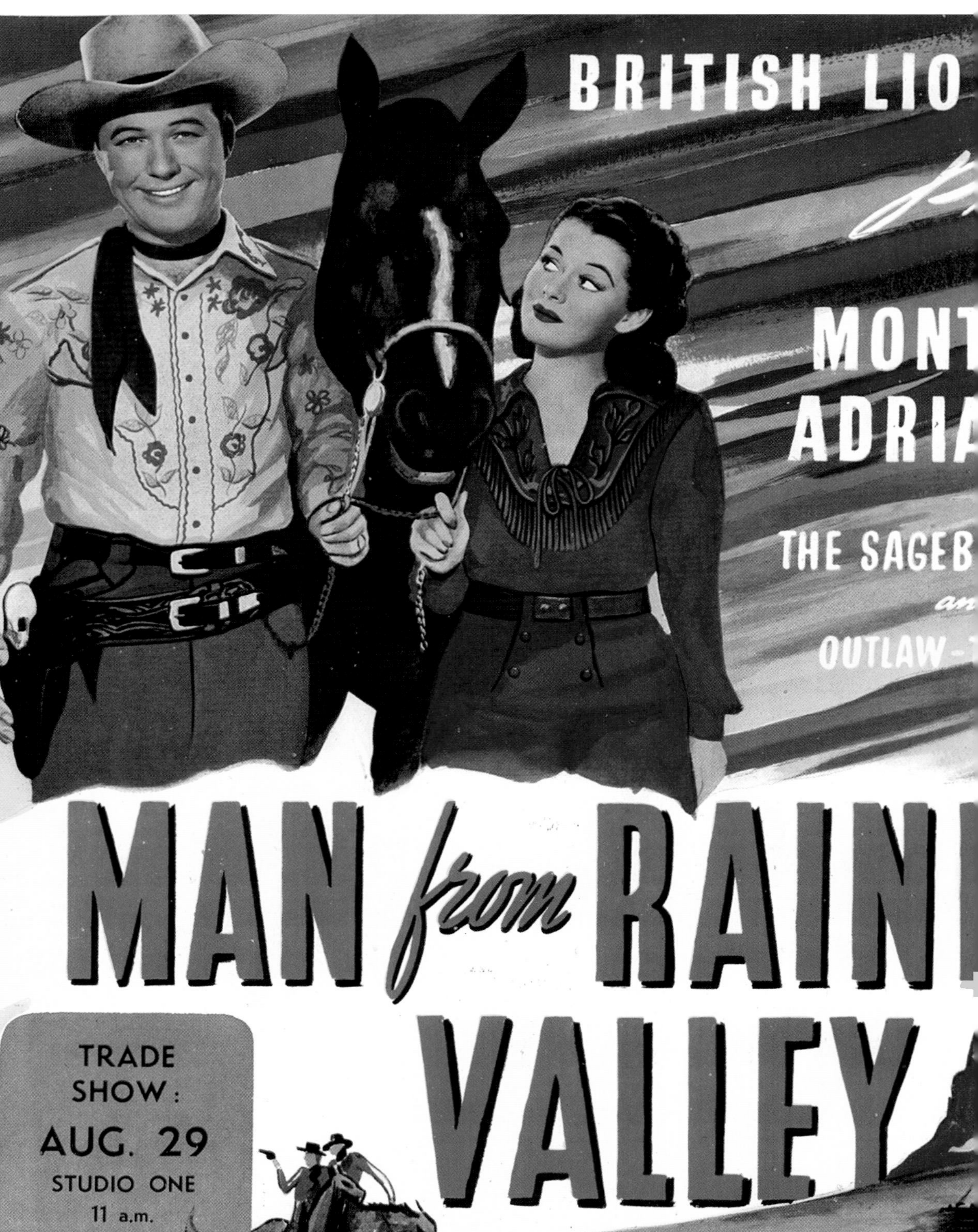
BRITISH LIO
MONT
ADRIA
THE SAGEB
OUTLAW-
MAN from RAIN
VALLEY
TRADE
SHOW:
AUG. 29
STUDIO ONE
11 a.m.

BRITISH LION
...ents
HALE
BOOTH
SERENADERS
...ring
...ILD HORSE
...OW
THE First OF A NEW SERIES
OF COLOUR WESTERNS
FROM REPUBLIC
IN
MAGNACOLOR
Greater THRILLS!
Greater ACTION!
Greater SPECTACLE!
REPUBLIC PICTURES
A MAGNACOLOR PRODUCTION

THE
"THE LONE RANGER
And The Lost City Of Gold"
starring
CLAYTON MOORE as THE LONE RANGER
JAY SILVERHEELS as TONTO
featuring DOUGLAS KENNEDY · CHARLES WATTS
with NOREEN NASH · LISA MONTELL
RALPH MOODY · NORMAN FREDRIC
Directed by LESLEY SELANDER
Produced by SHERMAN A. HARRIS
Written by ROBERT SCHAEFER and ERIC FREIWALD
Based upon the LONE RANGER LEGEND
A JACK WRATHER Production
COLOR BY EASTMAN COLOR
CAMPAIGN...IT'S YOUR BIG JUNE MONEYMAKER...
THRU UA

CHAPTER ONE

West of the Merrimac River: How a Massachusetts Boy Aspired to Become Rowdy Yates

Growing up as I did in the sleepy (all right, let's be honest—boring) post-industrial town of Haverhill, Massachusetts, during the Eisenhower fifties, it almost goes without saying that the stampede of westerns that permeated the popular culture of that sublime decade—the TV shows, of course, but also the movies, comic books, toys, and children's books—made up the warp and woof of this red-blooded boy's young life, even in the (sometimes) frozen Northeast.

I lived just seventeen miles from the New Hampshire seacoast, with only the humble Merrimac River to stand in for the Colorado in my febrile imagination (the poor Merrimac, at the time a polluted mess after half a century of being abused by the shoe factories lining its shores). Lobster rolls and steamed clams had to stand in for barbequed beef and beans—not much of a hardship, to be honest—but something else was going on at that time that had nothing to do with life in New England, and I could recognize a good thing when I saw it. Good things like a nice set of toy six-guns (with maybe a cowboy hat on the side), a stack of *Lone Ranger* comic books, chased down by three straight hours of assorted cattle-driving, bullet-whizzing, fist-fighting western TV shows—my typical daily dose of television viewing (interrupted only by *Leave It to Beaver*, to the best of my recollection).

My indoctrination into the vision of the Old West began in the mid-fifties with the recycled adventures of the holy trinity—Gene, Roy and Hoppy—all of whom had been canny enough to sell their salad-days B-

movies to television in the late 1940s, ensuring that, a few years later, I too could be exposed to the extremely mild thrills of these low-budget oaters during their endless recycling on Saturday and weekday afternoon programming. (I like to think that I knew even then that these shows were actually pretty sorry stuff—but Hoppy's cool all-black fightin' duds made up for a lot.)

One of the high points of being a little boy in 1955 was experiencing firsthand the craze for Davy Crockett that captured all of America for one brief but shining moment. Launched via *The Wonderful World of Disney* in three self-contained mini-movies that aired in December 1954, January 1955, and February 1955 (the Alamo episode), Davy was our King of the Wild Frontier, even if the boundaries of that frontier kept changing from episode to episode. I was just as driven to get one of those coonskin caps as thirty million other kids were—and by gosh, get one I did!

DELL
NO. 639
10¢
Walt Disney's
Davy Crockett
AT THE
ALAMO
FESS PARKER AS DAVY CROCKETT
© COPYRIGHT WALT DISNEY PRODUCTIONS

BRITISH LION presents
Gene AUTRY
SERENA
OF THE
A SUPREME AUTRY PRODUC
Smiley BURNETT
Fay McKENZI
BRITISH LION
A REPUBLIC Picture
BRITISH LION FILM COR
76-78 WARDOUR S
BRITISH LION presents
Roy ROGERS
RED RIVER VALLEY
GEORGE "Gabby" HAYES
SALLY PAYNE
Trade Show
BRITISH-LION
Private Theatre
Wed. MAY 27TH
11 A.M.
REPUBLIC PICTURES
A REPUBLIC Picture
BRITISH LION FILM CORPORATION LIMITED,
76-78 WARDOUR STREET, W. 1.
MANAGING DIRECTOR · S. W. SMITH
'GRAMS - "BRILIONFIL, RATH. LONDON"

Too, there was our own humble local programming cashing in on the western craze. For the Boston television market in the mid-fifties, that motivation translated into a tepid children's show called *Boom Town,* featuring a benign, buckskin-fringed fellow named Buffalo Bob as the host of the morning activities (and I use the word "activities" loosely). Banal to the extreme, yes—but we loved the guy anyway.

I didn't want to live in Boom Town, though, which appeared to be even more boring than 1958 Haverhill. Instead, I wanted to be Rowdy Yates. For the uninitiated: Rowdy was the second-in-command character on the prime-time series *Rawhide*, embodied in the person of a twenty-something Clint Eastwood, then at his most supernaturally gorgeous. Long before anyone could have known that he would grow into an international superstar on the strength of his "spaghetti" western trilogy, Eastwood embodied everything a Massachusetts boy might have associated with a successful adulthood—a manly profession (herding cattle across state lines), an ability to enter into fistfights whenever necessary (though recent viewings on DVD compilations of the series indicate that Rowdy lost an alarming number of these encounters), an utter lack of a girlfriend or wife, and—most impressively, to me—the best head of hair on the North American continent. Heck, it may well have been the best head of hair ever. In one episode, a bucket of water was thrown over Rowdy's head to revive him after another one of his unsuccessful bouts of fisticuffs, and his hair was *still* perfect even after being drenched. (Plus he had cool sideburns, not seen in my little world much except on the Brylcreamed heads of Haverhill's many aspiring juvenile delinquents.)

But if I couldn't grow up to be Rowdy Yates, I was willing to settle for being Sugarfoot, the charmingly sheepish character played by Will Hutchins on the eponymous ABC-TV series. *Sugarfoot* alternated with the even more popular *Cheyenne,* which featured the much more imposing form of the 6'7" Clint Walker in the title role of a brooding loner. Even at the age of seven, I was able to intuit that I was unlikely to grow up into a latter-day version of Cheyenne Bodie, a frankly scary giant of a man—but I could handle charmingly sheepish, even if I wasn't blessed with Hutchins' artlessly mussed-up blond locks. It has always been a grave disappointment to me

S1910
SIGNET
35¢
BOOKS
FRANK C. ROBERTSON
RAWHIDE
A novel based on the top
CBS Television Network
series starring Eric Fleming
as Gil Favor
Gil Favor hires on to beat a rival
cattle drive to Sedalia—a cattle
drive headed by an outlaw . . .
and a killer
A SIGNET BOOK

that, some fifty years on in my life, I didn't quite pull off this transformation either. At this point, I would happily settle for someone just referring to me as Sugarfoot (and what the heck did that sobriquet mean, anyway? I will pay ten dollars to the first person who can tell me how Will Hutchins earned that name).

And if even being Sugarfoot was beyond my capabilities, then as a last resort I was willing to step into the shoes of Johnny Crawford, the lucky lad who got to play Mark McCain, the son of big Lucas McCain (Chuck Connors), on *The Rifleman*. This was the first father-son western on network TV, running from 1958 to 1963, and the show was made more profound by the absence of a mother in the McCain family. (Sorry, Mom.) I know it helped Mark want to obey Lucas when he looked up and noticed he was 6'6" (sorry, Dad—but the guy *had* actually played for the Celtics!) and also had a modified Winchester that he could cock and shoot faster than any man could draw his pistol. Or so the writers on the series maintained. I also admired Crawford's pop hit "Cindy's Birthday," (which he did not get to sing à la Ricky Nelson on the show).

20c
Frontier Stories
TRADE MARK REG.
OF PIONEER DAYS
FICTION HOUSE MAGAZINES
A MAGAZINE DEDICATED TO THE ADVENTURES OF THE DAUNTLESS MEN AND WOMEN WHO CARVED A NEW EMPIRE-THE WEST
Vol. 13 No. 12
FRONTIER STORIES
SUMMER ISSUE
1938
APACHE!
LONG RIFLES DEFY THE RED SCOURGE OF THE PLAINS
by RAY NAFZIGER
WAGON TRAIN WEST
by TED FOX
WELLS-FARGO AMBUSCADE
by J. E. GRINSTEAD
SCOOP: MY LIFE STORY by JESSE JAMES

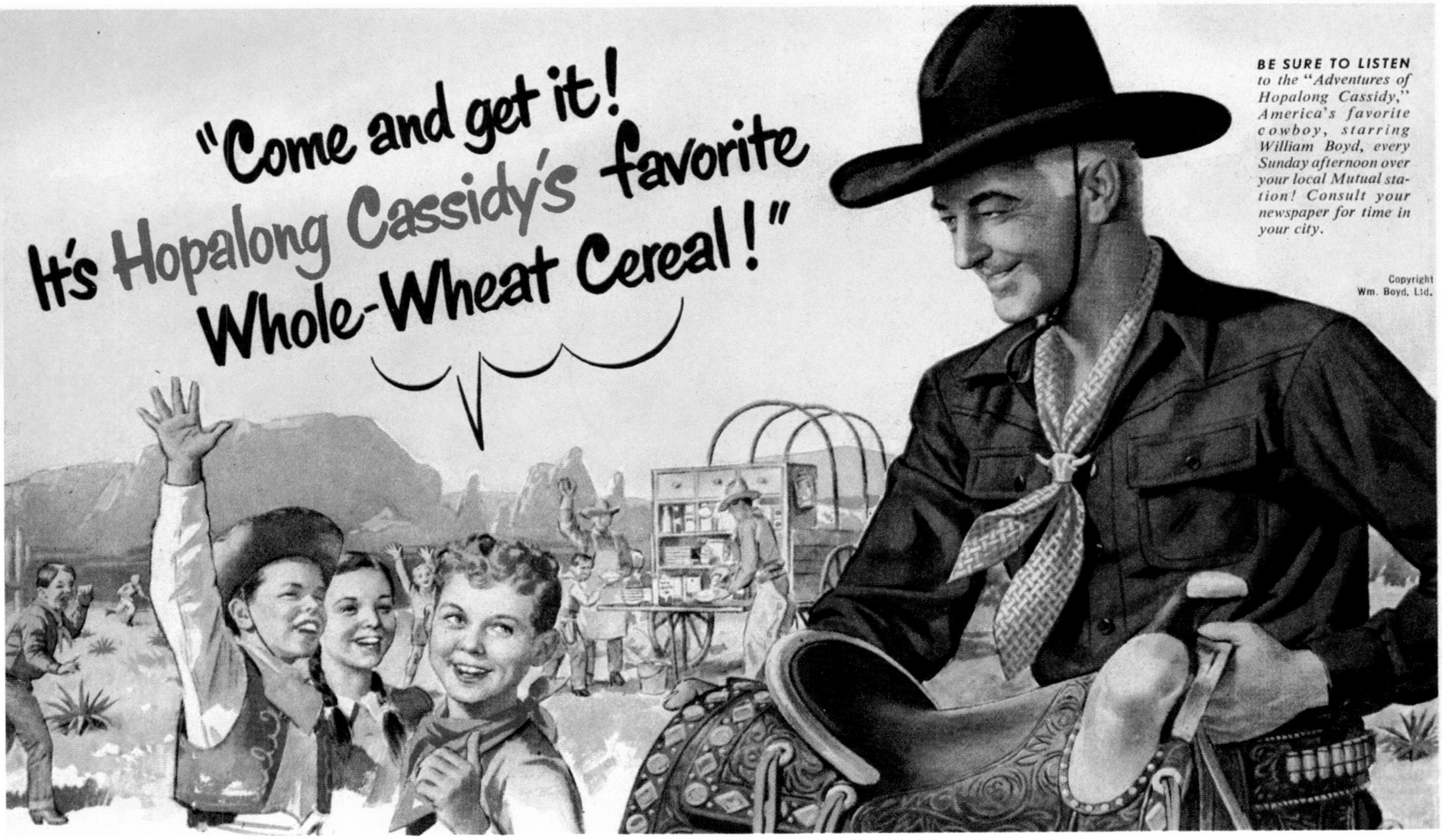

"Come and get it!
It's Hopalong Cassidy's favorite
Whole-Wheat Cereal!"

BE SURE TO LISTEN to the "Adventures of Hopalong Cassidy," America's favorite cowboy, starring William Boyd, every Sunday afternoon over your local Mutual station! Consult your newspaper for time in your city.

Copyright
Wm. Boyd, Ltd.

Another formative experience for me was seeing a show on television which I now believe was the 1950 film *Broken Arrow*. In this classic, James Stewart convincingly plays army scout Tom Jeffords (an actual person, about whom more later in this book) who befriends the noble Apache chief Cochise (played by Jewish Brooklyn-born actor Jeff Chandler) to the point where Jeffords is essentially adopted into the tribe, even taking the chief's lovely daughter as his bride. Although the story ends in betrayal and tragedy (both for Jeffords, whose wife is killed by soldiers, and for Cochise and his Apache people), I was deeply affected by the friendship of the two men and their effort to bridge their clashing cultures, at a time when to do so was viewed as an act of treason. In fact, I was so deeply imprinted by *Broken Arrow* that, ever afterward, I felt more than a little uncomfortable watching programs, or reading books or comics that portrayed the Indian characters as villains.

But *Broken Arrow* also thrived as a television series for three years, from 1956 to 1959, so it is entirely possible I am remembering that version of the story. If so, it is worth noting that the role of Cochise was now played by Michael Ansara, an actor born and raised in the ex-shoe town of Lowell, Massachusetts, just twenty miles down the Merrimac River from Haverhill. Hanta Ho!

As the fifties gave way to the sixties, the stranglehold that westerns had held on America's popular imagination began to loosen, and I could have served as Exhibit A. Even though such TV shows as *Bonanza, Gunsmoke,* and *The Virginian* were still riding high in the ratings, I had long since switched my viewing over to programs like *The Man from U.N.C.L.E.*, *The Mod Squad,* and *Star Trek.* My comic book reading had also shifted to the booming superhero scene, and the paperbacks I bought eschewed frontier adventures for those set on other planets. Spy and sci-fi flicks filled my

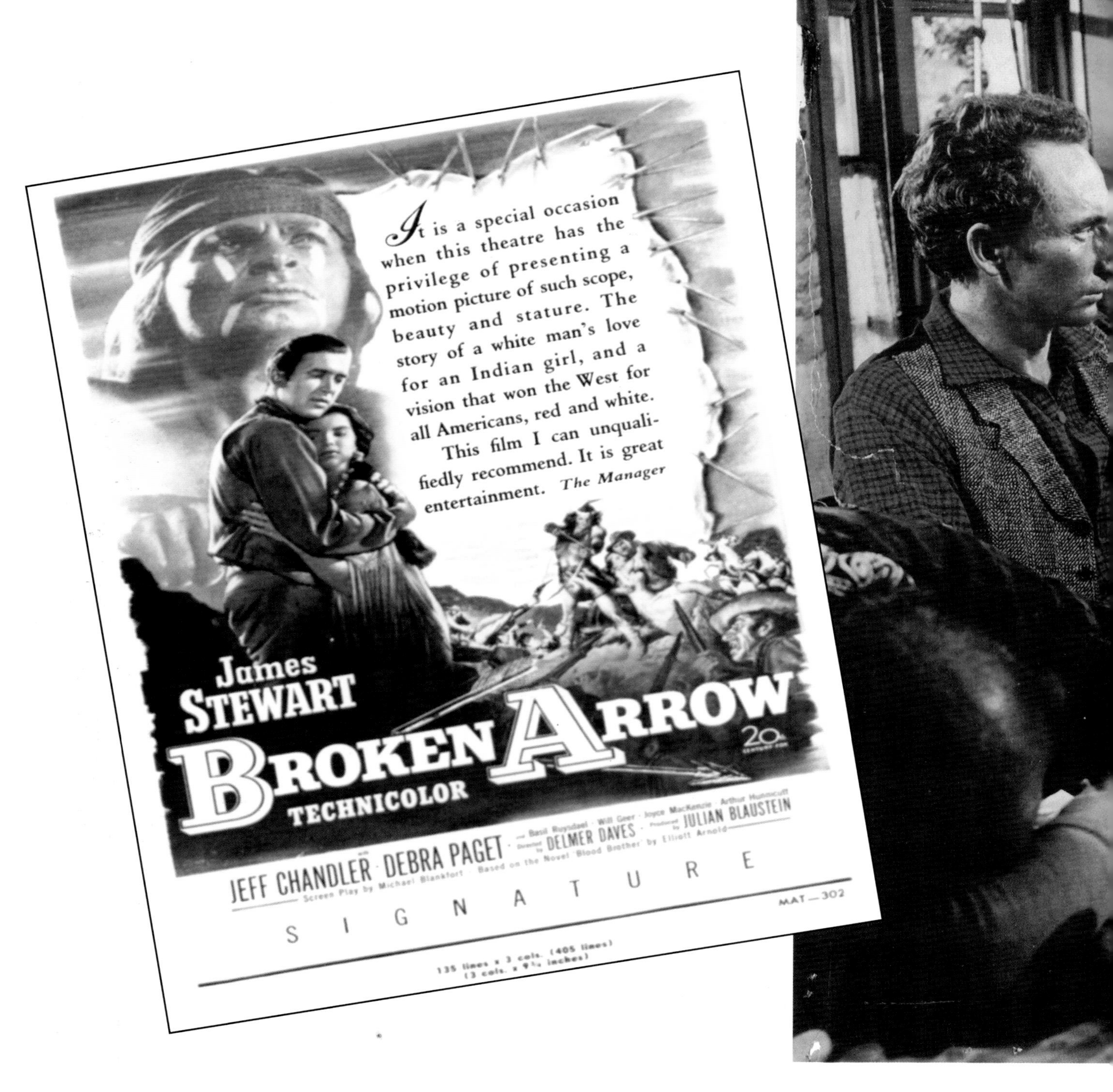
It is a special occasion when this theatre has the privilege of presenting a motion picture of such scope, beauty and stature. The story of a white man's love for an Indian girl, and a vision that won the West for all Americans, red and white.
This film I can unqualifiedly recommend. It is great entertainment. The Manager
James STEWART
BROKEN ARROW
20th
TECHNICOLOR
JEFF CHANDLER · DEBRA PAGET · Basil Ruysdael · Will Geer · Joyce MacKenzie · Arthur Hunnicutt
DELMER DAVES · JULIAN BLAUSTEIN
Screen Play by Michael Blankfort · Based on the Novel 'Blood Brother' by Elliott Arnold
SIGNATURE
MAT—302
135 lines x 3 cols. (405 lines)
(3 cols. x 9⅝ inches)

JAMES STEWART
BROKEN ARROW
Color by Technicolor
JEFF CHANDLER · DEBRA PAGET
BASIL RUYSDAEL WILL GEER
JOYCE MacKENZIE ARTHUR HUNNICUTT
20th CENTURY-FOX
DELMER DAVES · BLAUSTEIN

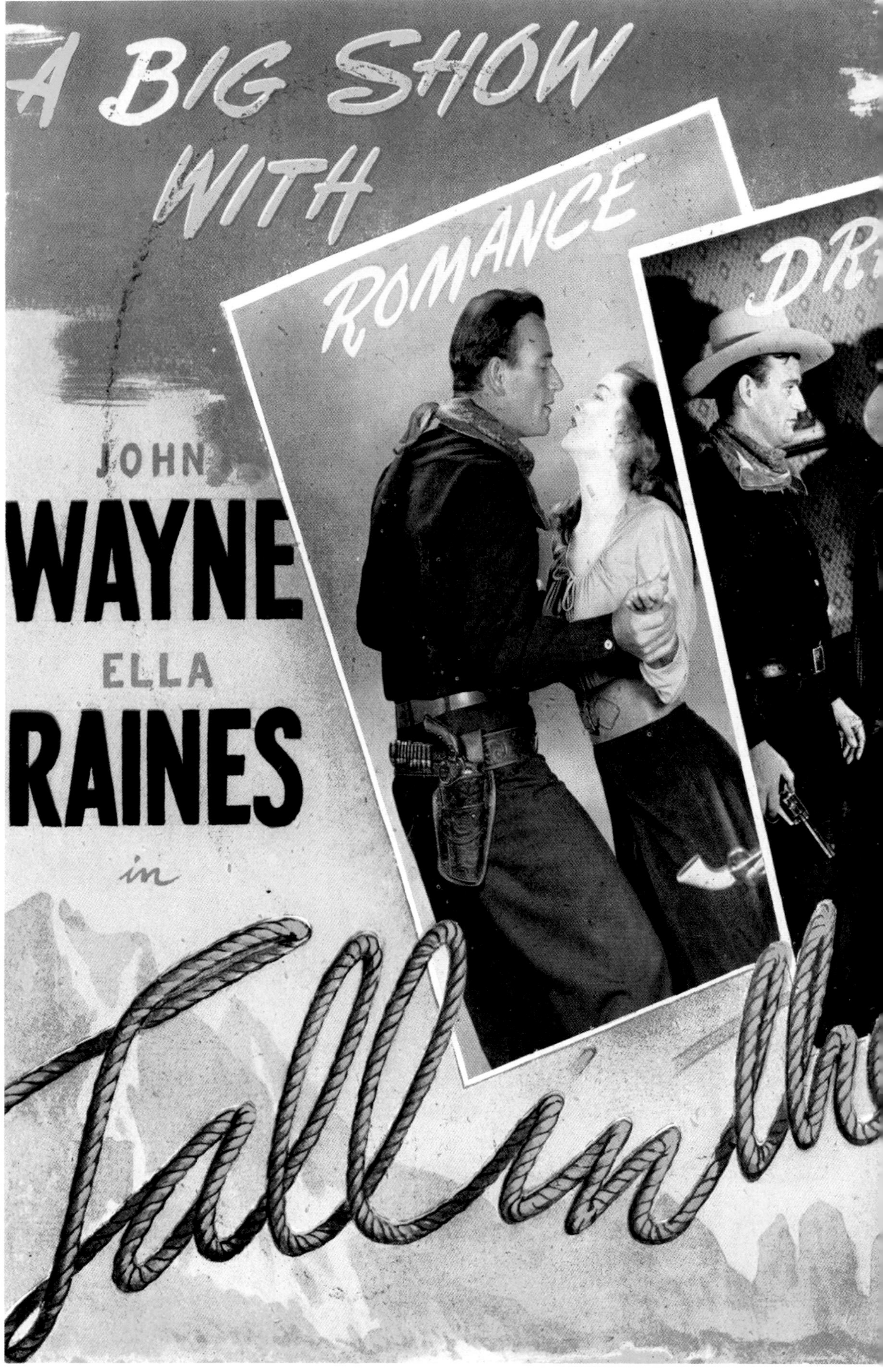
A BIG SHOW
WITH
ROMANCE
JOHN
WAYNE
ELLA
RAINES
in

RKO
RADIO
PICTURES
THRILLS
ACTION AND SUSPENSE!
"A draught of fresh air . . . Rousing drama, served up in de luxe fashion."
Daily Film Renter
"Non-stop action . . . Suspenseful romance, diverting comedy. Excellent, out of the common rut."
Cinema

movie-going afternoons, the excellent westerns that were being produced then wholly ignored—I never even knew about the Eastwood spaghetti westerns until years after the fact. In short, by the time I was a teenager I no longer gave a thought to my past days as a devotee of westerns.

But, like the old-timers say, life has a funny way of turning back in on itself. I have come to realize that those countless hours spent soaking up the world of the Old West during my formative days as a young'un had more to do with shaping the person I finally became than I ever might have guessed. Half a century later, my travels over the past couple decades have taken me through a good portion of the "real" West—Texas, of course, along with stops in Wyoming, Oregon, Washington, California, the Dakotas, Colorado, and Arizona—so I no longer have to rely on my imagination and the work of novelists, comic book artists, and filmmakers to see what all the fuss was about.

But when it comes to appreciating the *true* West—say, the West of 1868, to pick one of a hundred possible focal points—no number of plane rides I might now take into the setting sun could hope to ever close that gap in understanding. So instead, I watch *Deadwood* on HBO, Netflix old Randolph Scott films that were far too adult for me to go see when they first came out (making me wonder: what other great stuff did I miss while immersing myself in the Marvel Comics universe?), and thrill to Kevin Costner and Robert Duvall in *Open Range* (see it! Really!). Read mid-period novels by Louis L'Amour—read him for the first time, in fact—along with the novel on which *Broken Arrow* was based, the amazing *Blood Brother* by Elliot Arnold, a copy of which I found last year left behind in a local Starbucks. (A Starbucks—talk about kismet.)

As Terrence Rafferty wrote with such insight in his *New York Times* story "Jesse James: An Outlaw for All Seasons," which greeted the release of the highly praised film *The Assassination of Jesse James by the Coward Robert Ford,* "Historical accuracy never really had much to do with the western's cultural value, or with our long affection for it. Westerns are the stories we used to tell ourselves about our origins, about the sources of our native pluck and resilience. They were part of the messy, improvisonal [*sic*] process by which Americans define—and revise, and define again—a national self-image, and one of the many reasons to regret the demise of westerns is that without them it's just a little tougher for us to figure out who we are. (These days we need all the help we can get.)"

And how does that demise affect me, personally? It means I have to try a little harder now to keep the faith. I attend a screening of the newly restored version of Sam Peckinpah's *Major Dundee* (verdict: still not a patch on *Ride the High Country*) and reread Larry McMurtry's *Lonesome Dove* (even greater than the wonderful 1989 television adaptation). I soak up the unexpectedly fine AMC miniseries *Broken Trail* with the incomparable Duvall and Thomas Haden Church, then steel myself to watch the miniseries of McMurtry's *Comanche Moon* (verdict: it's no *Dove*, not by a mile). I see the advance publicity for the film version of Robert B. Parker's bestseller *Appaloosa,* and count the months until it reaches the theaters (and thank you for that lovely foreword to this volume, Bob).

All of that is what spurred me on to create *True West.* I wanted to have a book that celebrated what to me—and, I suspect, to millions of other lads and lasses who were fated to live ten states away from Texas—had always been the *true* West, the West of our collective imaginations and impressionable minds. This book attempts to gather all of the wonderful flotsam and jetsam that, to this New England-bred boy, constituted the reality of the Old West more vividly than any twenty history texts ever could have.

"Howdy Pardner

how'd you like to win a Hoppy bike, or cowboy outfit, or shootin' irons, absolutely free? they're just a few of the 4,000 wonderful prizes in my contest—and you can be a winner eight times! turn to page 40, and I'll tell you how to do it!"

CHAPTER TWO

Cowboy Cornucopia: Gene, Roy, and the Whole Darned Gang

Even the first moviemakers understood the fascination Americans had with the Old West—which, at the dawn of the twentieth century, wasn't even particularly old. Thomas Edison famously chose that scenario for his proto-film release in 1903, *The Great Train Robbery,* filmed so realistically that audiences (especially in the East, one presumes) literally jumped out of their seats at different points. In that first decade of the new century, most of the studios were based in the East, in parts of New York City like Astoria. So it was considerably more trouble to film a story set in the West than one set in someone's parlor or on the streets of New York.

But once the studios began to relocate to the Los Angeles area, the equation changed—now there was exotic scenery for the filming within an hour's ride, opening up a thousand possible scenarios for movie shorts set in the Old West. In those nascent days of the industry, before feature-length films had become the norm, there weren't many established stars, just actors who worked on dozens of short films, year in and year out. But by the mid-teens, longer films began to appear, allowing a star system to develop. Though some of the "star" actors from that period have since been lost to the shadows of time—anyone remember Jack Hoxie, "The Western Dynamo," who starred in the 1919 serial ("The Greatest Serial Ever Made," according to the Arrow Film Corporation advertising) *Lightning*

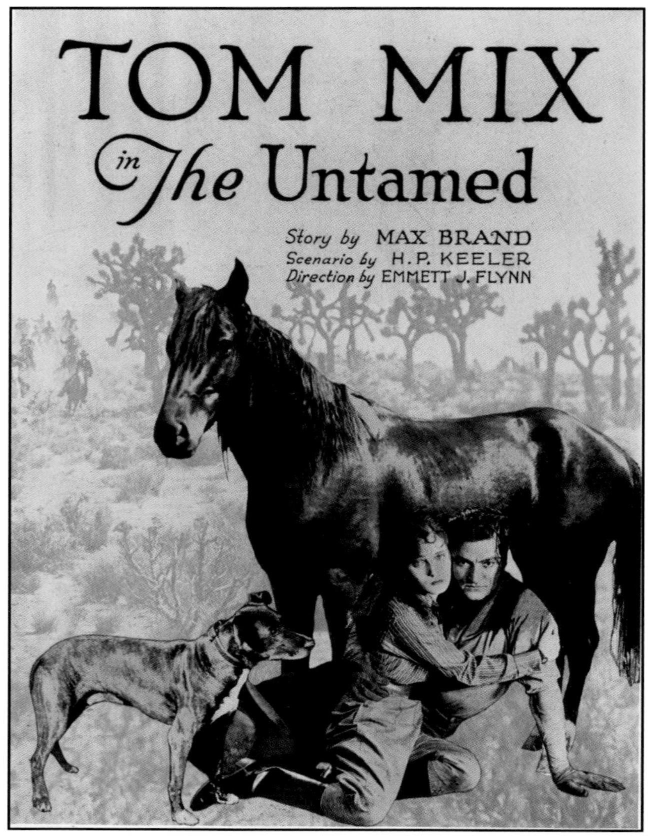

Bryce? How about William Desmond, who starred in *A Sagebrush Hamlet* ("Men—Women—Horses—Guns" was its tagline) that same year? No, I didn't think so. . . .

Soon, though, one name rose to the fore in the realm of westerns: William S. Hart. A former Shakespearean actor who had starred on Broadway in the original production of *Ben-Hur,* Hart began to act in films in 1914 and quickly gravitated toward westerns, a lifelong love of his. (In fact, Hart cultivated a friendship with the long-retired Bat Masterson and Wyatt Earp and supposedly owned a pair of Billy the Kid's six-guns.) The dour Hart's first big hits were the 1917 films *The Cold Deck* and *The Bargain,* and he soon earned the nickname "Two-Gun Bill." Hart quickly established himself as one of Hollywood's biggest stars of the silent era. Probably his signature film was *Tumbleweeds,* a big hit in 1925, when Hart was sixty-one. He retired from acting soon after.

Into Hart's shoes stepped Tom Mix, who had already been making films himself since the early teens, though for many years those were of a docu-

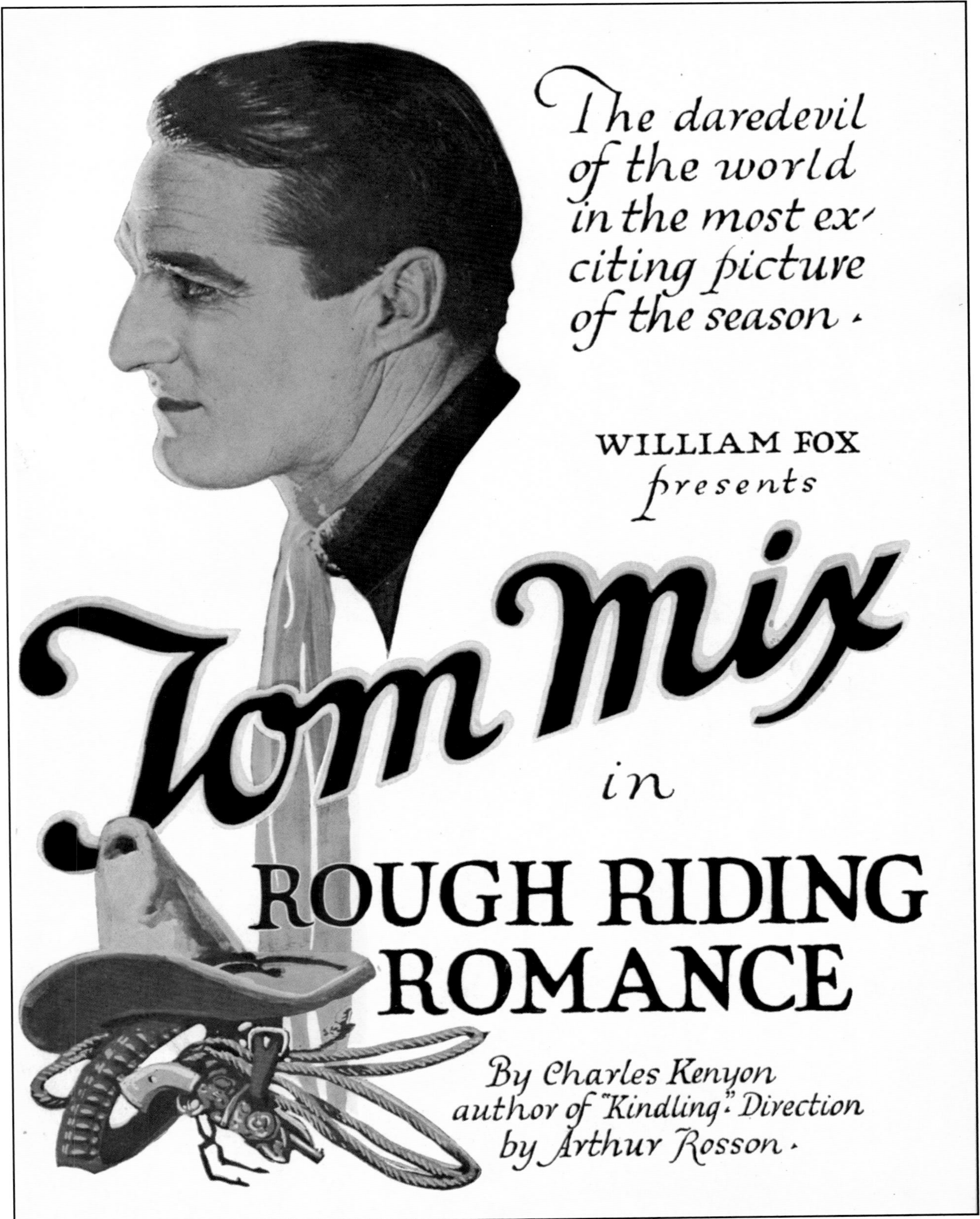
The daredevil of the world in the most exciting picture of the season.
WILLIAM FOX presents
Tom Mix
in
ROUGH RIDING ROMANCE
By Charles Kenyon author of "Kindling." Direction by Arthur Rosson.

mentary nature on riding, wrangling, and the like. (Mix had won the 1909 national Riding & Rodeo Championship, so he could perform his own stunts most convincingly.) In 1916, *The Golden Thought* became one of his early hits, and pictures like Zane Grey's *The Lone Star Ranger, Riders of the Purple Sage* (a Zane Grey classic), *King Cowboy, The Great K&A Train Robbery,* and *The Last Trail* followed throughout the twenties. Mix's cowboy action Bs were by then so popular that he was earning $7,500 a week from the Fox studio, a fortune by today's standards.

By one count, Mix had made nearly 330 silent films by 1929, when he semi-retired to run his own circus (where he earned even more per week than he did in films!). But he was lured out of retirement by Universal Studios, who wanted him to make talkies for them. Mix did make nine of them, an amazing six in 1932 alone, including *Flaming Guns* (perhaps the inspiration for the title of Mel Brooks' classic parody, *Blazing Saddles*) and his own version of the Max Brand classic, *Destry Rides Again.* But now in his fifties, Mix didn't recover so well from the spills he took doing his own stunts and served notice that he was done. In reduced circumstances, thanks to multiple divorces and various reversals, Mix came out of retirement one last time to make a fifteen-chapter serial, *The Miracle Rider,* for Poverty Row-studio Mascot. His lucrative deal in 1933 with the Ralston-Purina company for the *Tom Mix Ralston Straight Shooters* radio show lived on long after he did; Mix died in October 1940 at age sixty, the victim of a car crash in Arizona. But the Ralston radio show, which always had used other actors' voices, lingered on into 1950.

The silent cinema could claim a handful of A-level westerns—epics like James Cruze's *The Covered Wagon* (1923), John Ford's *The Iron Horse* (1924), and the Zane Grey adaptation *The Vanishing American,* starring Richard Dix. But the era was better known for producing a veritable stampede of cowboy stars, both major and minor, most of whom lasted well into the thirties. There was Harry Carey (*The Fox, West is West*), Hoot Gibson (*The Saddle Hawk, Ride for Your Life*), Buck Jones (*Hearts and Spurs, Men Without Law*), Ken Maynard (*The Royal Rider, Tombstone Canyon*), Richard Arlen (*Under the Tonto Rim*), Tom Tyler (*Idaho Red, Trigger Tom*), Tim McCoy (*Fighting for Justice, Man of Action*), and Tom Keene (*The Cheyenne Kid, Ghost Valley*), among many, many others.

With the benefit of hindsight, we know that out of this pack of cowboy personalities, one giant in particular emerged—John Wayne, who spent almost the entire decade of the thirties making six or seven low-budget pictures each year, none of them any better (or worse) than the rest of the product being churned out in those days for Saturday matinee viewing. With the exception of his 1930 Raoul Walsh epic *The Big Trail,* Wayne was seen strictly as a B-picture player, and so he was relegated to the assembly churning out those sixty-minute wonders. Consider this representative group, all released in 1934: *West of the Divide, The Trail Beyond, Randy Rides Alone, 'Neath Arizona Skies, The Man from Utah, The Lawless Frontier, Blue Steel.* That year was almost indistinguishable from the ones just before it and just after it. Then came 1939 and John Ford's *Stagecoach,* a film that would change everything about the movie career of John Wayne. More about that development anon.

But long before the ascension of John Wayne, another movie cowboy struck pay dirt in a manner that quickly cut him out from the rest of the herd. William "Bill" Boyd had been a jack-of-all-trades actor since the twenties, appearing in a wide variety of adventures and dramas, including *King of Kings, The Painted Desert* (likely his first western, 1931), and *Lucky Devils.* His big break was being cast in Paramount's adaptation of Clarence Mulford's character in the 1935 film *Hop-A-Long Cassidy*—only as the villain. But when the first choice for the hero's role dropped out—diminutive hard-boiled New Yorker James Gleason—the Oklahoma-raised Boyd happily became Hoppy. That first adventure led to two sequels in 1935, *The Eagle's Brood* and *Bar 20 Rides Again,* with several other follow-ups released in 1936: *Hopalong Cassidy Returns, Heart of the West, Call of the Prairie,* and *Three on the Trail.* Boyd now *was* Hoppy in the hearts and minds of moviegoers, going on to make a total of sixty-six Hoppy films over a twelve-year period.

Boyd's true genius lay in having the foresight to purchase the rights to the character for himself in 1946 from the Mulford estate. The original idea was to continue making the films under his own auspices, but after a dozen unremarkable entries, the series petered out in 1948. But this was also the period when the dawning television industry was desperately in need of content to fill its day-and-night scheduling, and Boyd was sitting in the cat-

bird seat, having also acquired the backlog of several dozen Hoppy features from Paramount, enabling him to sell the entire batch of Hoppy films to TV for syndication in 1949. To prep the episodes for airing in half-hour slots, Boyd edited them and even shot some new scenes (this while in his fifties!) to ensure that they ran smoothly. The result was that Hopalong Cassidy became one of the first television superstars, with a blizzard of promotional and product tie-ins further feathering Boyd's nest. He retired a few years later as a multimillionaire.

There were other cowboy stars emerging in the mid-thirties, but none would have the impact of the two singing cowboys whose careers started then. First was the advent of Gene Autry, who made his way to Hollywood in 1934 after Will Rogers gave him an introduction, having heard him sing on the radio in Oklahoma. Gene was given a number to perform in the Ken Maynard film *In Old Santa Fe* and then launched his starring career in modest fashion in 1935, with the fifteen-chapter serial *The Phantom Empire,* made by Poverty Row's Mascot Pictures (yes, the same Mascot for whom

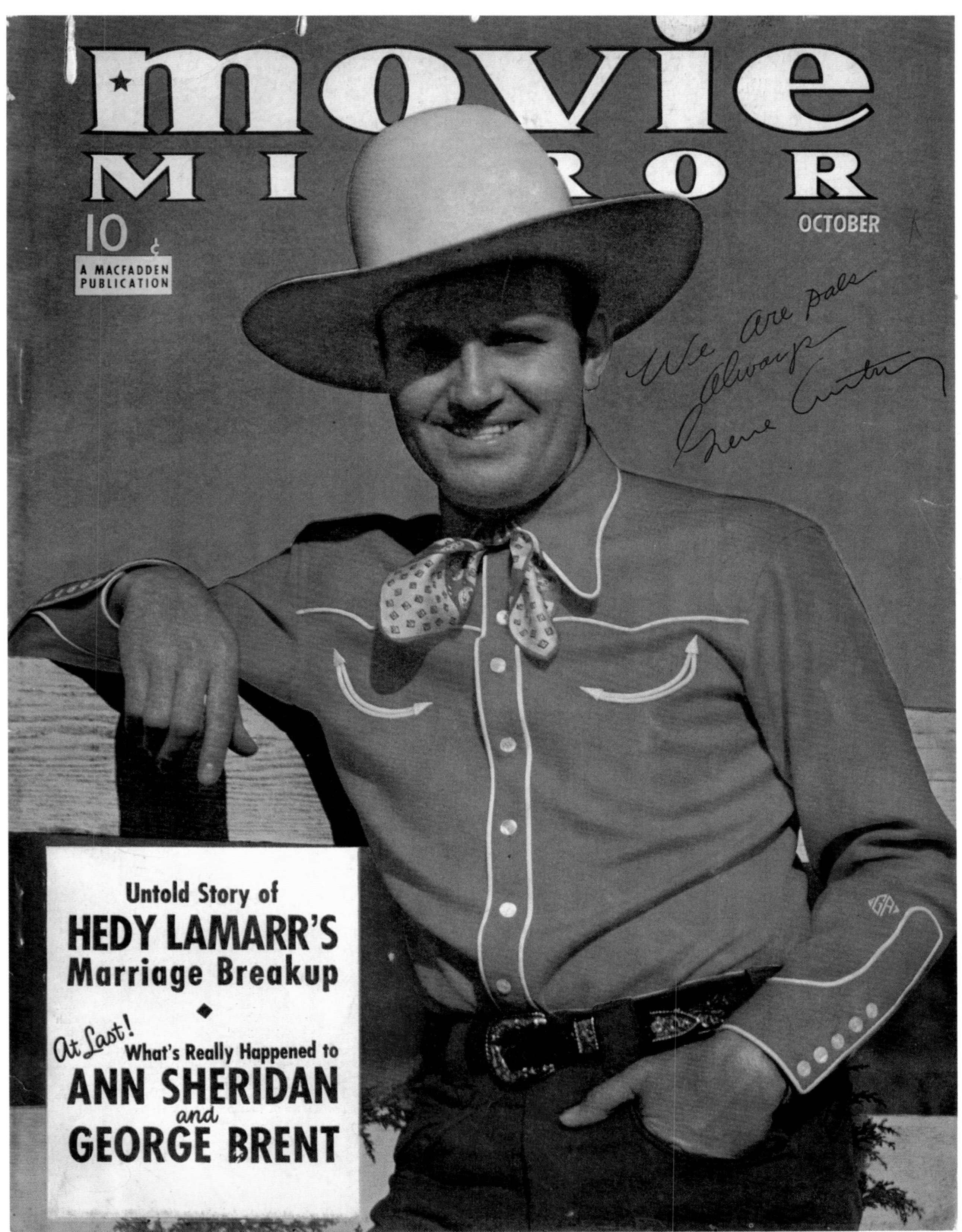
movie
MIRROR
10¢
A MACFADDEN PUBLICATION
OCTOBER
We are pals always Gene Autry
Untold Story of
HEDY LAMARR'S
Marriage Breakup
At Last! What's Really Happened to
ANN SHERIDAN
and
GEORGE BRENT

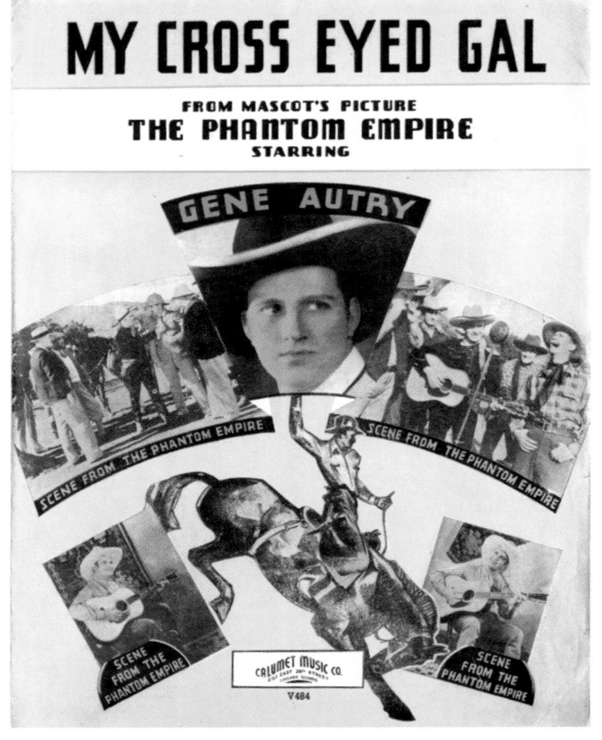
MY CROSS EYED GAL
FROM MASCOT'S PICTURE
THE PHANTOM EMPIRE
STARRING
GENE AUTRY
SCENE FROM THE PHANTOM EMPIRE
SCENE FROM THE PHANTOM EMPIRE
SCENE FROM THE PHANTOM EMPIRE
SCENE FROM THE PHANTOM EMPIRE
CALUMET MUSIC CO.
V484

GENE AUTRY
"Trail of Terror"
10¢
No. 66
DELL

WANTED
BY EVERY MOTION PICTURE PRODUCER!
The producers of Hollywood have joined the exhibitors of America in clamoring for GENE AUTRY, Singing cowboy No. 1 of the screen. They all recognize the box office magic of the AUTRY name. The trade and daily papers have been full of this and that company negotiating for the services of REPUBLIC'S singing-action star.
Despite anything you may read or hear, and to set you straight...GENE AUTRY is under long-term, exclusive contract to REPUBLIC.
If you want the new GENE AUTRY 1937-38 series of Four Jubilee Specials and Four Musical Westerns (and who doesn't!) you can get them, as usual, from
Gene Autry
4 JUBILEES . . . 4 MUSICAL WESTERNS
CALLING ALL COWBOYS
BOOTS AND SADDLES
ROLL, WAGON, ROLL
The OLD BARN DANCE
PUBLIC COWBOY No. 1
CALGARY OR BUST
SADDLE PALS
MAN—MUSIC MOUNTAIN

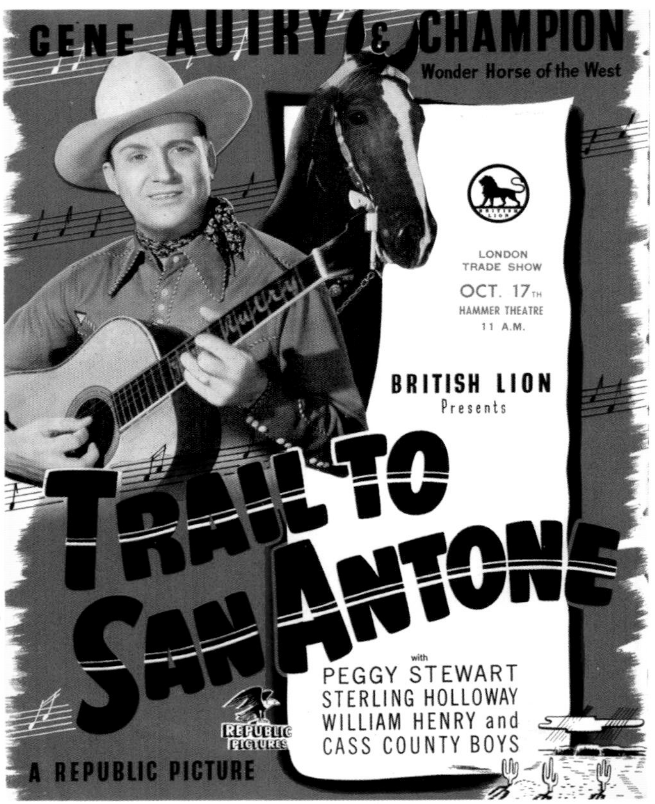
GENE AUTRY & CHAMPION
Wonder Horse of the West
LONDON TRADE SHOW
OCT. 17TH
HAMMER THEATRE
11 A.M.
BRITISH LION
Presents
TRAIL TO SAN ANTONE
with
PEGGY STEWART
STERLING HOLLOWAY
WILLIAM HENRY and
CASS COUNTY BOYS
REPUBLIC PICTURES
A REPUBLIC PICTURE

Gene Autry
AND THE
THIEF RIVER OUTLAWS
AUTHORIZED EDITION

GENE AUTRY
and the GOLDEN LADDER GANG

BRITISH LION presents
A Gay, Exciting New
GENE AUTRY
DE LUXE MUSICAL
EXCITEMENT
ROMANCE
COMEDY
GAY SONG HITS
"DOWN MEXICO WAY"
A REPUBLIC PRODUCTION with SMILEY BURNETTE
Fay McKenzie
LONDON
TRADE SHOW
Feb. 9th. 2·30 p.m
at
Cambridge Theatre
to be preceded by
"MEET THE STARS"
One Reeler
BRITISH LION
REPUBLIC PICTURES
BRITISH LION FILM CORPORATION LIMITED,
76-78 WARDOUR STREET, W. 1.
'GRAMS "BRILIONFIL, RATH, LONDON" ★ MANAGING DIRECTOR · S. W. SMITH ★ 'PHONE GERRARD 2682-5

BRITISH LION'S All-Action We

A Great Melody-Thrill Adventure

"Sunset in Wyoming"

With
SMILEY BURNETTE
MARIS WRIXON
GEORGE CLEVELAND

LONDON TRADE SHOW
Monday January 19 - 10.30 am
G-B PRIVATE THEATRE

A Whirlwind
Ron

"UN
FIES
ST

With
SMILEY B
CAROL HUG
FRANK DAR

Starring
GENE AUTRY
WORLD'S No. 1 WESTERN STAR
REPUBLIC PRODUCTIONS

BRITISH LION

BRITISH LION FILM CORPORATION LIMITED,
76-78 WARDOUR STREET, W.1.

Tom Mix did his final screen work that same year). Set in the underground land of Murania, the film is one of the few to offer both a lost civilization and a singing cowboy. (The big hit was Gene's "Silver-Haired Daddy of Mine.")

By the time the serial ran its course, Autry had made his first feature, *Tumbling Tumbleweeds* (poetic title, that), for Republic Pictures; complete with six songs, it billed Gene on its posters as "The Screen's New Singing Cowboy Star." Now Gene had a guitar, a pleasant (if unremarkable) voice, a horse named Champion, and a sidekick by the name of Smiley Burnette—everything a singing Texan required to attain stardom.

His next hits were *The Big Show* and *The Singing Cowboy* (also 1936), which established Gene's calling card. But another of the movies Gene made that year, *The Old Corral,* was even more interesting, including as it did the musical group The Sons of the Pioneers, who then featured a young singer named Dick Weston, later to be known as Roy Rogers; he loses a fist-fight to Gene in the course of the action, but their real battle for western screen supremacy was yet to unfold.

Public Cowboy #1 (set in contemporary times) and *Git Along Little Dogies* followed in 1937, and in their wake came literally dozens of other hits: *Gold Mine in the Sky* (1938), *Colorado Sunset* (1939), *Down Mexico Way* (1940), and *Ridin' on a Rainbow* (1941) were but a few of the many musical adventures Gene made in those pre-war years. During this time, his recording career became so successful that Gene Autry would be honored today just for that body of work, had it been his only contribution to the western in the popular arts.

Once World War II broke out, Gene enlisted in the Air Transport Command and served his country for the next several years. But Republic Studios barely missed a beat, already having established Roy Rogers as the other Greatest Cowboy Singing Sensation. Roy Rogers, born Leonard Slye (near Cincinnati, of all places!) four years after Autry, had been in California since age nineteen. He eventually formed a singing group called The Rocky Mountaineers, a band that evolved into The Sons of the Pioneers, just as Len Slye decided to evolve into Dick Weston. In 1935 the Sons got the call from Hollywood to perform in a short subject and made enough of an impression to get more work spot-singing in feature films. Their cameo in

Autry's 1936 feature *The Old Corral* paid off in spades two years later when Republic held auditions for a singing cowboy who could replace the (briefly, as it turned out) striking Gene Autry. "Dick Weston" won the job, was renamed Roy Rogers, and launched his career as a frontline western star in the 1938 film *Under Western Stars*—in which he played a singing congressman.

Public reception was positive, and Republic put him on the same B-picture treadmill that Autry had endured. Aided and abetted by irascible, bearded George "Gabby" Hayes, Roy starred in *Shine on Harvest Moon, In Old Caliente, Young Buffalo Bill, Young Bill Hickok, Jesse James at Bay,* and *In Old Sacramento* over the next few years. (A less happy choice was the 1939 misfire *Wall Street Cowboy,* which made the fatal mistake of leaving Roy songless, not to mention devoid of fistfights.)

Then the war broke out—and Roy kept right on making pictures for Republic, unlike Gene. *Sunset on the Desert, Heart of the Golden West,* and *Ridin' Down the Canyon* were followed by his 1943 signature film, *King of the Cowboys* (which, oddly, had Autry's former second-banana Smiley

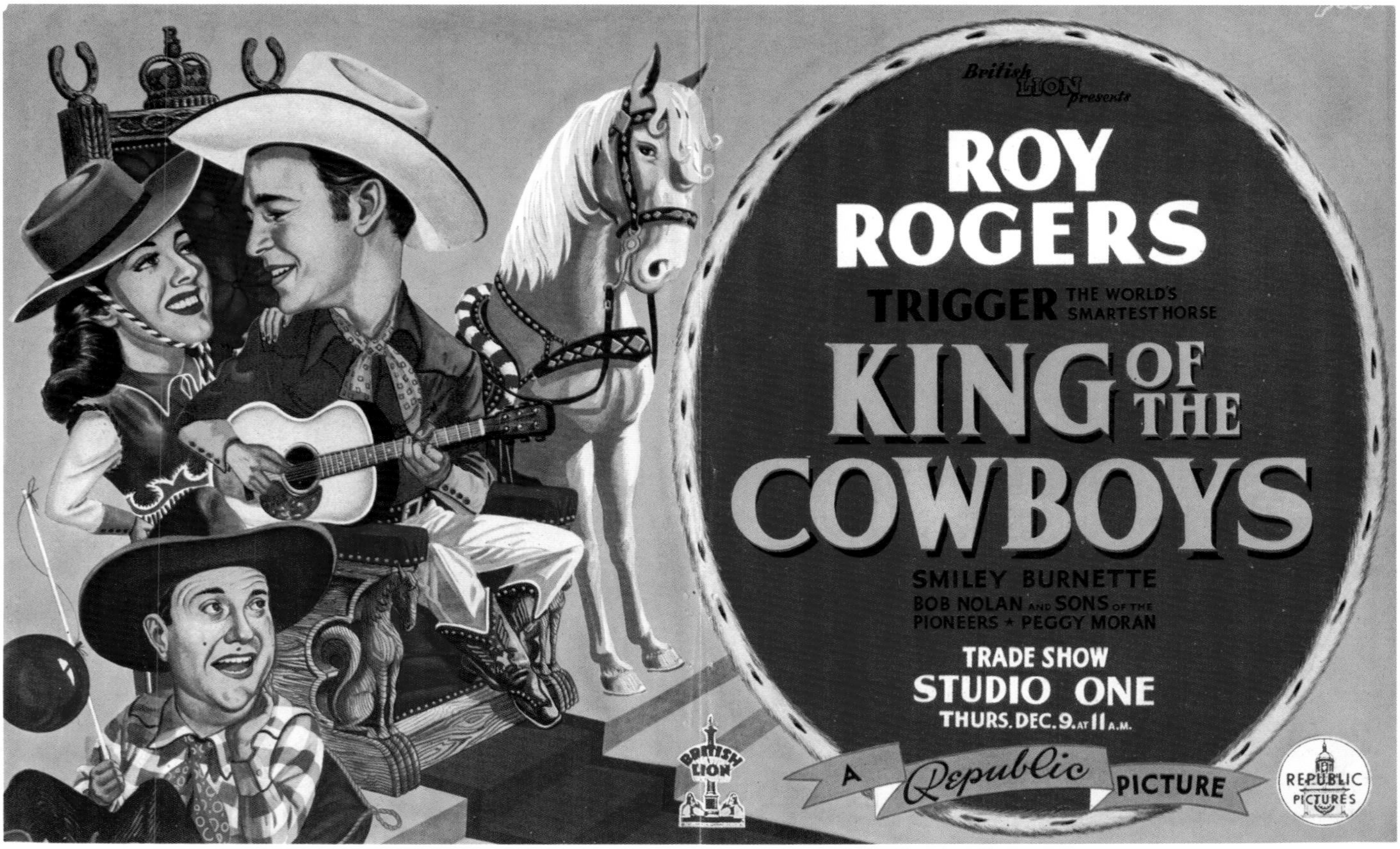
British LION presents
ROY ROGERS
TRIGGER THE WORLD'S SMARTEST HORSE
KING OF THE COWBOYS
SMILEY BURNETTE
BOB NOLAN AND SONS OF THE PIONEERS ★ PEGGY MORAN
TRADE SHOW
STUDIO ONE
THURS. DEC. 9. AT 11 A.M.
BRITISH LION
A Republic PICTURE
REPUBLIC PICTURES

British LION presents
ROY ROGERS King of the Cowboys
"TRIGGER" THE WORLD'S SMARTEST HORSE
SONG OF TEXAS
SHEILA RYAN • BARTON MacLANE • HARRY SHANNON
PAT BRADY ARLINE JUDGE
BOB NOLAN AND THE SONS OF THE PIONEERS
★ TRADE SHOW RIALTO
THURS. NOV. 25. AT 10-45 A.M.
A Republic PICTURE
BRITISH LION
REPUBLIC PICTURES

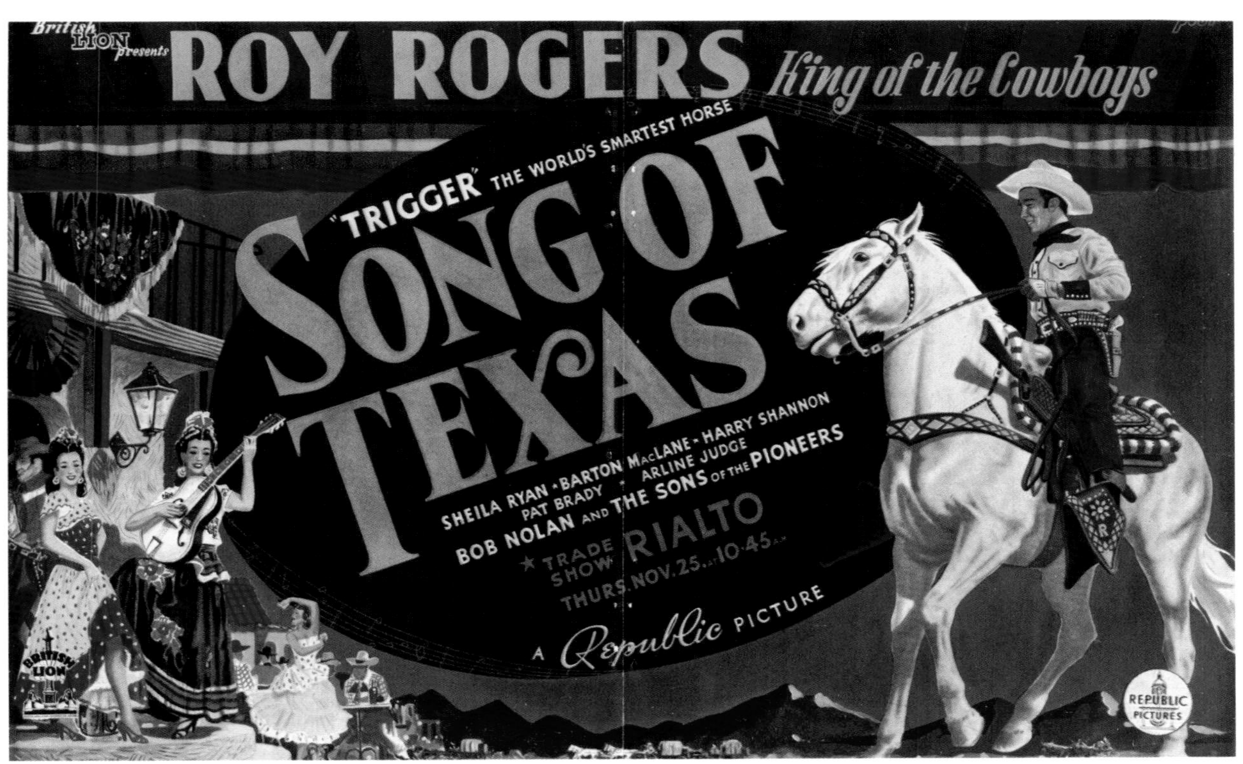

WHO'S WHO IN
western stars
25¢
DELL
ROY ROGERS
REX ALLEN
GENE AUTRY
RANDY SCOTT
ROCKY LANE
BILL BOYD
BILL ELLIOTT
500
OTHERS
Roy Rogers

BRITISH LION Presents
ROY
ROGERS
KING OF THE COWBOYS
TRIGGER
SMARTEST HORSE IN THE MOVIES
in
Home in
OKLAHOMA
REPUBLIC PICTURES
LONDON TRADE SHOW
JUNE 17
HAMMER THEATRE
11 a.m.
featuring GEORGE "GABBY" HAYES with DALE EVANS
BOB NOLAN & THE SONS OF THE PIONEERS

NEW EXCITEMENT...
NEW THRILLS...
NEW ADVENTURE!
BRITISH LION PRESENTS
ROY
ROGERS
in
ROMANCE ON THE
RANGE
with GEORGE (GABBY) HAYES
SALLY PAYNE • LINDA HAYES
A REPUBLIC PICTURE
TRADE SHOW
STUDIO ONE
WEDNESDAY-17 MARCH
11 A.M.
BRITISH LION FILM CORPORATION LIMITED

British LION presents
A Republic
PICTURE
ROY ROGERS
KING OF THE COWBOYS
WITH
GEORGE "Gabby" HAYES
IN
RIDIN'
DOWN THE
CANYON
TRADE SHOW RIALTO TUES. JULY 20. AT 11 A.M.

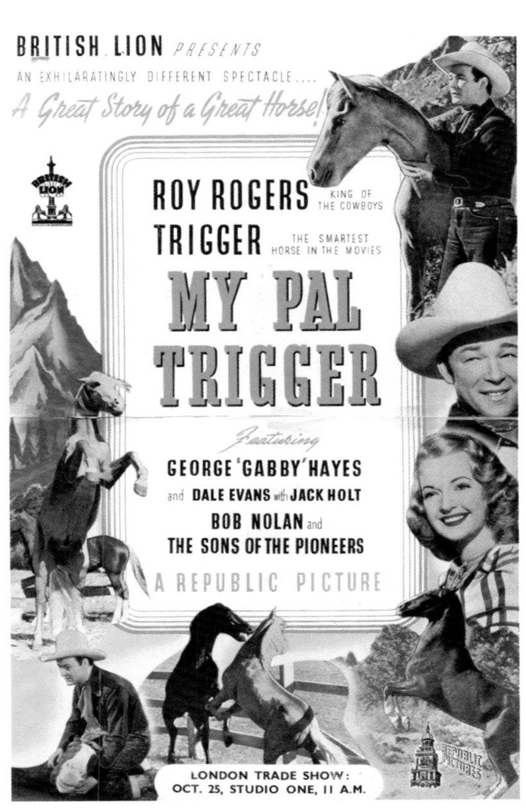
BRITISH LION PRESENTS
AN EXHILARATINGLY DIFFERENT SPECTACLE....
A Great Story of a Great Horse!
ROY ROGERS KING OF THE COWBOYS
TRIGGER THE SMARTEST HORSE IN THE MOVIES
MY PAL TRIGGER
featuring
GEORGE 'GABBY' HAYES
and DALE EVANS with JACK HOLT
BOB NOLAN and
THE SONS OF THE PIONEERS
A REPUBLIC PICTURE
LONDON TRADE SHOW:
OCT. 25, STUDIO ONE, 11 A.M.

50¢
ROY ROGERS
Official
SOUVENIR
PROGRAM

BRITISH LION presents
ROY ROGERS King of the
featuring GEORGE "GABBY" HAYES
DALE EVANS · BOB NOLAN and
the SONS OF THE PIONEERS
Directed by
FRANK McDONALD
A REPUBLIC PICTURE

Cowboys
TRIGGER Smartest Horse in the Movies
in
UNDER
NEVADA SKIES
LONDON TRADE SHOW
WEDNESDAY, FEB. 19
STUDIO ONE 11 a.m.

Burnette in place of Gabby Hayes). *The Cowboy and the Señorita* in 1944 offered a more palpable portent, however—an actress named Dale Evans was Roy's costar, a role she would fill many, many more times, both before and after Roy married her.

Of course, Roy Rogers didn't have the wartime playing field all to himself when it came to making cowboy movies. Names like Tex Ritter (another mighty fair singer), Tim Holt, Don "Red" Barry, Sunset Carson, Wild Bill Elliot (as Red Ryder, straight out of the Sunday funnies), Charles Starrett (as The Durango Kid), Smith Ballew, Bob Crosby ("The Singing Sheriff"), Allan "Rocky" Lane, Monte Hale, and George O'Brien all starred in multiple B-pictures each year—all of them feeding into what seemed to be the nation's insatiable appetite for uncomplicated movies about good-hearted, law-abiding heroes who forever rode across the silver screen on golden (or snow-white) steeds, perpetually in search of justice for the defenseless, unencumbered by anything resembling the actual realities of daily life (by either the standards of the Old West or present-day America). But by the standards of ten-year-old boys (and girls?) everywhere, they were akin to gods.

Then the war ended, which meant that Gene Autry would be returning to Hollywood and to Republic Studios, to pick up where he left off—and so he did, with pictures like *Sioux City Sue*. Roy continued his own skein of hits with *Under Nevada Skies* and *Roll on Texas Moon*. But there must not have been quite enough elbow room at Republic with both Gene and Roy vying for top dog status, because a year later, Gene departed for new pastures, making his home at Columbia Pictures. There he made movies like *The Cowboy and the Indians* and *Sons of New Mexico* (both 1949), their posters bearing the legend "A Gene Autry Production"—a rare perk for the day, though increasingly common for stars as the years went by.

This Mexican standoff between the royalty of movie cowboys entered a new arena at this time, as television was beginning to make its presence felt, and no doubt both Gene and Roy had taken note of the first strike recently made by Bill "Hoppy" Boyd, as well as the instantaneous success of ABC's *The Lone Ranger*. While they continued to make B-pictures for their respective studios, the superstars realized it was time to expand their quest for world domination to this new medium as well.

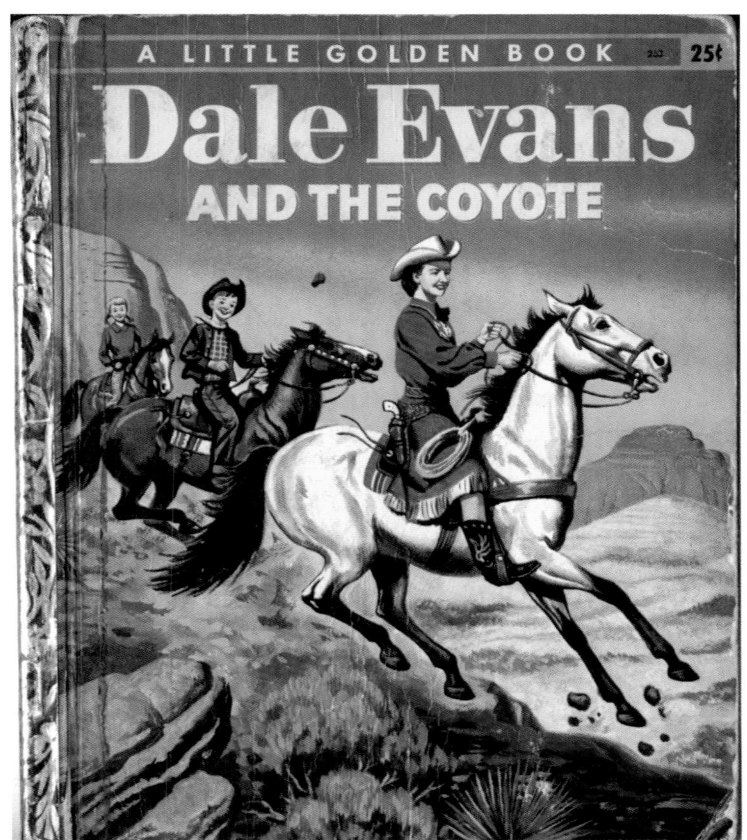
A LITTLE GOLDEN BOOK
25¢
Dale Evans
AND THE COYOTE

Roy Rogers
and Dale Evans

British LION presents
ROY ROGERS
KING OF THE COWBOYS
TRIGGER
SMARTEST HORSE IN THE MOVIES
HANDS ACROSS THE BORDER
RUTH TERRY
BOB NOLAN AND THE SONS OF THE PIONEERS
TRADE SHOW
Rialto
TUES. MAR. 21.
at
11. A.M.
A Republic PICTURE

"Best Wishes"
Roy Rogers, Dale Evans
&
Trigger

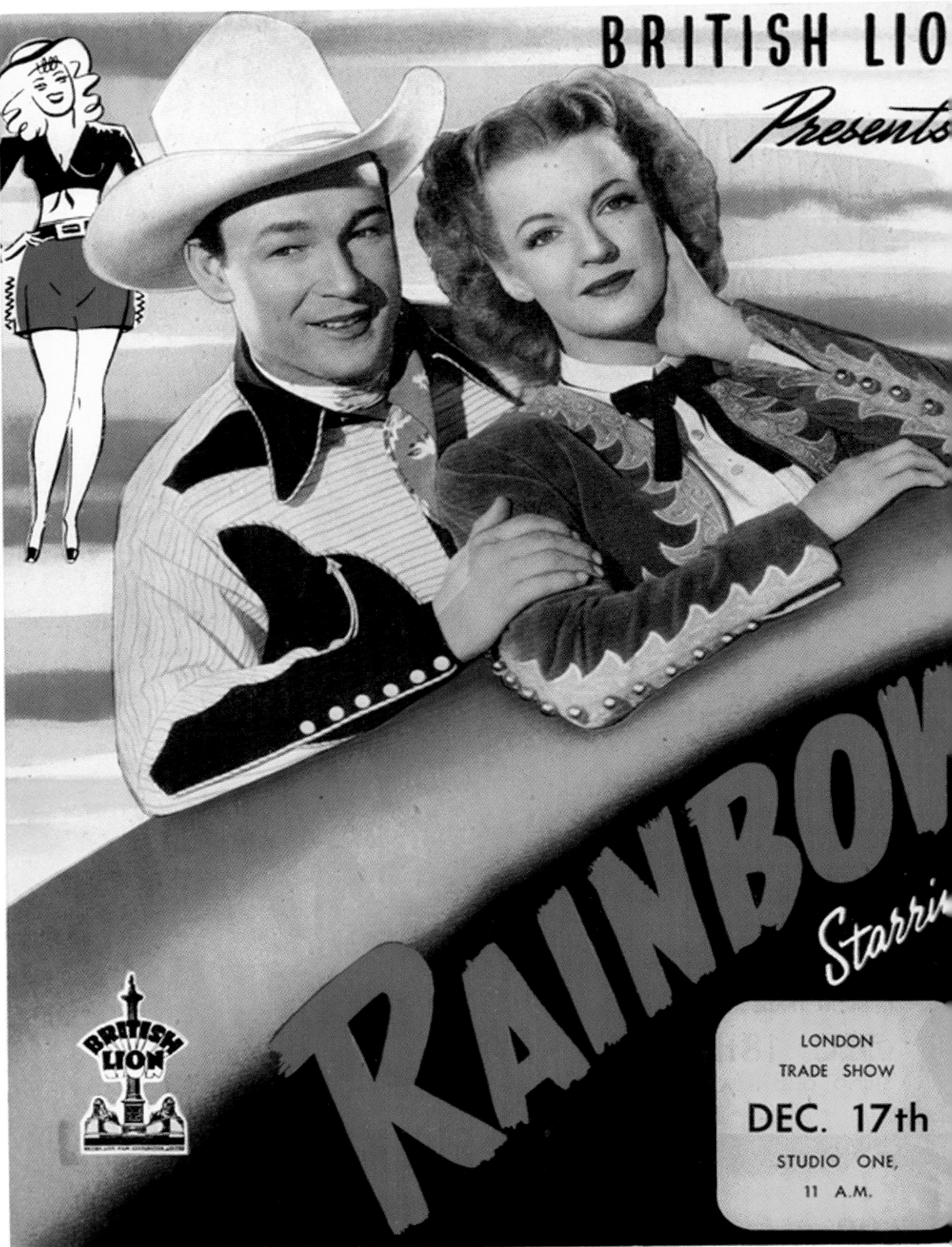

BRITISH LIO
Presents
RAINBOW
Starri
BRITISH LION
LONDON
TRADE SHOW
DEC. 17th
STUDIO ONE,
11 A.M.

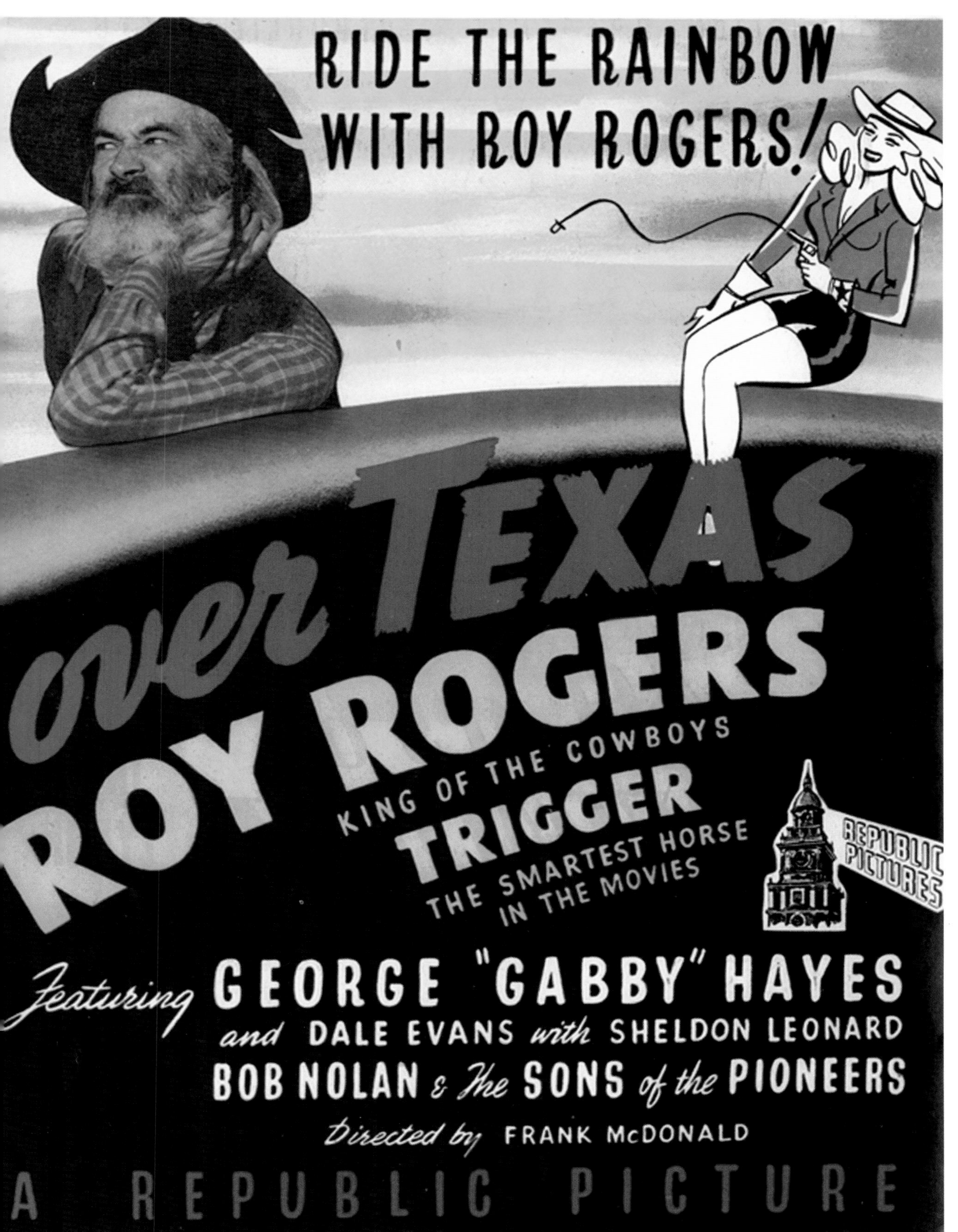
RIDE THE RAINBOW
WITH ROY ROGERS!
over TEXAS
ROY ROGERS
KING OF THE COWBOYS
TRIGGER
THE SMARTEST HORSE
IN THE MOVIES
REPUBLIC
PICTURES
Featuring GEORGE "GABBY" HAYES
and DALE EVANS with SHELDON LEONARD
BOB NOLAN & The SONS of the PIONEERS
Directed by FRANK McDONALD
A REPUBLIC PICTURE

Gene made it onto the air first, debuting on CBS in July 1950 with *The Gene Autry Show,* accompanied by Pat Buttram, his signature theme song "Back in the Saddle Again," and, of course, Champion. For some reason it took Roy quite a spell to get . . . cooking, but *The Roy Rogers Show* finally appeared on NBC on December 30, 1951, almost a year and a half later than Gene's debut. Gene's show ran into the summer of 1956 and Roy's until 1957, at which point the aging stars likely realized they could just as easily let their fortunes collect interest, instead of working so hard on weekly TV. But Roy did return for a few months in 1962 with *The Roy Rogers & Dale Evans Show*, a musical variety program whose guests included (of course) The Sons of the Pioneers.

By this point, the rest of the cowboy heroes had either followed Gene and Roy's transition from movies to television or been put out to pasture. Films were no longer the coin of the B-cowboy realm—the widespread adoption of location shooting in the bigger-budget westerns of the early fifties (such as *Broken Arrow, The Naked Spur, Shane,* and *Hondo,* to name just a few of the most memorable) had raised the stakes, making films that were shot on the cheap look patently ridiculous more often than not. Maybe it would be the deserts of Utah standing in for those of Arizona, or the mountains and forests of Canada standing in for Wyoming's, but by gum, that spectacular scenery was going to be as real as the grimy stubble

on the stars' formerly clean-shaven kissers. Which was fine for elite western stars like Jimmy Stewart, John Wayne and their like but hardly could be supported by their lessers—the cowboy stars who had once been idolized by generations of movie-going youngsters, but who now simply didn't possess the acting chops, or the screen presence, to carry an adult western film shot with an A-level budget and Academy Award aspirations.

So it was on to the wonderful world of television for a great many of those second- (and third-) tier cowboy actors. There, the cobbled together sets of plywood saloons and cardboard cactus would be less likely to disrupt the enjoyment of the audience, most of which (it must be remembered) was watching the proceedings on a humble twelve-inch screen in black-and-white. (Color TV was not widely accepted into American households until the sixties, and many programs continued to be shot in black-and-white until well into the latter half of the decade.) Those erstwhile cowboy heroes of the cheerfully tacky 58-minute B-pictures now would have a smaller, less grand range to ride. But even with those lowered expectations, many of this new breed of TV cowboys managed to ride their way into a stardom that came to rival that of their lionized big-screen brethren

And so ended the golden era of the cowboy star.

Until we meet again—Happy trails to you all!!

Raoul
The BIG
With JOHN WAYNE
MARGUERITE CHURCHILL • EL BRENDEL
TULLY MARSHALL • DAVID ROLLINS
• TYRONE POWER
and 20,000 others in an all-talking movietone romance
OREGON CITY
OLD FORT WALLA WALLA
FORT BOISE
FORT HALL
FORT BRIDGER
FOX

Walsh's
TRAI
Young love and courage sweep on to triumph in this
story of the winning of the West. Twenty thousand pioneers
magnificent migration, vanquishing Indian, bear, buffalo,
thrills await you in this, the most important picture ever
FORT LARAMIE
CHIMNEY ROCK
FORT KEARNEY
INDEPENDENCE

"CIM" BOOMS AHEAD
ROARS DOWN
SHOW TRAIL
TO ETERNAL
GLORY OF THE
SCREEN!
DON'T PULL
YOUR PUNCHES
when you play RKO-Radio's mammoth super attraction . . . now rushing headlong to record grosses in the subsequent runs.
CIMARRON
RICHARD
DIX
IRENE
DUNNE
AND
SUPERLATIVE
CAST . . . .
DIRECTED BY
WESLEY
RUGGLES
Nine smash weeks at the Globe New York at $2 with thousands still clamoring for admission . . . Terrific grosses in all keys . . . Start your pre-advance campaign NOW. Don't pull your punches when you work on "Cim". . .

William Fox presents
The Cisco Kid
"Be a good bandit, Cisco Kid, and let's be friends."
"How so, Sergeant?"
"You take my money and I'll take your girl."
That first outdoor talking feature, IN OLD ARIZONA, was just a sample of the vigorous outdoor action and panorama of scenery which only the technically perfected Fox Movietone can capture on film.
Here the Cisco Kid, played by WARNER BAXTER, attempts to outwit Serjeant Mickey Dunn, as played by EDMUND LOWE. Audiences are already waiting for this one.
Dialog by TOM BARRY
Directed by RAOUL WALSH

CHAPTER THREE

Hollywood Rides the Range: 101 Great Western Films

There are numerous silent-era westerns that were acclaimed in their day—films like *The Covered Wagon* (1923), *The Iron Horse* (1924) and *Riders of the Purple Sage* (1925), to name but three of dozens of worthies. But despite their pedigree—these were the A-list productions of the various studios, featuring bankable stars and a serious level of promotion—these movies are rarely seen today, and some of the most famous examples may not even exist anymore. Thus, the list that follows indicates my choices of what I would argue are the 101 most significant western films (leaving aside any of the cowboy hero B-pictures already discussed) of the sound era, with fledgling transitional efforts like *In Old Arizona* (the first Cisco Kid picture, adapted from O. Henry by director Raoul Walsh) and the creaky *The Virginian* (Gary Cooper acting—and speaking—in excruciating slow motion) discounted on the theory that no one today could bear to actually sit through them.

1) ***The Big Trail*** (1930)—The first major role for John Wayne, who immediately returned to a steady diet of B-pictures for the next nine years. This sprawling, expensive epic about a wagon train traveling the Oregon Trail was directed by Raoul Walsh, one of the five top directors of westerns during Hollywood's golden age—but it was not a financial success, despite heavy promotion.

2) ***Cimarron*** (1931)—Edna Ferber's 1930 bestseller was the basis for this A-list production, which covers the triumphs and travails of an

Oklahoma family between 1890 and 1915, when the territory was trying to attain statehood. One of the very few westerns ever to win the Academy Award for Best Picture, *Cimarron* starred Richard Arlen and Irene Dunne as the enterprising husband and wife who face a hundred obstacles. The film is best remembered today for its land-rush sequence, filmed outdoors with the proverbial cast of thousands.

3) ***Annie Oakley*** (1935)—George Stevens directed this winning (if highly imaginative) telling of the Oakley legend, with Barbara Stanwyck supplying the star power (in lovely cowgirl outfits) and Preston Foster as her sharpshooting beau. (Historical photographs of Oakley indicate she bore very little resemblance to Stanwyck, it should be noted.)

4) ***Last of the Mohicans*** (1936)—Not really a western? True—but at the time of its action, the French-Indian wars of the 1760s, even upper New York State and southern Quebec counted as the frontier. Randolph Scott is excellent as James Fenimore Cooper's archetypal Hawkeye, and Bruce Cabot is surprisingly effective as the evil Magua. Michael Mann's sumptuous 1992 version certainly plays as more authentic, but for the time it was made, this version is just fine.

5) ***The Plainsman*** (1936)—Gary Cooper has one of his signature roles in Cecil B. DeMille's typically overblown but highly entertaining recalibration of history—here a fanciful presentation of the adventures of Wild Bill Hickok and Calamity Jane. Let it be noted, as above with Annie Oakley, that (according to the historical photographs that have survived) Calamity Jane looked about as much like star Jean Arthur as Walter Brennan did. James Ellison portrays the dashing Buffalo Bill, while an obscure actor named John Miljan impersonates a noble George Custer. The two leads look as beautiful together as they did that same year in *Mr. Deeds Goes to Town*.

6) ***Rhythm on the Range*** (1936)—Bing Crosby got to indulge his true love of the West here by playing a ranch hand who croons to both cattle and the lovely Frances Farmer in this musical comedy. The Sons of the Pioneers back up the Bingster on his hit tune "I'm an Old Cowhand (from the Rio Grande)," and who is there amongst those singing Sons but young Leonard Slye, aka Dick Weston, aka (two years later) Roy Rogers.

7) ***Harlem on the Prairie*** (1937)—The first black-cast western, this oddity starred Herb Jeffries, formerly a vocalist with Duke Ellington's

AN A·B·F·D RELEASE
HARRY M. GOETZ presents
J. FENIMORE COOPER'S Immortal Romance
THE LAST OF THE MOHICANS
Directed by GEORGE B. SEITZ
Produced by EDWARD SMALL
with
RANDOLPH SCOTT
BINNIE BARNES
HENRY WILCOXON
BRUCE CABOT
HEATHER ANGEL
Trade Show: TUESDAY, DEC. 1ST at 11 a.m.
STUDIO ONE

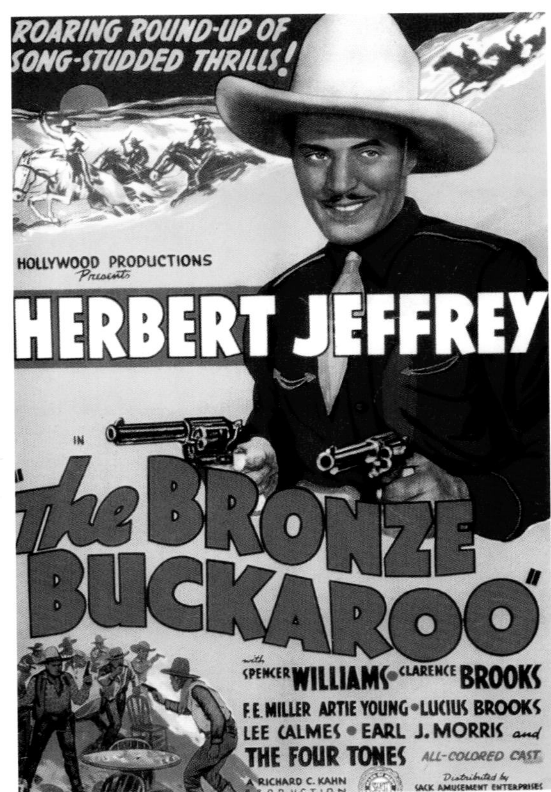
ROARING ROUND-UP OF SONG-STUDDED THRILLS!
HOLLYWOOD PRODUCTIONS Presents
HERBERT JEFFREY
IN
"The BRONZE BUCKAROO"
with
SPENCER WILLIAMS • CLARENCE BROOKS
F.E. MILLER ARTIE YOUNG • LUCIUS BROOKS
LEE CALMES • EARL J. MORRIS and
THE FOUR TONES
ALL-COLORED CAST
A RICHARD C. KAHN PRODUCTION
Distributed by SACK AMUSEMENT ENTERPRISES

WHEN HE'S Not Singin', HE'S Shootin'
WHEN HE'S Not Shootin', HE'S Lovin'—
ASTOR PICTURES Presents
"Two Gun" Louis
JORDAN
and his T-6
"LOOK-OUT Sister"
11 GREAT SONG HITS
Starring
SUZETTE HARBIN · MONTE HAWLEY
with
GLENN ALLEN · TOMMY SOUTHERN · JACK CLISBY
and introducing THE CHAMPION COWBOY
BOB SCOTT
Directed by BUD POLLARD
Produced by BERLE ADAMS

renowned band, who here handles both the horses and the crooning just fine. Later entries in the "race pictures" genre would include *Harlem Rides the Range* and *The Bronze Buckaroo* (both with Jeffries) and *Look-Out, Sister* (starring "jump" band leader Louis Jordan, of all people). Are these "great" westerns? No. But for African Americans at the time, this is what Hollywood gave them to call their own.

8) ***Way Out West*** (1937)—Laurel and Hardy were still among the top screen comedians when they made this gem. Set in Brushwood Gulch, the intrepid but wholly inept duo try to bequeath the deeds to a gold mine they are carrying to the daughter of their late partner. Needless to say, the bad guys intercede and give our lads a run for that money before Laurel and Hardy triumph. Considerably superior to the lone forays into the Old West by either The Marx Brothers (*Go West*) or W.C. Fields (*My Little Chickadee*), though both of the 1940 releases have their moments.

9) ***Wells Fargo*** (1937)—Joel McCrea is in peak form as one of the founders of that historic line, faced with a major problem when, during the Civil War, gold shipments being transported for the Union armies are intercepted by the Rebs. His chief suspect is his wife, a Confederate sympathizer, played by Frances Dee—McCrea's real-life wife at the time.

10) ***The Lone Ranger*** (1938)—This well-regarded fifteen-chapter Republic serial marked the first screen appearance of radio's star masked man; it starred the now-obscure Lee Powell as the Lone Ranger and Chief Thundercloud as Tonto. The serial was edited into a feature version for release two years later. Followed in 1939 by the less effective *The Lone Ranger Rides Again.*

11) ***Destry Rides Again*** (1939)—James Stewart was one of Hollywood's top leading men when he made this extremely loose adaptation of the Max Brand evergreen. The gimmick is that Stewart's deputy sheriff Destry refuses to wear a gun and orders only milk when he sidles up to the bar. Dancehall queen Marlene Dietrich has one of her most fondly recalled roles as Frenchy, the girlfriend of bad-guy Brian Donlevy; she soon falls for the soft-spoken Destry and serenades him with the unforgettable "See What the Boys in the Back Room Will Have." (Dietrich's mannerisms and enunciation were skillfully mocked by Madeleine Kahn in Mel Brooks' *Young Frankenstein* years later.)

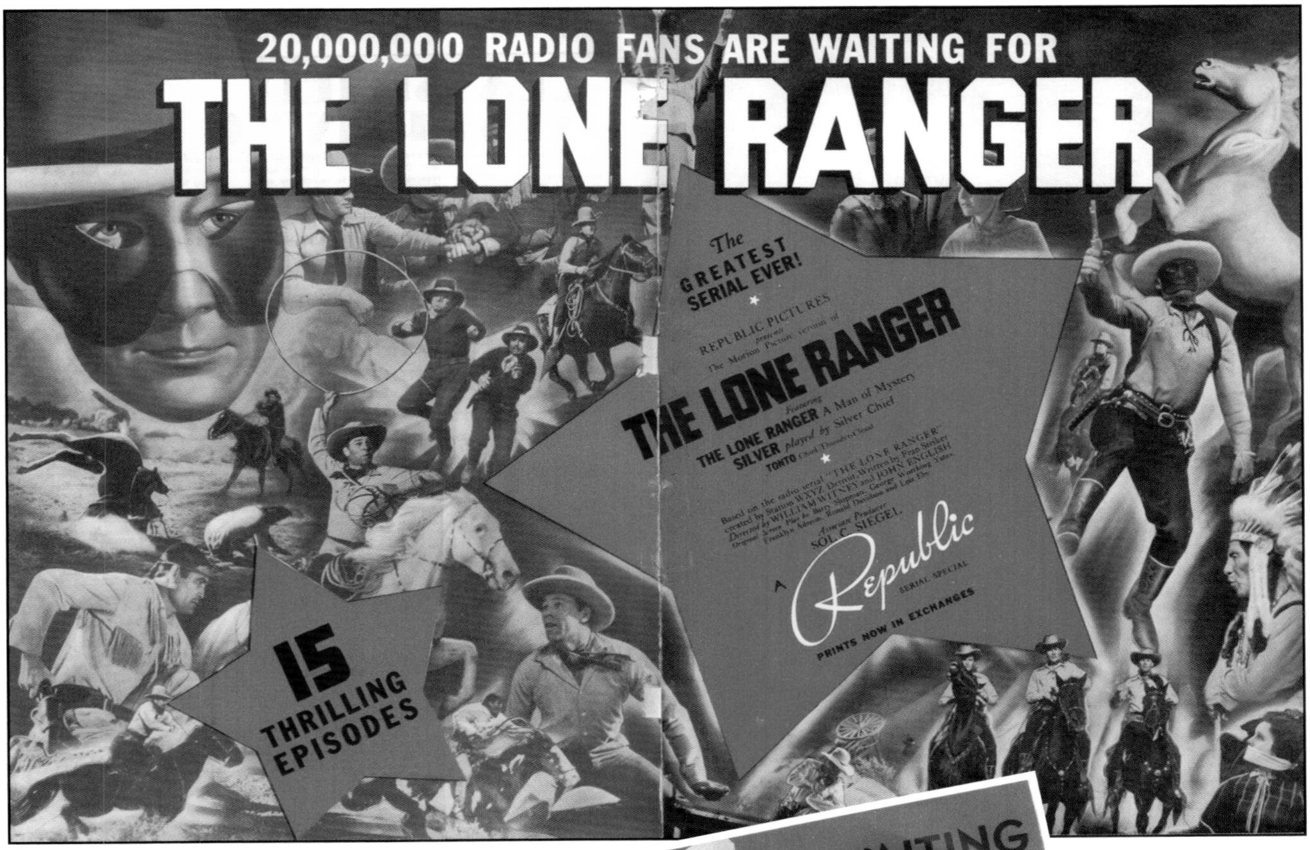
20,000,000 RADIO FANS ARE WAITING FOR
THE LONE RANGER
The GREATEST SERIAL EVER!
REPUBLIC PICTURES
presents
The Motion Picture version of
THE LONE RANGER
featuring
THE LONE RANGER A Man of Mystery
SILVER played by Silver Chief
TONTO Chief Thunder-Cloud
Associate Producer
SOL C. SIEGEL
A Republic SERIAL SPECIAL
PRINTS NOW IN EXCHANGES
15 THRILLING EPISODES

AFTER 4 YEARS OF WAITING
The picture with a four-year advance publicity and advertising campaign behind it!
Radio's greatest show is now the screen's greatest thrill sensation. All your phantom favorites brought to vital screen life. Just announce this one and your selling campaign is half done. But there's a 24-page campaign book, loaded with ready-made national tie-ups
HEIGH-YO, Silver!
REPUBLIC PICTURES
PRESENTS THE
MOTION PICTURE
VERSION OF
The
LONE
RANGER
WHO IS
THE LONE
RANGER?
Based on the radio serial "The Lone Ranger"
Created by Station WXYZ Detroit,
and written by Fran Striker
15
EPISODES
TONTO
A Republic SERIAL SPECIAL
Directed by
WILLIAM WITNEY
and JOHN ENGLISH
Original screen play by
Barry Shipman, Franklyn
Adreon, Ronald Davidson
and Lois Eby
Associate Producer
SOL. C. SIEGEL
with
THE LONE RANGER
A Man of Mystery
SILVER
Played by Silver Chief
TONTO
Chief Thunder-Cloud
and a supporting cast of screen favorites

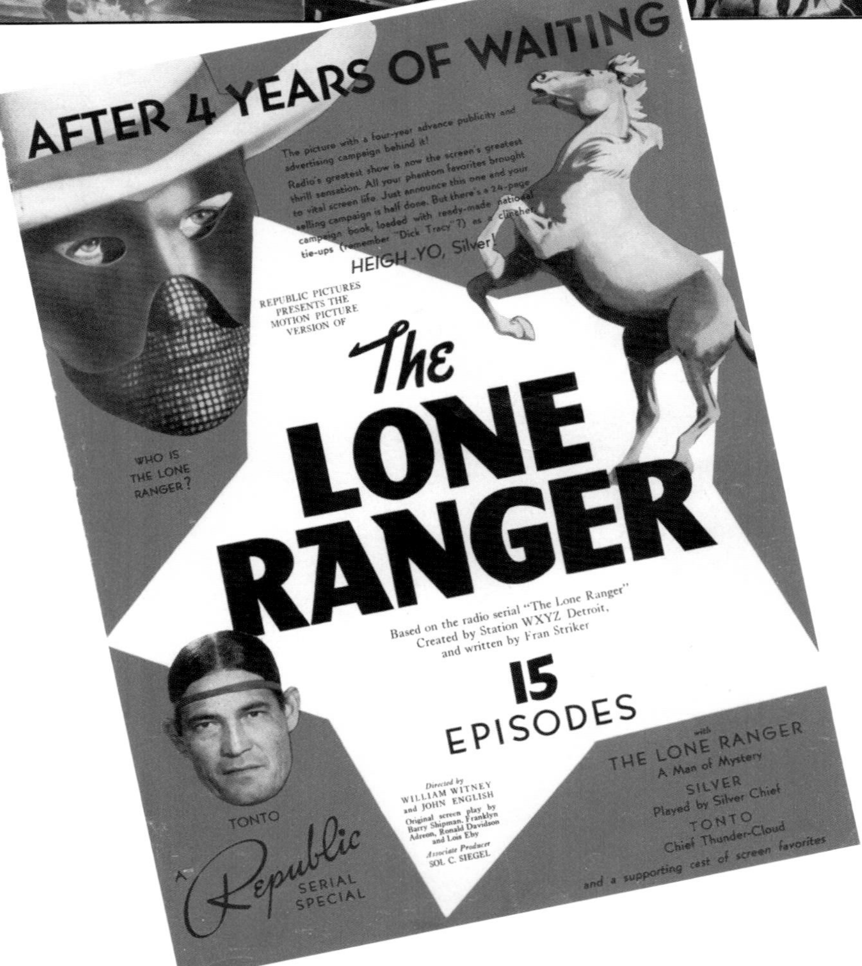

"West Of Chicago, There's No Law...West Of Dodge City, No God!"
ERROL FLYNN
DODGE CITY
in TECHNICOLOR
OLIVIA de HAVILLAND · ANN SHERIDAN
BRUCE CABOT · FRANK McHUGH · ALAN HALE · JOHN LITEL · HENRY TRAVERS
VICTOR JORY · WILLIAM LUNDIGAN
Directed by MICHAEL CURTIZ · ORIGINAL SCREEN PLAY BY ROBERT BUCKNER
MUSIC BY MAX STEINER
A WARNER BROS. PICTURE
THE GREATNESS OF AMERICA TODAY SPRANG FROM THOSE WHO BUILT IT!
The dashing sweethearts of 'Robin Hood' now face their most thrilling adventure!...
DODGE CITY Wide-Open Babylon of America... Hell-hole of the West!
SEE DREADED 'HELL STREET'... PAVED WITH HUMAN BLOOD!
SEE THE FEARFUL LONGHORN STAMPEDE, CRUSHING ALL LIFE BEFORE IT!
SEE DODGE CITY'S NOTORIOUS HOT SPOT...THE GAY LADY SALOON!
SEE THE WALKING GOLD OF TEXAS... BOOTY OF 100 BLOODY RANGE WARS!

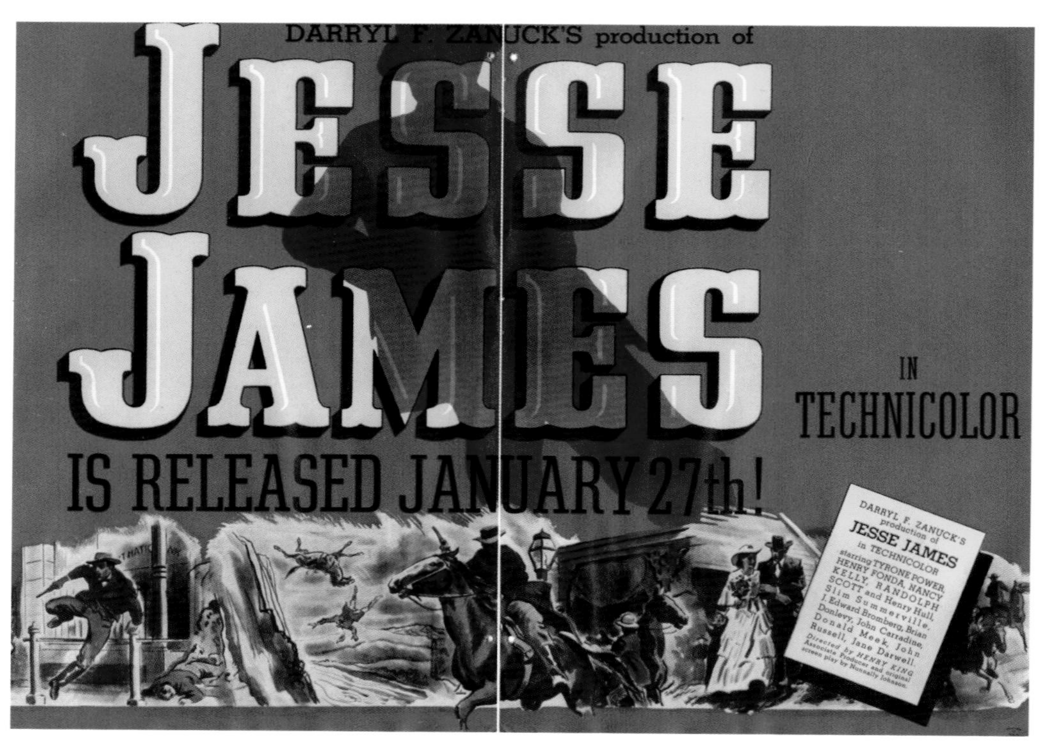
DARRYL F. ZANUCK'S production of
JESSE JAMES
IN TECHNICOLOR
IS RELEASED JANUARY 27th!
DARRYL F. ZANUCK'S production of
JESSE JAMES
in TECHNICOLOR
starring TYRONE POWER
HENRY FONDA, NANCY
KELLY, RANDOLPH
SCOTT and Henry Hull,
Slim Summerville,
J. Edward Bromberg, Brian
Donlevy, John Carradine,
Donald Meek, John
Russell, Jane Darwell
Directed by HENRY KING
Associate Producer and original
screen play by Nunnally Johnson

12) ***Dodge City*** (1939)—One of Errol Flynn's best movies, from perhaps the greatest year ever for Hollywood films, this is yet another epic saga based on the Wyatt Earp story. Ably helmed by top Warner's director Michael Curtiz, the film has a splendid cast that includes Olivia DeHavilland (always Flynn's most persuasive romantic interest), Ann Sheridan, and Bruce Cabot.

13) ***Drums Along the Mohawk*** (1939)—Like *Last of the Mohicans,* the setting of this pre-Revolutionary War picture is the Northeast, and so might seem to be out of place in this discussion. But for the settlers living in those then-remote outposts, days away from civilization, it sure must have *felt* like the frontier! Henry Fonda and Claudette Colbert are persuasive as the couple trying to homestead in the midst of Indian attacks and assorted other hardships. Based on the bestselling novel by Walter Edmonds and ably directed by John Ford. Edna May Oliver and John Carradine provide colorful support.

14) ***Jesse James*** (1939)—Matinee idol Tyrone Power was perhaps one of the least likely Hollywood superstars to be chosen to portray the legendary bandit, but he tried his best to downplay his ridiculously good looks to give a (rather far-fetched) portrayal of James as a misunderstood knight taking on corrupt railroad agents. Henry Fonda was cast as Frank James, and John Carradine as a memorable Bob Ford. The film's huge commercial success led Fox to assign Fonda immediately to the sequel, *The Return of Frank James.*

Many versions of Jesse's life and legend would follow, including Sam Fuller's 1949 directorial debut, *I Shot Jesse James,* and Nicholas Ray's 1957 *The True Story of Jesse James,* which, true to the zeitgeist of the day, gives the tale a juvenile delinquent spin.

15) ***Stagecoach*** (1939)—One of John Ford's greatest achievements, this historic drama, based on a short story by Ernest Haycox, presents a motley group of passengers who are making their way via stagecoach across a peril-packed route (shot on location in Monument Valley) to the town of Lordsburg. One of them is the Ringo Kid (memorably played by John Wayne), an ex-con and the only one among the group who possesses the survival skills to keep them all alive. Claire Trevor, John Carradine, and

Thomas Mitchell (who won an Oscar) also excel as members of this band of flawed travelers.

Generally considered one of the most important westerns ever made, *Stagecoach* not only rescued Wayne from his B-picture purgatory but also demonstrated to the Hollywood studios that there was a viable audience for quality adult westerns. That in turn led to a reapportioning of Hollywood's acting, directing, and writing talent, thus opening the doors wide for the making of more A-list westerns.

16) ***Union Pacific*** (1939)—Another epic from the hyperbolic imagination of Cecil B. DeMille. Joel McCrea, barely recovered from establishing the Wells Fargo line, here portrays the overseer of the Union Pacific company's Herculean effort to build the first transcontinental railroad—still one of the most staggering achievements in the history of America. Barbara Stanwyck lends her usual firecracker support, and Brian Donlevy plays a gambler who wants that effort to fail. One of the film's highlights is a spectacular train wreck that probably only DeMille would have had the sand to attempt staging.

17) ***The Dark Command*** (1940)—Raoul Walsh's version of the Quantrill's Raiders saga, complete with the razing of the town of Lawrence, Kansas, with Walter Pidgeon (here called "Cantrill" for some reason) as the leader of the Confederate guerrilla band and John Wayne as the marshal sworn to bring him to justice. Claire Trevor is the love interest for both men, but the film's big surprise is that her quick-gun brother is played by Roy Rogers. Even Gabby Hayes is along for the ride, this being a Republic film.

18) ***Geronimo*** (1940)—Chief Thundercloud, recently seen in the two Lone Ranger serials as Tonto, here became the first Native American to be cast as the (at least nominal) protagonist in a Hollywood movie. Unfortunately, his Geronimo was on screen far less than Paramount contract players Preston Foster and Ellen Drew. Another biopic by the same name was released in 1962, with Chuck (*The Rifleman*) Connors absurdly cast as the legendary Apache warrior. Probably the best version to date is the 1993 TNT movie directed by Walter Hill, with Wes Studi quite fine as Geronimo, supported by Gene Hackman as General Crook and Robert Duvall as an Indian scout.

19) ***The Mark of Zorro*** (1940)—Still the best of the many permutations of Zorro movies, even after all these years, thanks to the derring-do of Tyrone Power (never better), the villainy of Basil Rathbone (never oilier), and the beauty of Linda Darnell (never lovelier). Director Rouben Mamoulian can take a lion's share of the credit for this one. There had been low-budget Zorro serials released in 1936 and 1937, as well as the famous silent film with Douglas Fairbanks.

20) ***Santa Fe Trail*** (1940)—Not the best of Errol Flynn's westerns for Warners, given his pallid characterization of Confederate General Jeb Stuart, but the film still rates a look for Raymond Massey's vivid portrayal of abolitionist John Brown, whose attack on Harper's Ferry is well staged by director Michael Curtiz. Lovely Olivia De Havilland is just window dressing here, however, and as for Ronald Reagan's cameo as the young George Custer—the less said the better.

A GREAT NEW SCREEN PERSONALITY! ...Miss GENE TIERNEY FLAMES TO STARDOM AS "THE BANDIT QUEEN"!
No woman was ever a more tender sweetheart...or a more relentless champion of right!
BELLE STARR
THE BANDIT QUEEN
RANDOLPH SCOTT
with
GENE TIERNEY
and
Dana Andrews • John Shepperd
Elizabeth Patterson • Chill Wills
Directed by Irving Cummings
Associate Producer Kenneth Macgowan
Screen Play by Lamar Trotti
Story by Niven Busch and Cameron Rogers
IN TECHNICOLOR
WATCH FOR TRADE SHOWING ANNOUNCEMENTS!

21) ***The Westerner*** (1940)—Gary Cooper had one of his best roles here as a drifter who wanders into the town run by Judge Roy Bean and lives to regret it. Walter Brennan won an Oscar for his indelible portrait of the murderously nutty Bean, whom Coop barely manages to outwit in the film's memorable conclusion. One could only wish that William Wyler—then at his artistic peak—had chosen to direct more westerns.

22) ***Belle Starr*** (1941)—The beautiful but stoic Gene Tierney is somewhat miscast here as the southern "Bandit Queen" of legend, who carries the fight to the carpetbagging Yankees in the years immediately after the Civil War, marrying Reb guerrilla fighter Randolph Scott in the process. The biopic trend in Hollywood was still picking up steam at this juncture.

23) ***Honky Tonk*** (1941)—Clark Gable seems to be having fun playing a con man who meets his match in the person of a young Lana Turner. The great Claire Trevor is here relegated to the thankless role of the dance-hall girl whom Gable ditches to take up with the more staid Lana. Gable would be given more and better roles in westerns as the fifties dawned.

24) ***They Died with Their Boots On*** (1941)—Flynn again, this time as General George Custer himself. As imagined by director Raoul Walsh, this well-barbered Custer was both a friend to the Indian as well as a man struggling with a deep identity crisis. (Well, one out of two isn't bad.) Leaving aside the hagiography typical of Hollywood movies of the time, this is an action-packed account of one of history's most controversial figures. De Havilland is cast again as Flynn's love interest, for the final time.

25) ***Western Union*** (1941)—Fritz Lang directed this thrilling account of the early days of Western Union's attempts to establish telegraph lines throughout the West. Randolph Scott is impressive as the ex-outlaw who scouts for them as the lines go up, while Barton MacLane excels as Scott's dastardly brother, who is bent on foiling the plans of the company. Robert Young costars but pales by comparison.

26) ***The Spoilers*** (1942)—John Wayne and Randolph Scott are colorful opponents in this third filming of the Rex Beach novel, with Marlene Dietrich back again as the dance-hall girl who ultimately decides to side with Right. The epic fistfight at the finale is the main reason to watch this picture today.

27) ***The Outlaw*** (1943/1946)—Though not really released until 1946, this legendary obsession of RKO Studio boss Howard Hughes began filming in 1941. Pneumatic teenager Jane Russell was rescued from obscurity to toil under Hughes' maniacally detailed eye for the next two years as the Mexican hottie who captures the eye of Jack Buetel, here a bit over his head as Billy the Kid. Old pros Walter Huston and Thomas Mitchell fare better as, respectively, Doc Holliday and Pat Garrett. Howard Hawks "co-directed" with Hughes—*that* must have been fun! But Jane was the entire focal point of the advertising—"Mean . . . Moody . . . Magnificent!" went one tagline. Billy the Who?

28) ***The Ox-Bow Incident*** (1943)—William Wellman's somber drama about the ugliness of the mob mentality was certainly the most serious western made in Hollywood to that point. Dana Andrews, Anthony Quinn, and Francis Ford play cowboys who are wrongly accused of cattle rustling and

hanged on the flimsiest of evidence by the outraged mob, as dissenters Henry Fonda and Henry Morgan stand by helplessly. It soon comes to light that the actual rustlers have been caught, and so the mob must face their own inhumanity. Criticized in some quarters as being pretentious, the film does retain its moral force today, however stilted it sometimes comes across.

29) ***Duel in the Sun*** (1946)—This over-the-top melodrama was David O. Selznick's vainglorious attempt to turn wife Jennifer Jones into the world's greatest—and most desirable—movie star. It was credited to director King Vidor, who actually quit partway through because of Selznick's endless interference, leading to a parade of replacement directors, supposedly including Selznick himself. This superheated lust-fest, said to have been the biggest box-office western of the decade, was based on the novel by Niven Busch. *Duel* featured brothers Gregory Peck and Joseph Cotten at each other's throats over the prospect of bedding down half-breed spitfire Jones, who leads them both to their doom (not to mention her own). Suffice it to say, there is no other western quite like *Duel,* for better or worse. Watching it today remains a genuine guilty pleasure.

30) ***My Darling Clementine*** (1946)—John Ford's elegiac and idiosyncratic telling of the Earp saga, based as so many of the Earp films were on the Stuart Lake novel, features Henry Fonda as Wyatt Earp, Victor Mature as consumptive Doc Holliday, and a wonderful supporting cast that included Walter Brennan, Tim Holt, Linda Darnell, Jane Darnell, and Ward Bond. The final shootout comes as almost an afterthought following Ford's masterly vignettes leading up to it. If this list was only ten films long, *Clementine* would still be present.

31) ***Pursued*** (1947)—Robert Mitchum had been acting in westerns for years, including the Zane Grey B-picture *Nevada,* but this was his first mature work in the genre. Perhaps the first truly psychological western, *Pursued* has director Raoul Walsh at the helm of Niven Busch's complex story, much of it told in flashback, with Mitchum's childhood trauma as the key to his recklessness and nihilism as an adult. Teresa Wright, Dean Jagger, and the always frightening Dame Judith Anderson lend the film overtones of Hitchcock's *Spellbound,* a hit two years earlier.

32) ***Blood on the Moon*** (1948)—Mitchum excels again in another proto-psychological western, this one directed by RKO's master of creepy atmos-

pherics, Robert Wise. Robert Preston plays Mitchum's twisted mentor, and Barbara Bel Geddes is the rancher who inspires Mitchum to renounce Preston for the forces of good. Walter Brennan and Tom Tyler furnished able support, but it's Mitchum's show all the way.

33) ***Fort Apache*** (1948)—John Ford's sublime trilogy about the cavalry begins with this dissection of a military martinet—convincingly rendered by Henry Fonda, in one of the least sympathetic parts of his career—who arrives at Fort Apache to take command, a task for which he is woefully unqualified. John Wayne, as his savvy second-in-command, does his damnedest to subtly teach him the ropes—but he might as well be talking to a block of granite and cannot stop the vainglorious, Custer-like Fonda from rushing to his doom and taking some unfortunate soldiers with him. Ford stock company hearties Ward Bond and Victor McLaglen are well supported here by John Agar and, in one of her first mature roles, Shirley Temple.

34) ***The Paleface*** (1948)—Bob Hope has rarely been better than in this satire, with Jane Russell as undercover government agent Calamity Jane, and Hope the hapless dentist (Painless Potter, to be precise) whom she marries as a cover while she tries to find the parties responsible for supplying guns to hostile Indians.

35) ***Red River*** (1948)—Borden Chase adapted his *Saturday Evening Post* story in this classic yarn about a cattle drive and a whole lot more. Howard Hawks directs John Wayne as an intractable blowhard of a father and Montgomery Clift as his adopted son, the two of them at constant loggerheads about how their huge herd of cattle should be driven to Abilene. An epic in every sense of the word.

36) ***Colorado Territory*** (1949)—Raoul Walsh's pure western version of W. R. Burnett's novel *High Sierra,* which Walsh had filmed in 1941 as a gangster movie that just happened to be set in the contemporary West. Joel McCrea here replaces Humphrey Bogart as the doomed criminal who is loved by a good woman (here, Virginia Mayo), but who just can't stay alive long enough to enjoy it. Shot by Walsh as more of a film noir than *High Sierra* was, this is a rare case of a major director rethinking one of his key works and then filming it again.

"Men are lost and gone forever
when they go for Clementine!"
Darryl F. Zanuck presents
JOHN FORD'S
MY DARLING
CLEMENTINE
HENRY FONDA · LINDA DARNELL · VICTOR MATURE
WITH WALTER BRENNAN · TIM HOLT · CATHY DOWNS
Directed by JOHN FORD · Produced by SAMUEL G. ENGEL
THE NEW 20th CENTURY-FOX HIT!

Duel in the Sun
The intensely dramatic novel of the American Southwest, from which
the David O. Selznick technicolor film was made, starring JENNIFER JONES,
GREGORY PECK & JOSEPH COTTEN. A Forum Motion Picture Edition.
Niven Busch

JOHN FORD'S MASTERPIECE OF THE FRONTIER!
JOHN FORD and MERIAN C. COOPER
present
JOHN WAYNE
HENRY FONDA
SHIRLEY TEMPLE
PEDRO ARMENDARIZ
FORT
APACHE
Directed by
JOHN FORD
Screen play by Frank Nugent
as suggested by The Saturday Evening Post
story "Massacre" by James Warner Bellah
AN ARGOSY PICTURE
Released thru RKO Radio Pictures, Inc.
A real picture and a great one. It's got sweep and scope, human scenes straight from the shoulder. There are long, lean cavalrymen . . . their women . . . fighting . . . humor. You can smell the heat and the dust. In other words, this is motion picture!
JOHN WAYNE as Capt. York
HENRY FONDA as Colonel Thursday
SHIRLEY TEMPLE as Philadelphia Thursday
PEDRO ARMENDARIZ as Sergeant Beaufort
WARD BOND as Sergeant O'Rourke
GEORGE O'BRIEN as Capt. Collingwood
VICTOR McLAGLEN as Sergeant Mulcahy
ANNA LEE as Mrs. Collingwood
IRENE RICH as Mrs. O'Rourke
DICK FORAN as Sergeant Quincannon
GUY KIBBEE as Dr. Wilkins
GRANT WITHERS as Meacham
MAE MARSH as Mrs. Gates
and introducing JOHN AGAR as Mickey O'Rourke

37) ***She Wore a Yellow Ribbon*** (1949)—The second of John Ford's cavalry trilogy, now with John Wayne as the wise commander of the post that has survived an endless number of Indian attacks. Wayne wants to talk peace, even if it means he has to risk his life by taking his offer directly to the Indians' camp. A stately, elegiac film that likely couldn't have been made even five years earlier. McLaglen is joined in supporting roles by the great Ben Johnson, John Agar, and Joanne Dru.

38) ***Annie Get Your Gun*** (1950)—It was a big deal to transfer Irving Berlin's smash Broadway musical to film, but the difficulties that plagued the production, with Judy Garland having to drop out due to one of her frequent bouts with illness, became almost as legendary as the show itself. But Betty Hutton does well enough as a hyperkinetic Annie Oakley, and Howard Keel is reliable as sharpshooter Frank Butler. MGM knew how to do this stuff, and here they did it well, again.

39) ***Broken Arrow*** (1950)—Based on the excellent novel by Elliot Arnold, this classic tale delineates the unique relationship between cavalry scout Tom Jeffords and Apache chief Cochise, as between them they try to tamp down the full-bore Indian war that threatens to break out almost monthly. The problem is the stifling policies of both the occupying soldiers and the politicians who gave them their marching orders, along with the hot-headed attacks on the settlers led by Geronimo and his band of hostile Apaches. In the course of coming to know Cochise (well played by Jewish actor Jeff Chandler), Jeffords is invited into the tribe and eventually marries Cochise's daughter (Debra Paget). But she is killed during a surprise attack by the cavalry forces, and Jeffords can only share in Cochise's grief. A moving film, effectively directed by Delmar Daves.

40) ***The Gunfighter*** (1950)—Gregory Peck has rarely been better than in this measured portrait of an aging gunfighter who has become sick to death of having to uphold his reputation. And now a cocky, new young gun wants to make his rep by taking out Peck's walking (but now weary) legend. The suspense as Peck sits in a saloon, awaiting the arrival of the kid, is masterful (direction by Henry King). The story belongs to director Andre de Toth, who himself made some fine, dark westerns during his long career.

In The John Ford Tradition of Greatness
JOHN FORD AND MERIAN C. COOPER
present
SHE WORE A YELLOW RIBBON
JOHN WAYNE
in his most heroic role as Captain Brittles of the U.S. Cavalry
Starring
JOHN WAYNE · JOANNE DRU · JOHN AGAR
BEN JOHNSON · HARRY CAREY JR.
with VICTOR McLAGLEN · MILDRED NATWICK · GEORGE O'BRIEN · ARTHUR SHIELDS
Story by JAMES WARNER BELLAH · Screen Play by FRANK NUGENT and LAURENCE STALLINGS
DIRECTED BY JOHN FORD
COLOR BY TECHNICOLOR
Produced by ARGOSY PICTURES CORPORATION · Distributed by RKO RADIO PICTURES

From those who have thrilled to its blazing action-the thunder of its drama-the sweep of its magnificent production... comes the word-
IN 25 YEARS-
ONLY THREE!
"COVERED WAGON" · "CIMARRON"
AND NOW-
HOWARD HAWKS' GREAT PRODUCTION
"RED RIVER"
"DON'T MISS RED RIVER!"
Monterey Productions presents
HOWARD HAWKS'
"RED RIVER"
starring JOHN WAYNE · MONTGOMERY CLIFT
WALTER BRENNAN · JOANNE DRU
With HARRY CAREY, Sr. · COLEEN GRAY · JOHN IRELAND · NOAH BEERY, Jr. · HARRY CAREY, Jr. · PAUL FIX
From the Saturday Evening Post story, "The Chisholm Trail", by Borden Chase · Screenplay by Borden Chase and Charles Schnee
Executive Producer, CHARLES K. FELDMAN · DIRECTED AND PRODUCED BY HOWARD HAWKS · RELEASED THRU UNITED ARTISTS
COMING TO YOUR FAVORITE THEATRE!

THE BIG TECHNICOLOR SPECTACLE!
A year in the making! Hundreds in the cast! A fortune to bring it to you!
SHE FOUGHT LIKE A TIGRESS ON HER WEDDING DAY!
The love story of the primitive Indian beauty and the white trapper is one of the screen's most exciting romances!
CLARK GABLE
M-G-M PRESENTS
ACROSS THE WIDE MISSOURI
ONLY THE BIG MOVIE SCREEN CAN PICTURE SUCH GIANT THRILLS!
AMBUSCADE
...Flaming arrows and merciless tomahawks.... the war cries of painted redskins...and the doughty band of frontiersmen is surrounded!
RACE FOR LIFE
Through a gauntlet of screaming savages and into greater peril .... the trackless wilderness!
RENDEZVOUS
Where roistering men revel through the night .... and a free-for-all is the smashing climax!
LOVE-VENGEANCE
...An embittered adventurer locks in deadly struggle with the red renegade.....Chief of the Blackfeet!
CO-STARRING
RICARDO MONTALBAN · JOHN HODIAK
with ADOLPHE MENJOU · J. CARROL NAISH · JACK HOLT
and introducing
MARÍA ELENA MARQUÉS
AN M-G-M PICTURE
GABLE...
As you like him best . . . rough, rugged, romantic in one of his greatest roles!
RICARDO MONTALBAN
JOHN HODIAK
ADOLPHE MENJOU
J. CARROL NAISH
Suggested by BERNARD DeVOTO's book

41) ***Wagon Master*** (1950)—John Ford is on record as calling this the favorite of all his works, and while few would agree that it deserves the very top spot, it is a fine piece of work. Ben Johnson gives a typically satisfying performance as the drifter who, with the help of partner Harry Carey, Jr. first rescues from outlaw hands and then leads out of the wilderness a band of Mormons who dream of settling in a community of their own. Ward Bond is a standout as the Mormon leader, and Ford favorite Joanne Dru is her usual spunky self.

42) ***Winchester '73*** (1950)—In one of James Stewart's landmark westerns, he teams for the first time with the director who in the fifties established himself as a master of the genre—Anthony Mann. The story is one of revenge, as Stewart is forced to chase down and then battle an array of very scary bad guys—first Steven McNally, who murders Stewart's dad and then steals his prize Winchester, then psycho-killer Dan Duryea, who has managed to acquire the precious rifle after McNally is vanquished. Hard as nails for ninety-two thrilling minutes, *Winchester '73* set a new standard for what the adult western could aspire to.

43) ***Across the Wide Missouri*** (1951)—Clark Gable is in fine fettle as a brawling fur trapper in 1820s Colorado, with Maria Elena Marques as the Blackfoot maiden he falls in love with and John Hodiak and Ricardo Montalban as, respectively, his friend and his foe. William Wellman pulls no punches in showing how the encroachment of the white man spoiled an (almost) virgin wilderness.

44) ***Rawhide*** (1951)—Tyrone Power has rarely been better than in this taut drama about a stagecoach way station held hostage by a band of murderous outlaws, the creepiest being Jack Elam at his psychopathic best (worst?). Susan Hayward registers well as the object of the outlaws' menacing leers. First-class suspense about people in serious jeopardy, expertly presented by veteran action director Henry Hathaway.

45) ***Bend of the River*** (1952)—James Stewart joins forces with Anthony Mann in crafting this first-class drama about an ex-outlaw (Stewart) who joins with his supposedly reformed partner (Arthur Kennedy) to help shepherd a group of would-be settlers to what they dream will be their promised land. A thousand hardships follow, the most perilous of which becomes the betrayal by Kennedy that leaves the settlers without food and Stewart

exposed to die on the top of Mt. Hood. One of the most eloquent arguments ever made for westerns to be shot entirely on location. (The river bend alluded to in the title is the Snake River.)

46) ***High Noon*** (1952)—Gary Cooper is most closely identified with his Oscar-winning role in this much-celebrated drama, though its reputation and awards have dulled somewhat since 1952. Even so, it is hard not to be caught up in the tension as the film unfolds in real time, as a ticking clock draws ever closer to the noon hour, when the gunman who has sworn to kill Coop—who sent him to prison—arrives on the train with his cohorts. Fred Zinnemann directed—none too subtly, typical of a Stanley Kramer production. Grace Kelly, as Coop's Quaker wife, appears a bit over her head here, in one of her first screen appearances. Tex Ritter sings the memorable, Oscar-winning theme song (but we prefer the Frankie Laine cover version).

47) ***The Lusty Men*** (1952)—Robert Mitchum has one of his best roles as an ex-rodeo rider who mentors newcomer Arthur Kennedy but then creates a mess when he finds himself attracted to Kennedy's wife, the feisty Susan Hayward. Nick Ray directed this, one of his rare westerns, with panache.

48) ***Rancho Notorious*** (1952)—Fritz Lang was hardly associated with the western genre, but this delirious exercise in revenge has deservedly become a cult favorite since it was released. Marlene Dietrich is at her florid best as Altar Keane, the proprietress of the outlaw hideout known as Rancho Notorious, and Arthur Kennedy is the man who infiltrates it on the pretense of being an outlaw in need of safe harbor—but who really only seeks revenge on the gunsels hiding out there who killed his wife. *Rancho* wasn't even shot on location—the cheapo sets are actually laughable at times—but oddly, the effect is to make the picture stick with you.

49) ***Viva Zapata!*** (1952)—Marlon Brando played the legendary revolutionary in this prestigious Elia Kazan picture, but it was Anthony Quinn who reeled in an Oscar for his performance as Zapata's thuggish brother. Made at the height of the HUAC investigations, the implicit socialist message was toned down dramatically by the powers at MGM, who didn't want to be accused of making Commie propaganda. John Steinbeck penned the screenplay and thus contributed directly to the undermining of his own novel.

50) ***Arrowhead*** (1953)—Charlton Heston is actually the heavy, here playing a nasty cavalry scout who faces off against an imposing Jack Palance as Toriano, chief of the Apaches who does not want his people transported to a reservation in Florida—sensibly enough. A fine, tough western, regrettably overlooked today, that was written and directed with authority by the reliable Charles Marquis Warren.

51) ***Hondo*** (1953)—John Wayne had one of his favorite roles in this very handsome Louis L'Amour adaptation and served as the producer as well. John Farrow, rarely associated with westerns, directed Wayne to good advantage, and the fine supporting cast included Geraldine Page, Ward Bond, and James Arness (a few years before the Duke proposed him for the lead role on *Gunsmoke*). Great location shooting in the deserts of New Mexico makes this one a keeper.

52) ***The Naked Spur*** (1953)—One of the very best psychological westerns of the decade. A high-water mark in the career of the great James Stewart, this Anthony Mann-directed classic features memorable villainy (the peerless Robert Ryan), conflicted heroism (Stewart himself, tortured as only he can play, à la *Vertigo*), and, as the nominal love interest, Janet Leigh in a rare bad-girl role. All this, and spectacular location scenery too, courtesy of the Rockies.

53) ***Shane*** (1953)—Highly praised at the time of its release, George Stevens' epic (some would say ponderous) adaptation of the wonderful Jack Shaefer novel from 1949 pumps up the mythic elements to an almost laughable level (at least to modern-day eyes). Let's start with the casting of 5' 6" Alan Ladd as the tall, dark, unconquerable brooder of the book—what was Stevens thinking? (And I won't even get into that pristine buckskin-fringed outfit of his . . .) Jean Arthur, always a fine actress, hardly strikes sparks with Ladd the way the film wants us to believe, but Van Heflin is very good as Brandon de Wilde's dad, and Jack Palance earned a permanent mark in cinema history as his black-clad, remorseless killer whom Shane must eventually confront, mano a mano. All in all, *Shane* is still worth seeing for its many virtues (location photography among them), but it sure helps if you are twelve years old during your first viewing.

54) ***Apache*** (1954)—Burt Lancaster has one of his best roles here, as an Apache renegade who once rode with Geronimo and now refuses to follow

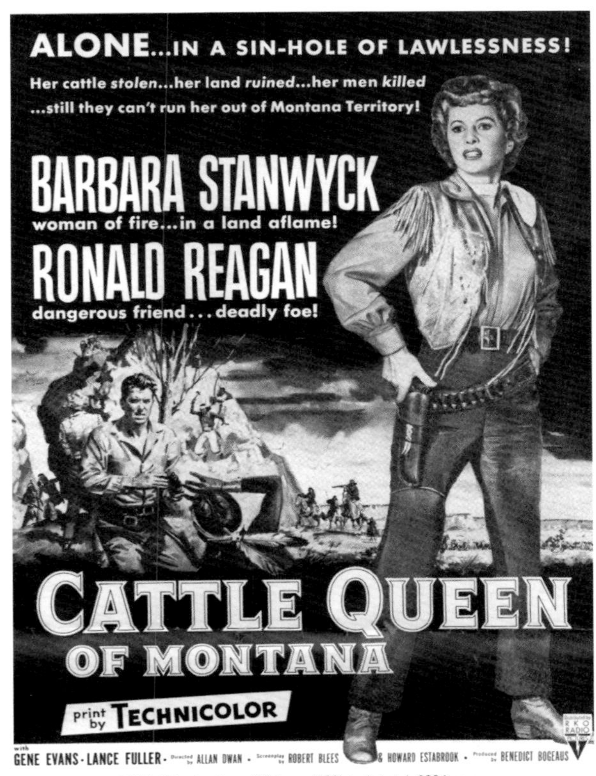

him into surrender and the reservation life. Robert Aldrich directs a fine cast that includes Jean Peters, John McIntire, and Charles Bronson. Odd to think of this progressive, pro-Indian feature being in theaters at the same time as the day's conventional savage-red-man-attacks pictures, but it was. From the novel *Bronco Apache* by Paul Wellman.

55) ***Cattle Queen of Montana*** (1954)—Barbara Stanwyck stars opposite Ronald Reagan—yes, himself, here as an undercover government agent—in this unpretentious yarn about knave Gene Evans trying to incite an Indian war as a cover to steal a cattle empire, established by Stanwyck's murdered father, out from under her. Choice back story: members of the Blackfeet Indians on the set (as extras) were so taken with Stanwyck's courage—she did many of her own stunts—that they bequeathed her the tribal name of Princess Many Victories and made her a blood sister. Directed by old-timer Allan Dwan in a classic, no-frills style.

56) ***Drum Beat*** (1954)—Alan Ladd fares well in this offbeat story, both written and directed by Delmer (*Broken Arrow*) Daves, about unsettled

relations between the white settlers and the Modoc tribe of Oregon, with Charles Bronson as their legendary leader, Captain Jack. It falls to Ladd (who also produced the film) to effect a peace between the two factions. Once again, terrific location vistas add much to the impact of the film.

57) ***Johnny Guitar*** (1954)—Joan Crawford enjoys one of her signature roles as the hostess of a gambling den in this quintessentially fifties hotbed of psychodrama, repressed sexuality, betrayal, and good old-fashioned six-guns. Johnny Guitar features wonderful—or at least wonderfully *odd*—performances by Sterling Hayden (as Joan's ex-lover), Mercedes McCambridge (quite frightening as a cattle queen), and tough guys Ward Bond, Ernest Borgnine, and Scott Brady. A cult following grew up around the film after its release and lives on to this day. Shot in TruColor by the great Nicholas Ray, who seems to have been in the midst of a fever-dream, for second-banana studio Republic.

58) ***River of No Return*** (1954)—Marilyn Monroe was at the peak of her stardom and physical beauty when she made this western for Otto Preminger, for once being given an equally formidable (and attractive) costar in the person of Robert Mitchum. Marilyn plays a saloon singer who is shanghaied and deserted in the wilds by gambler Rory Calhoun, while Mitchum is the resourceful farmer who gallantly risks his all to get them both back to civilization. Way more fun than MM's other western, the heavy-handed *The Misfits.*

59) ***Seven Brides for Seven Brothers*** (1954)—Stanley Donen directed this colorful, energetic rethinking of a story by Stephen Vincent Benét. Howard Keel and Jane Powell star as frontier newlyweds whose happiness inspires Keel's six roughneck younger brothers (including Russ Tamblyn) to abduct six prospective brides from town for themselves. MGM at the height of its movie musical powers, with singing and dancing that has yet to be topped (thank you, Michael Kidd).

60) ***The Far Country*** (1955)—The Anthony Mann/James Stewart combination had already proven itself at the box-office, so it was no surprise that this vehicle, scripted by Borden Chase, was also well received. That said, this is not one of their most potent works. John McIntire is convincing enough as the villain and Ruth Roman an acceptable romantic interest for the self-sufficient cattleman Stewart plays. But having Walter Brennan

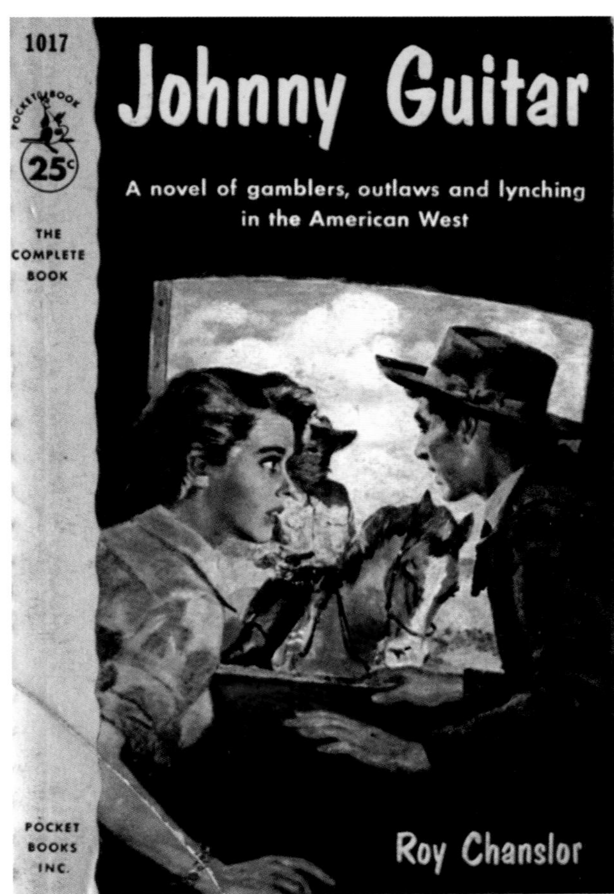

cast as Stewart's cantankerous (what else?) partner in driving a herd of cattle into Alaska (where beef is such a rarity) has the effect of lowering the dramatic stakes, rather than raising them.

61) ***The Man from Laramie*** (1955)—The final collaboration of director Anthony Mann with James Stewart is one of the most intense. Here Stewart is fueled by a desire for revenge on the varmint that sold rifles to Indian marauders, who used them to kill Stewart's brother, a cavalryman. The trail leads Stewart to the Waggoman spread, kingdom of near-blind ranching mogul Donald Crisp and his two guard-dog sons (Alex Nichol and Arthur Kennedy). They try to put off Stewart, but in his righteous rage he will not be denied, and it is not long before the blood begins to flow—first Stewart's, and then each of the Waggoman's. Hard-boiled vengeance at its grandest.

62) ***Oklahoma!*** (1955)—When the Rogers & Hammerstein show opened on Broadway on the last day of March in 1943, few could have

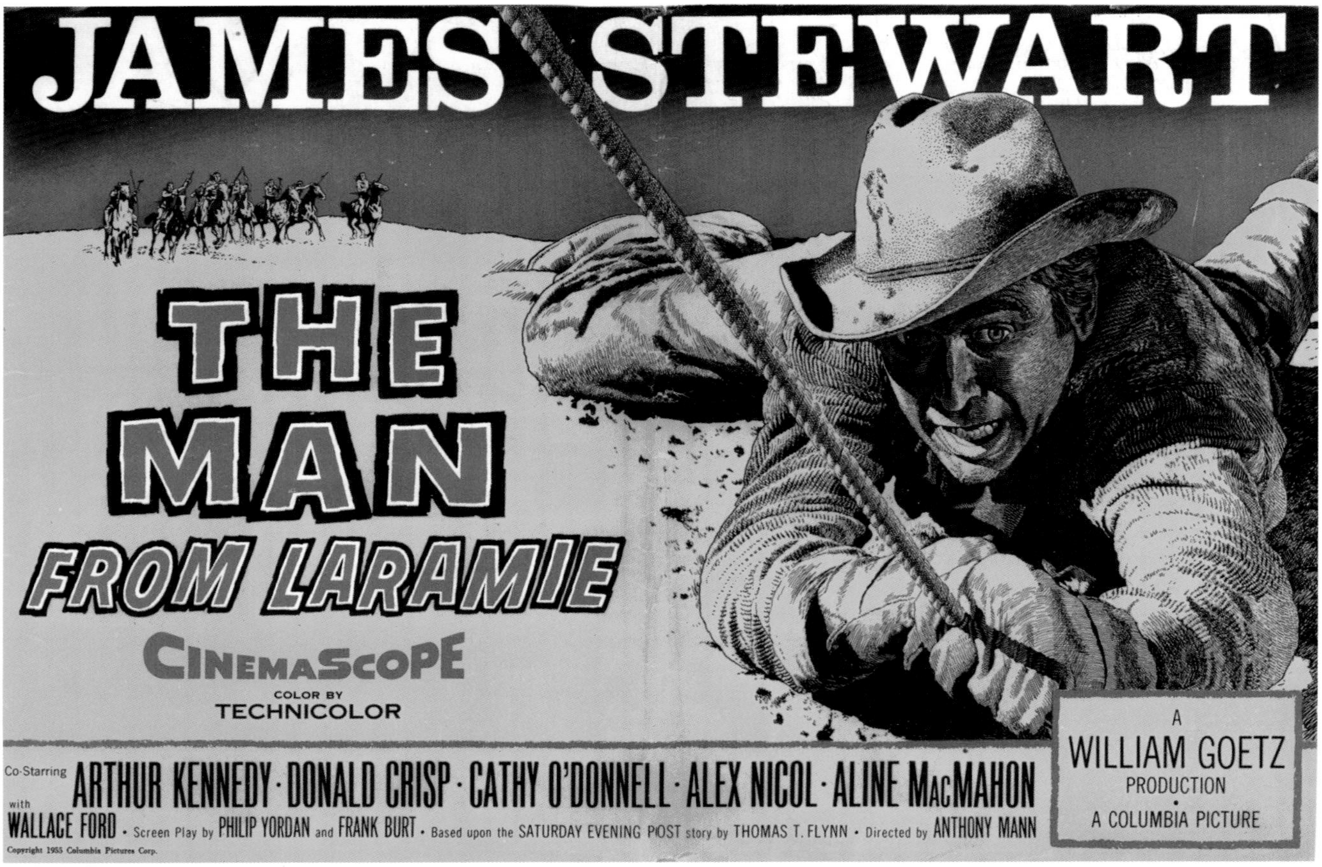
JAMES STEWART
THE MAN FROM LARAMIE
CINEMASCOPE
COLOR BY TECHNICOLOR
Co-Starring ARTHUR KENNEDY · DONALD CRISP · CATHY O'DONNELL · ALEX NICOL · ALINE MacMAHON
with WALLACE FORD · Screen Play by PHILIP YORDAN and FRANK BURT · Based upon the SATURDAY EVENING POST story by THOMAS T. FLYNN · Directed by ANTHONY MANN
Copyright 1955 Columbia Pictures Corp.
A WILLIAM GOETZ PRODUCTION
A COLUMBIA PICTURE

Selections from
THE THEATRE GUILD MUSICAL PLAY
Decca RECORDS
OKLAHOMA!
featuring members of the ORIGINAL NEW YORK PRODUCTION
Music by RICHARD RODGERS Lyrics by OSCAR HAMMERSTEIN II
Production directed by ROUBEN MAMOULIAN
ALFRED DRAKE · JOAN ROBERTS · HOWARD daSILVA · CELESTE HOLM · LEE DIXON
with "OKLAHOMA" Orchestra and Chorus directed by JAY BLACKTON
OVERTURE • OH, WHAT A BEAUTIFUL MORNIN' • SURREY WITH THE FRINGE ON TOP
KANSAS CITY • I CAIN'T SAY NO • MANY A NEW DAY • PEOPLE WILL SAY WE'RE IN LOVE
PORE JUD IS DAID • OUT OF MY DREAMS • ALL ER NOTHIN' • OKLAHOMA • FINALE
DECCA 33⅓ RPM LONG PLAY
DECCA LONG PLAY MICROGROOVE UNBREAKABLE RECORD— 8000

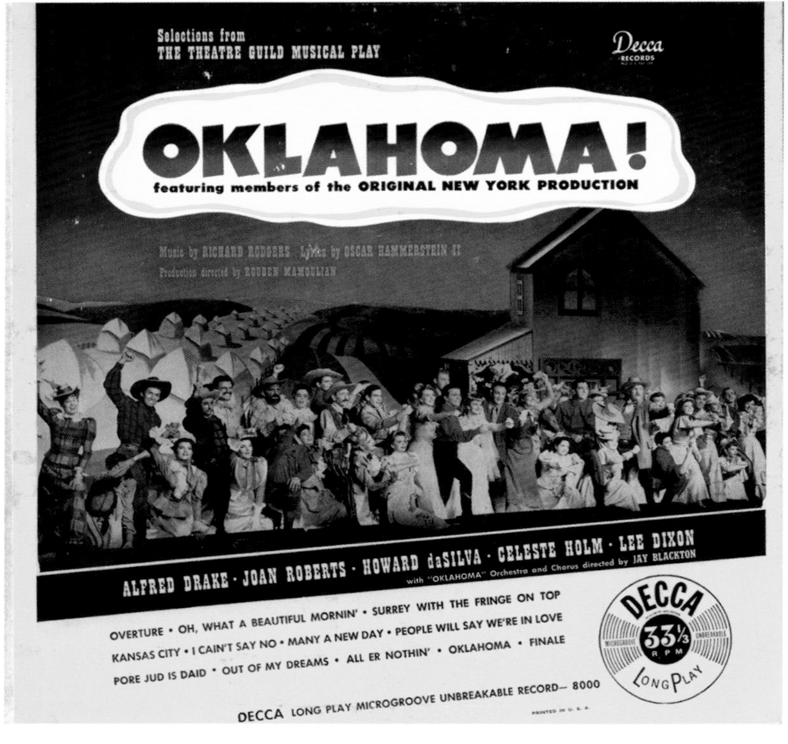

guessed it would play some 2200 times over a span of five years. But it took another seven years for the beloved musical to make it to the big screen. The classic songs (like "Oh, What a Beautiful Morning!") survived just fine, but Gordon MacRae is a tad stiff as the cowboy lead and Shirley Jones only adequate as his beloved. The film springs to life whenever Rod Steiger—chewing the scenery with unalloyed relish—and Gloria Grahame are onscreen. Fred Zinneman directed in a workmanlike fashion.

63) ***The Tall Men*** (1955)—Raoul Walsh has a fine time here with his lively cast, which finds Clark Gable jousting with blowhard Robert Ryan for the hand of curvaceous Jane Russell during a cattle drive from Texas to Montana. By this juncture, real-life outdoorsman Gable had reinvented himself as one of the finest of Hollywood's western stars, and one wonders what fine work he might have submitted if not forced to serve in all those melodramas and romantic comedies by MGM over the first twenty years of his career.

64) ***Giant*** (1956)—Shot on location in and around Marfa, Texas, which in another millennium would provide the appropriately bleak settings for both *No Country for Old Men* and *There Will Be Blood*, this sometimes ponderous adaptation of Edna Ferber's epic novel famously starred James Dean in his final screen performance, along with old-school stars Rock Hudson and Elizabeth Taylor (who both perform quite well). At 201 minutes of running time, there is much that is very good here—particularly the first half of Dean's mercurial performance as a roughneck who suddenly is transformed into an oil baron—but also a whole lot that makes you want to stick a pitchfork into plodding director George Stevens (who actually won an Oscar). Certainly worth at least one viewing, especially for fans of epics set in Texas.

65) ***Jubal*** (1956)—Heavy on the psychology, this brooding drama offers Rod Steiger in one of his patented Evil Creep roles, as he brilliantly manipulates ranch hand Glenn Ford and jealous boss Ernest Borgnine into fighting to the death for the favors of Borgnine's wife, the hot-to-trot Valerie French. It has been remarked that the movie plays like *Othello* on the open range, but Shakespeare didn't have the luxury of having his Iago shot full of hot lead, as Ford has the pleasure of doing in his final duel with the vile Steiger.

66) ***The Searchers*** (1956)—There isn't much new that can be said about this powerful, unforgettable drama, except that more critics seem to have chosen this as the best western movie than any other. Based on the excellent 1953 novel by Alan Lemay and adapted by screenwriter Frank Nugent, *The Searchers* represents the summit of the John Ford collaborations with John Wayne, whose character here, the revenge-driven, Indian-loathing Ethan Edwards, surely must count as his least sympathetic role—and also his most powerful.

And yet it is also one of his most heroic, as Ethan spends five long, hard years searching for niece Natalie Wood, abducted by Apaches as a girl. Hearing she has become the squaw to Apache leader Scar (Henry Brandon), Ethan sets himself two goals—find the tribe that has her and then kill both Scar and his tainted niece, too unclean ever to rejoin white society. But her adoptive brother, half-breed Jeffrey Hunter, who has joined Ethan on the quest, soon realizes it is squarely up to him to keep Ethan from exacting that vengeance when they do finally locate her . . .

More has been written about this film than perhaps any other western, but the fact is, if you have read this far in *True West,* you are probably already well acquainted with this masterpiece.

67) ***Seven Men from Now*** (1956)—Randolph Scott was once one of the handsomest men in Hollywood, a fact which allowed him to act not only in westerns and other adventure films but also in romantic comedies and the like. As Scott got older, though, his features hardened, giving him a stern, weathered cast. That newborn toughness served him in good stead when he started his cycle of westerns with director Budd Boetticher and screenwriter Burt Kennedy. The films they made were simple—B-pictures, with no pretensions otherwise—but they had true sticking power. Scott usually played a man drawn against his will into taking violent action, which in *Seven Men from Now* finds him tracking the outlaws who have murdered his wife. One of those outlaws is played by Lee Marvin, who had only recently begun to establish himself as the big screen's pre-eminent bad guy, and Scott must eventually confront and kill him in order to save victim Gail Russell.

The formula varied a bit, but there is no mistaking the Boetticher/Kennedy touch on the subsequent films they made with Randolph Scott—

JOHN WAYNE
DANS
LA PRISONNIÈRE
DU DÉSERT
The Searchers
AVEC
JEFFREY HUNTER · VERA MILES
WARD BOND · NATALIE WOOD
VISTAVISION
TECHNICOLOR
Mise en scène JOHN FORD
WB
DE ZWARTE VALK

RUN OF THE ARROW
TECHNICOLOR®
STARRING
ROD STEIGER
SARITA MONTIEL
BRIAN KEITH and
RALPH MEEKER with
JAY C. FLIPPEN
CHARLES BRONSON
OLIVE CAREY
Written, Produced and Directed by
SAMUEL FULLER

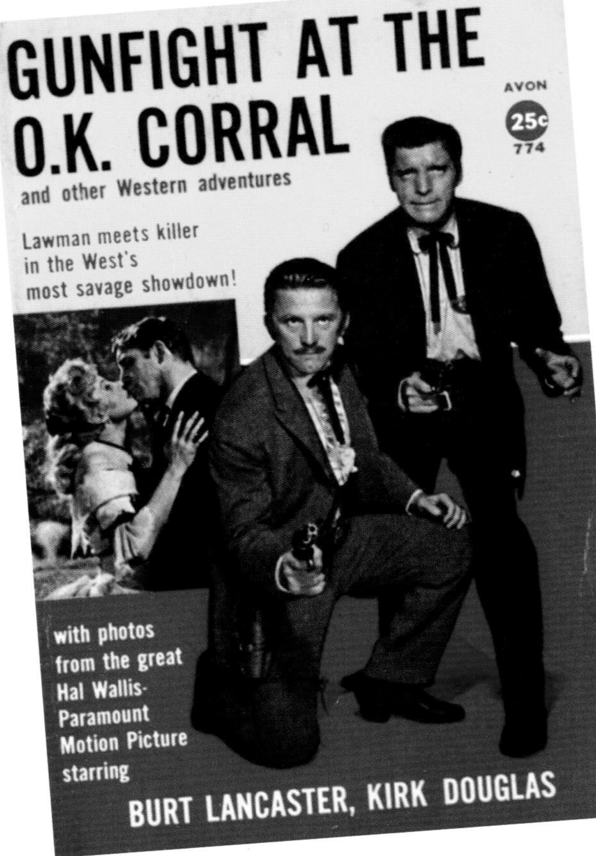
GUNFIGHT AT THE
O.K. CORRAL
and other Western adventures
AVON
25c
774
Lawman meets killer
in the West's
most savage showdown!
with photos
from the great
Hal Wallis-
Paramount
Motion Picture
starring
BURT LANCASTER, KIRK DOUGLAS

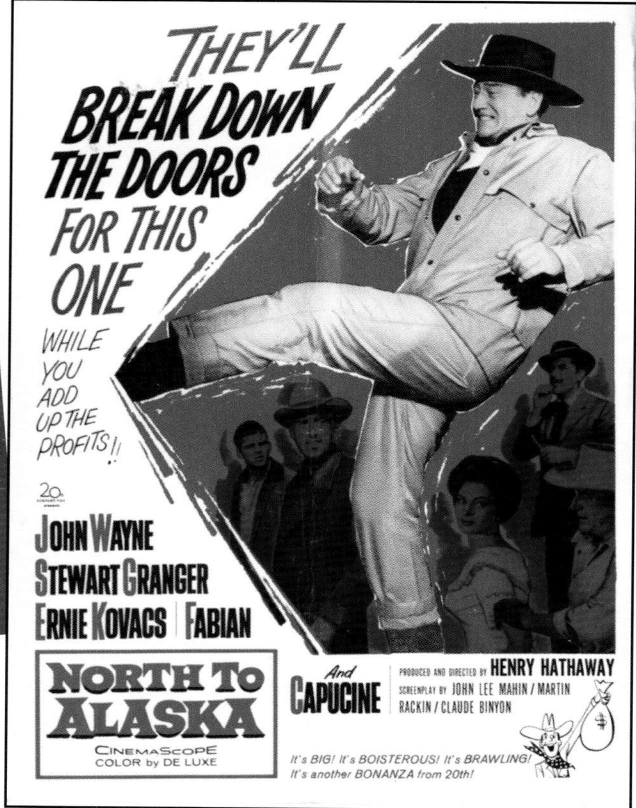
THEY'LL
BREAK DOWN
THE DOORS
FOR THIS
ONE
WHILE
YOU
ADD
UP THE
PROFITS!!
JOHN WAYNE
STEWART GRANGER
ERNIE KOVACS | FABIAN
NORTH TO ALASKA
CINEMASCOPE
COLOR by DE LUXE
And
CAPUCINE
PRODUCED AND DIRECTED BY HENRY HATHAWAY
SCREENPLAY BY JOHN LEE MAHIN / MARTIN
RACKIN / CLAUDE BINYON
It's BIG! It's BOISTEROUS! It's BRAWLING!
It's another BONANZA from 20th!

first *The Tall T* (1957; from an Elmore Leonard short story), then *Ride Lonesome* (1959), and finally *Comanche Station* (1960). Though each presents its own set of challenges and offers up its own distinctive bad guys (Richard Boone, Lee Van Cleef, James Coburn, Claude Akins), the constant is always the indomitable Scott—unyielding, unforgiving, and, in the end, always the baddest man left standing.

68) ***Run of the Arrow*** (1957)—Rod Steiger here assumes a complex role as an ex-Confederate soldier who joins a tribe of Sioux rather than admit that the South lost the Civil War. Both written and directed by Sam Fuller, *Run* has a fine cast that includes Ralph Meeker, Brian Keith, and erstwhile cowboy star Tim McCoy (here playing an army officer who ultimately must persuade the Sioux to sign a peace treaty). Like most of Fuller's films, *Run* isn't exactly like any other western—which becomes part of the pleasure of watching it.

69) ***Gunfight at the O.K. Corral*** (1957)—A tale oft told, this John Sturges-directed version of the famous conflict and gun battle between Wyatt Earp, Doc Holliday, and the Clanton gang stars Burt Lancaster as Wyatt and Kirk Douglas as the afflicted Doc, with Rhonda Fleming drafted for window dressing. Truth to tell, the movie lacks the visual poetry and other subtleties present in John Ford's 1946 film, but it still does a good enough job of presenting the legendary confrontation. Screenplay by Leon Uris, of all people, with a pedestrian theme song by Frankie Laine.

70) ***3:10 to Yuma*** (1957)—The 2007 remake starring Russell Crowe and Christian Bale became the focal point of a surprisingly heated debate—did the latter-day filmmakers make a better movie by "opening up" the action in the manner they did, or was Delmer Daves' black & white (and much more trim) original, largely set indoors, the superior work? On the one hand you have the intensity of Russell Crowe—perhaps our best actor today—as the captured gunslinger; on the other, the taciturn Glenn Ford. And yet, Ford's quiet, congenial menace somehow carries as much of a punch as Crowe's more expansive, even quirky interpretation of the role. And then there is the conundrum of Christian Bale in the 2007 version playing the citizen who assumes the perilous task of delivering the gunman to the train that will transport him to the prison in Yuma, versus Van Heflin in the original. Bale is a revelation, but Van Heflin's coiled performance is flawless.

In the end, then, the verdict must be: see both. This is the rare case of a remake re-imagining an excellent original without diminishing it one iota. Kudos to both creative teams for expanding the source material, a short story penned by Elmore Leonard, in distinctly different but equally effective fashions.

71) ***Man of the West*** (1958)—Anthony Mann had completed his cycle of films with star James Stewart, so for this extremely intense film, he recruited Gary Cooper for the role of the (quasi-) hero and Lee J. Cobb, playing his father, to hold forth as the (quasi-) villain. In fact, as scripted by Reginald Rose, author of many of the fifties most prestigious television dramas, this feels less like a western of the day than a variation of *The Desperate Hours*, with Coop held hostage by the paranoid visions of dear old nutty dad—not to mention menacing brother Jack Lord. Songstress Julie London does well in support, but it is really Cobb's show all the way—maybe his best performance after *On the Waterfront*.

72) ***Rio Bravo*** (1959)—Howard Hawks' hugely enjoyable "answer" to *High Noon*. Where in the earlier film we see Gary Cooper spending 90 percent of the film fruitlessly seeking aid from the townspeople, in Hawks' vision, sheriff John Wayne not only refuses to ask for any help, he loudly rejects it even when it is offered with no strings attached. And yet, despite himself, Wayne ends up with that much-needed help, in the form of teen gunslinger Ricky Nelson, rehabilitated drunk Dean Martin (in perhaps the best role of his screen career), and the inevitably cantankerous, constantly complaining Walter Brennan. The delightful Angie Dickinson parries and thrusts Wayne's stubborn idiocies with an aplomb not seen since Hawks put young Lauren Bacall through her paces in *To Have and Have Not* and *The Big Sleep* (the latter sharing the same screenwriting team, Jules Furthman and Leigh Brackett). *Rio Bravo* appears on just about everyone's list of Ten Best Westerns, and each repeated viewing illustrates why.

73) ***Heller in Pink Tights*** (1960)—Louis L'Amour's novel *Heller with a Gun* is given a lively ride by director George Cukor, on whose distinguished and lengthy résumé this remains the only western. Sophia Loren plays the grand diva of a theatrical troupe that barnstorms through the West in the 1860s, and Anthony Quinn plays the long-suffering guy who can

only love her from afar. Inspired by the legend of real-life actress Adah Isaacs Menken.

74) ***North to Alaska*** (1960)—Made the same year as John Wayne's self-directed, grandiose epic *The Alamo,* this rollicking adventure is ten times more fun—and forty minutes shorter. Guided by the capable hands of director Henry Hathaway, Wayne and Stewart Granger play cohorts who strike it rich in the gold mines of Alaska and then have to outwit, and out-fight, each other in their dual pursuit of the beauteous Capucine. Ernie Kovacs is amusing as a con man, and teen idol Fabian does his best as an ornament to increase the box-office, (but we prefer Ricky Nelson's teen gunslinger, Colorado, from *Rio Bravo).* Lots of fun, muddy fistfights ensue, with none of *The Alamo's* ponderous speechifying.

75) ***The Magnificent Seven*** (1960)—Famously adapted by John Sturges from Kurosawa's 1952 classic *Seven Samurai,* this transposition to the American West works surprisingly well. One principal reason is the phenomenal cast Sturges is given to work with. Yul Brynner is cast as the cool-as-a-cucumber leader of the band of professional gunmen who have hired themselves out to a village that is being victimized by a fearsome group of banditos (led by the marvelous Eli Wallach). He is supported by expert gunmen (and knife-throwers, in one case) James Coburn, Steve McQueen, and Charles Bronson. (Robert Vaughn's Nervous Nellie gunman is another matter entirely.) A huge international hit, with a theme song for the ages (thank you, Elmer Bernstein!). Sequels would follow, as would a TV series, but this is the only required entry.

76) ***The Unforgiven*** (1960)—Alan LeMay's fine novel is mounted impressively by director John Huston, who rarely deigned to make a western. The fine cast includes Burt Lancaster, Charles Bickford, and Lillian Gish, but a problem exists with the casting of Audrey Hepburn, who plays the key role of the young woman who has been raised in Lancaster's family as white ever since she was found alone on the plains as a girl. But now Indians have come calling who claim that she is actually a member of their tribe, taken from them wrongfully. Hepburn turns in a well-modulated performance as the confused foundling, but it requires a huge suspension of disbelief to accept her as a Native American. On the other hand, Audie

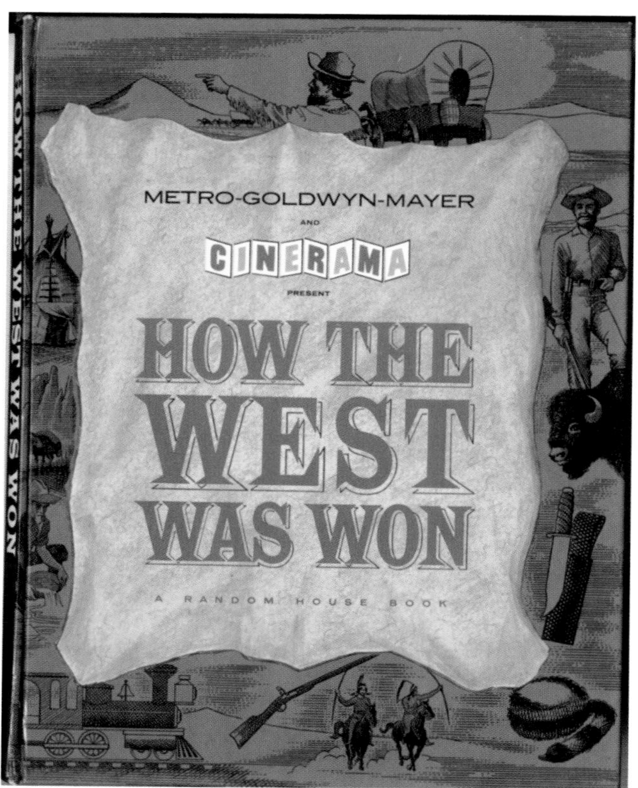

Murphy is simply terrific as her racist adoptive brother. An interesting postscript to *The Searchers,* which LeMay authored several years earlier.

77) ***One-Eyed Jacks*** (1961)—Marlon Brando was not the first major star to direct himself in a western—John Wayne had accomplished that feat a year earlier with *The Alamo*—but he raised the stakes by first firing Stanley Kubrick from the assignment. What Brando then wrought is pretty much a fascinating mess, but the nearly two-and-a-half hours that remain of what was once a five-hour cut (edited once by Brando and then again by Paramount) still contains several scenes that are either powerful, or beautiful, or even funny. The fact that they don't match up with each other very smoothly can be laid at Brando's feet, no doubt—but at the same time, he earns kudos for eliciting mesmerizing performances out of both himself and Karl Malden, whose work as the film's chief villain is one of the best of his career.

78) ***How the West Was Won*** (1962)—MGM's Cinerama spectacular must have seemed like a great idea at the time, but the years have not been kind to it. The gimmick of having three directors—John Ford for one segment (set during the Civil War), Henry Hathaway for three parts, and George Marshall for one—virtually guarantees that the segments are not going to mesh, and

445-02542-060
60c
"To be compared to Salinger's Catcher in the Rye"
—Best Sellers
HUD
by Larry McMurtry
The brilliant novel that became a powerful film starring Paul Newman with an Academy Award-winning performance by Patricia Neal
WINNER OF THE JESSE H. JONES AWARD FOR FICTION
(Original title: Horseman, Pass By)

YUL BRYNNER
MAGNIFICENT
Seven who fought like seven hundred!
MAGNIFICENT
Seven notches above the ordinary!
MAGNIFICENT
The stand they made!
CHARLES BRONSON · ROBERT VAUGHN · BRAD DEXTER
JAMES COBURN
and INTRODUCING HORST BUCHHOLZ
Filmed in Panavision · Color by DeLuxe

even the *Who's Who* of Hollywood superstars (James Stewart, John Wayne, Henry Fonda, Gregory Peck) and second-level stars (George Peppard, Richard Widmark, Karl Malden, Lee J. Cobb) don't mesh. At nearly three hours running time, the film does offer much of merit, but its everything-plus-the-kitchen-sink approach diminishes its impact (which, granted, is already diminished by watching it on DVD rather than on the special Cinerama screen for which it was intended).

79) ***The Man Who Shot Liberty Valance*** (1962)—Deceptively simple, right down to its use of black and white cinematography and artificial sets, this latter-day work by John Ford, adapted from a short story by Dorothy Johnson, is surely one of his very best. John Wayne has never been in better dyspeptic form than here, playing a hard-as-nails rancher who can only look askance at James Stewart's hapless tenderfoot lawyer. Stewart naturally runs afoul of town bully Liberty Valance (Lee Marvin, in his defining role), while almost inadvertently stealing away the heart of Wayne's enamorata (Vera Miles). What then transpires demonstrates Ford's absolute mastery, as Stewart, Marvin, and Wayne are placed on a collision course that none of them can avoid. It is impossible not to be moved by the elegiac ending. The terrific theme song was composed by the Bacharach-David team and sung by Gene Pitney. Given what was wrought, who would ever have thought that Ford and Wayne were at each other's throats for almost every moment of the filming?

80) ***Ride the High Country*** (1962)—Sam Peckinpah here directs one of the finest westerns ever made—quite an achievement for the former television director so early in his career. Now in the September of their years, veteran cowboy stars Joel McCrea and Randolph Scott play a pair of aging gun hands who agree to help shepherd a shipment of gold from a mining camp to the safety of the bank back in town. But Scott has no intention of letting the gold get that far—he intends to take it for himself, even if it means betraying his old partner. McCrea tips to that scheme, so now he has to transport the gold and the now-handcuffed Scott back to civilization. Just one complication: a band of angry miners is hot on their trail, for stealing away the unwilling bride (Mariette Hartley) they rescued from the mining camp. Wonderful location photography by Lucien Ballard enhances this unforgettable saga.

81) ***Hud*** (1963)—A contemporary western that fans of westerns love to hate. Larry McMurtry's searing novel *Horseman, Pass By* was brought to the screen by director Martin Ritt, who elicited a convincing performance from star Paul Newman as the iconic Hud. Over the next two hours Hud demonstrates beyond a shadow of a doubt why he must be considered the meanest s.o.b. in Texas—and likely on the entire planet. Melvyn Douglas won an Oscar as Newman's (justifiably) irascible father, and Patricia Neal took the Best Actress Oscar for her indelible performances as the housekeeper exploited by Hud. Brandon De Wilde also scores as Hud's younger brother, whose idolization of him has shattered into a million pieces by the film's end. Stunning cinematography by James Wong Howe.

82) ***A Fistful of Dollars*** (1964)—Clint Eastwood had long since established himself as a major television star on the CBS-TV series *Rawhide* at the time he was offered the lead role in Sergio Leone's *A Fistful of Dollars,* which was to be shot in Italy with an international cast. Eastwood's fee? The princely sum of $15,000. (Which was why Leone's first and second choices, James Coburn and Charles Bronson, reputedly had passed.) A reworking of the 1961 Kurosawa classic *Yojimbo,* the film positions Eastwood as The Man with No Name, a cigar-chomping, cynical cipher who is possessed of almost supernatural skills and cunning. Leone's distinctive treatment of his amoral cast of characters and the film's stylized violence (not to mention the haunting score by Ennio Morricone) made a huge impact on audiences both in the U.S. and around the world. Eastood was transformed into a truly international movie star almost overnight.

The follow-up entries in what became Leone's trilogy, *For a Few Dollars More* (1965) and *The Good, the Bad & the Ugly* (1966), were even better than *Fistful.* In the former, Eastwood's mysterious Man now faces Lee Van Cleef's formidable The Major as his doppelganger to up the dramatic stakes. And then in the final chapter, Van Cleef is joined in the cast by the dynamic (and utterly loathsome) Eli Wallach. The setting is now some ravaged, nameless Civil War battlefields, amid which the three hard-bitten men try to outwit each other as they search for a trunk full of Confederate gold. Released in a nearly three-hour cut, *Good/Bad/Ugly* was a smash hit in the U.S. during the summer of '66 and bestowed a new iconic status on Eastwood. The Eastwood/Leone partnership proved to be nothing less

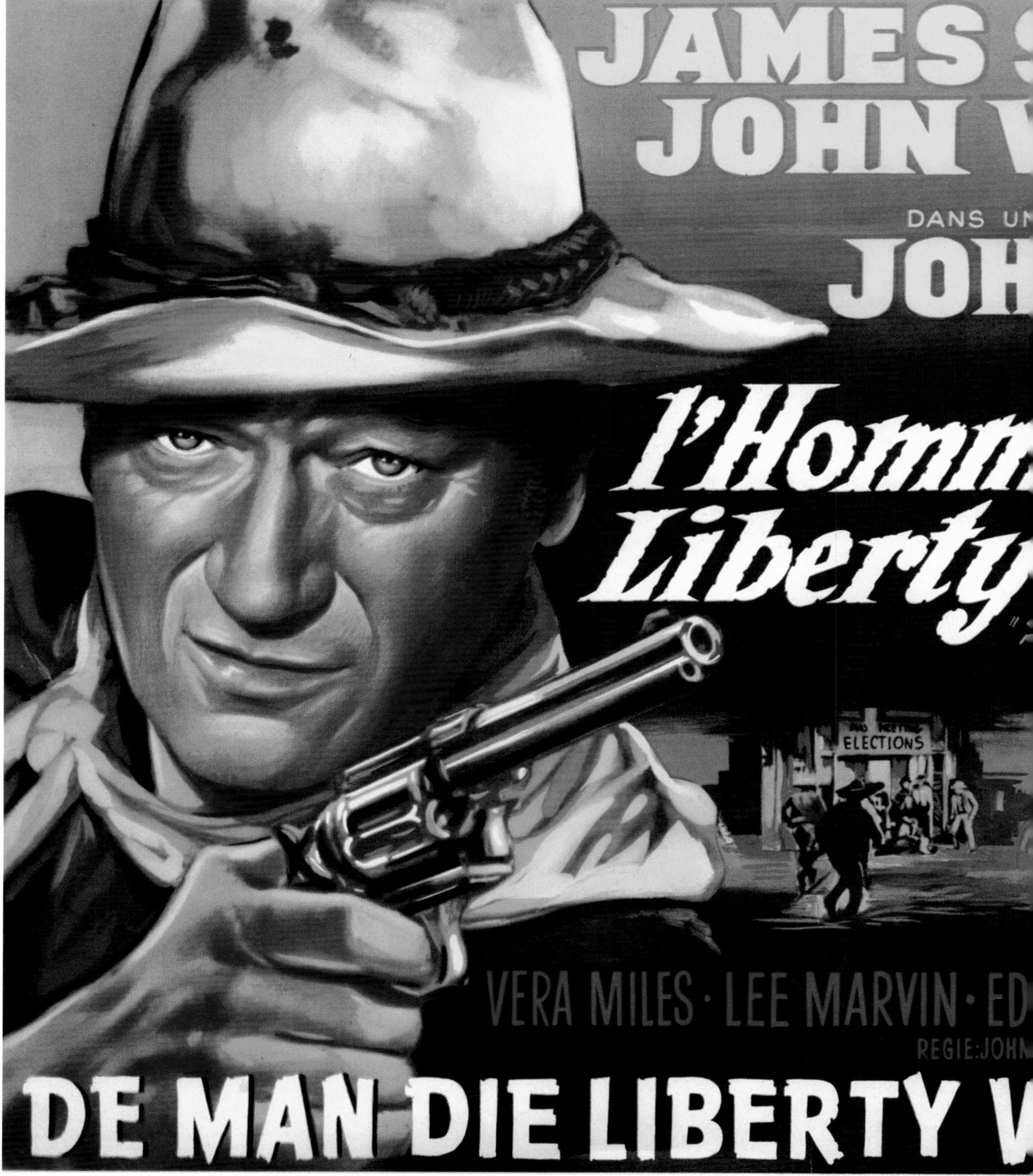
JAMES
JOHN
DANS
ELECTIONS
VERA MILES · LEE MARVIN ·
DE MAN DIE LIBERTY

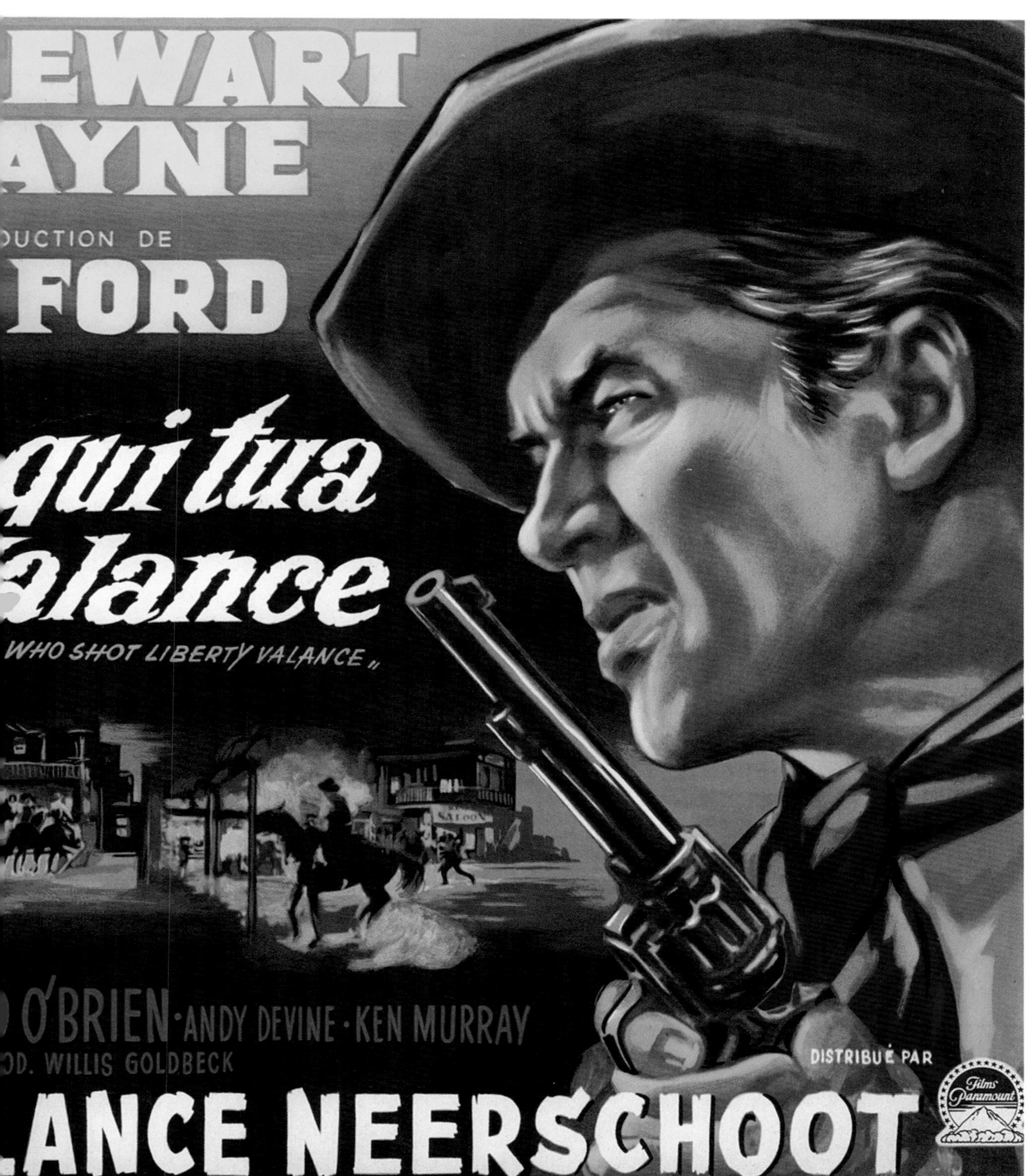
EWART
AYNE
DUCTION DE
FORD
qui tua
alance
WHO SHOT LIBERTY VALANCE"
SALOON
O'BRIEN · ANDY DEVINE · KEN MURRAY
OD. WILLIS GOLDBECK
DISTRIBUÉ PAR
Films Paramount
LANCE NEERSCHOOT

than a cultural milestone, the reverberations of which can still be felt after all these decades.

83) ***Cat Ballou***—It's now hard to believe, but this enjoyable trifle was an international smash. Jane Fonda plays the eponymous Cat, an erstwhile schoolteacher who throws away her books to help revenge the brutal death of her father at the hands of sadistic killer Lee Marvin. (Has there ever been any screen actor who was better at this sort of thing than Marvin?) To that end, she wires dime novel hero Kid Sheleen, who upon arrival is drunk as a skunk (and is also played by Lee Marvin, in one of the film's more delicious twists). Marvin, who won the Oscar for his dual performances, has a field day parodying both his Liberty Valance gunslinger image and the boys'-book heroism of the hopelessly soused Kid. Not as funny as it thinks it is but still a film that is worth seeing, if only for Marvin.

84) ***Major Dundee***—Peckinpah labored long and hard on this sprawling Civil War-era adventure, with Charlton Heston as a Union officer haunted by a past disgrace. Now he is charged with crossing into Mexico to chase down a band of marauding Apache. To that end he gathers a motley crew of Confederate prisoners to swell his numbers, the most interesting of whom is Richard Harris, himself a disgraced officer, though a curiously noble one. (James Coburn, Warren Oates, and Jim Hutton are also excellent in supporting roles.) Their mission is eventually completed, but along the way the film follows numerous diversions, including Heston suffering a full-blown identity crisis. Famously trimmed by Columbia with a hacksaw for its release, the film was recently restored to something much closer to what Peckinpah intended. Even so, it doesn't carry the emotional weight, or the grandeur, of either *Ride the High Country* or *The Wild Bunch.*

85) ***The Professionals*** (1966)—Burt Lancaster is in fine fettle here as an explosives expert who is recruited during the time of the Mexican Revolution to join a band of experts in other useful professions—Woody Strode as an archer par excellence, Robert Ryan as a horse wrangler—along with steely soldier of fortune Lee Marvin, who years earlier had joined with Lancaster in aiding Pancho Villa. Their mission: one of Villa's veteran revolutionaries (Jack Palance, appropriately charismatic) has absconded with the beauteous wife (Claudia Cardinale at her most glorious) of wealthy

American Ralph Bellamy. Now the four of them must penetrate his remote Mexican desert fortress, rescue her, and bring her back to the States. Director Richard Brooks, who also wrote the screenplay, does a wonderful job of dramatizing both the camaraderie of the quartet and the excruciating hardships they must endure to execute the mission. The film's twist ending is a satisfying cherry on top. A true gem, about which you hear little today.

86) ***Hang 'Em High*** (1967)—The first of Eastwood's American westerns following his blockbuster trilogy for Sergio Leone, this picture is credited to director Ted Post—but with the benefit of forty years hindsight, we can see Clint's hand everywhere here. Eastwood plays a deputy sheriff bent on revenging his near-hanging by nine men who sentenced him to death, led by Pat Hingle's evil judge. At the same time, he aids beautiful widow Inger Stevens, who is searching for the men who cruelly murdered her husband. Ben Johnson, Bruce Dern, and Dennis Hooper are present and always welcome. By no means the strongest of his oeuvre—Clint is clearly still feeling his way here—the film remains historically important for what it helped launch, among other thing's Eastwood's Malpaso production company.

87) ***Will Penny*** (1968)—Charlton Heston has rarely been better than in this reflective portrait of an aging cowboy loner, who finds himself attracted to lovely Joan Hackett while he is protecting her from the dangerous Bruce Dern and Donald Pleasance. Directed with a sure hand by Tom Gries, who also wrote the screenplay.

88) ***Once Upon a Time in the West*** (1968)—The greatest Sergio Leone film not to star Clint Eastwood, this is a majestic, stately epic—and I do not employ that term loosely—on the one hand detailing the first exhilarating moments of civilization finally reaching the West and on the other rendering one man's meticulously plotted course for revenge—for what, we do not know for over two hours. (The movie was released with a 144-minute running time, longer than most westerns, but still twenty-four minutes shorter than the version Leone intended to be seen. It took another fifteen years for that version to be released in the U.S.)

The man seeking vengeance is Charles Bronson, who manages his mysterious role with simmering intensity, as bit by bit the puzzle of his life and thus his desire for revenge, is revealed. In the course of teasing out the mys-

There were three men in her life. One to take her...
one to love her –and one to kill her.
PARAMOUNT PICTURES PRESENTS
A SERGIO LEONE FILM
CLAUDIA CARDINALE
HENRY FONDA
JASON ROBARDS
CHARLES BRONSON
ONCE UPON A TIME IN THE WEST
GABRIELE FERZETTI
WOODY STRODE
JACK ELAM · LIONEL STANDER · PAOLO STOPPA · FRANK WOLFF · KEENAN WYNN
EXECUTIVE PRODUCER BINO CICOGNA · MUSIC BY ENNIO MORRICONE · A RAFRAN-SAN MARCO PRODUCTION · TECHNISCOPE · TECHNICOLOR · A PARAMOUNT PICTURE
THE BRILLIANT NEW SCREENPLAY BY
WILLIAM GOLDMAN
AUTHOR OF "BOYS & GIRLS TOGETHER"
BUTCH CASSIDY
AND THE
SUNDANCE KID
PLUS A PORTFOLIO OF
ON-LOCATION PHOTOGRAPHS
AWARD BOOKS
A464X 60¢ MAC
They were the last of the West's legendary lawless breed—savage men who lived to kill... and killed to live!
The Wild Bunch
Starring William Holden, Robert Ryan, Ernest Borgnine
A major motion picture from Warner Bros.—Seven Arts
Brian Fox

UNFORGIVEN
Aug. 7
R

tery, Leone introduces a fascinating set of supporting characters, ranging from the dyspeptic thief Jason Robards to the ice-cold killer Henry Fonda to the luscious ex-prostitute Claudia Cardinale, who in the end is the only one willing and able to embrace the advent of that new, civilized world. But it is the enigmatic, iconic Bronson on whom the power of the film truly relies, and you will never come to know anyone's eyes more intimately than you do his after observing his steely gaze for nigh on three hours. A rewarding viewing experience, though patience is helpful.

89) ***Butch Cassidy and the Sundance Kid*** (1969)—One of the year's biggest hits, this was also one of the most popular westerns of the decade, proving that there was still commercial life in the genre. Of course, it helped to have two of the day's most glamorous leading men, Paul Newman and relative newcomer Robert Redford, on hand to strike sparks off each other and lovely costar Katherine Ross as well. George Roy Hill's deft direction and William Goldman's clever screenplay had much to do with the wide appeal of the film; Goldman's ability to inject post-modern banter into even the most suspenseful scenes gave the film a fresh feel. That screenplay won an Oscar and so did the lovely cinematography of Conrad Hall, the smash Bacharach-David theme song "Raindrops Keep Fallin' on My Head," and the score by Bacharach. And of course, the film sent Redford's career into orbit.

90) ***True Grit*** (1969)—Charles Portis' well-received novel, narrated in the vernacular of the day by a teenage girl, was the basis for this enormously enjoyable, and hugely popular, adventure. The hero is an eye-patched, hard-drinking, overweight, grizzled John Wayne in the role that would (finally!) win him his Oscar, Marshal Rooster Cogburn. Kim Darby plays the hilariously obnoxious girl who hires him to bring in the man who killed her father (outlaw leader Robert Duvall), and Glen Campbell is barely adequate as the Texas Ranger who deals himself into the play. Director Henry Hathaway makes the picture run like a Swiss watch, though complaints echo to this day that the whole thing is just too lightweight. That may be, but if there is anything more thrilling than the film's climactic encounter—the Duke riding full tilt across a field straight into Duvall's band of outlaws, reins held in his teeth to keep both hands free with rifle and pistol blasting merrily away—I have yet to come across it.

91) ***The Wild Bunch*** (1969)—That 1969 was some kind of year for westerns, wasn't it? Sam Peckinpah hadn't made a film since the studio butchered *Major Dundee* four years earlier, so few were prepared for the raw power of this alternately lyrical and bloody masterpiece when it arrived. Set in the West of 1912, in and around the border territory where the Mexican Revolution was still in its first bloom of passion, *The Wild Bunch* stars William Holden as the world-weary leader of a rag-tag band of veteran mercenaries, cutthroats and thieves who have signed on with him to make one last big score. (The band includes just about every great supporting actor in Hollywood: Warren Oates, Ernest Borgnine, Ben Johnson, Strother Martin, and L.Q. Jones.) But their plan runs into major complications when they learn that Robert Ryan, Holden's former partner, has been retained to track them down and bring them in—dead or alive, naturally.

The acting is uniformly excellent, and Lucien Ballard's cinematography is a major element in conveying the nasty, brutish, and short aspect of the West in which these men exist. The then-shocking ending, with the band being shot down in slow motion by a veritable blizzard of bullets, has now become a venerable cliché—but at the time Peckinpah devised it, the technique was still fresh.

Peckinpah followed this true epic with the very enjoyable, far lighter *The Ballad of Cable Hogue* (1970), which starred Jason Robards and Stella Stevens and featured barely a drop of blood. But like *Bunch,* it too was a commentary on the closing of the frontier—or, if you will, the death of the *true* West.

92) ***Little Big Man*** (1970)—Arthur Penn had already established his reputation as an iconoclast via Bonnie and Clyde a few years earlier, so no one should have been surprised by the irreverence that fuels this terrific adaptation of the 1964 Thomas Berger novel. Essentially, this is the counterculture version of *How the West Was Won,* with Dustin Hoffman's 121-year-old Indian narrator framing the revisionist history lesson that is about to follow. And what a lesson it is. Calder Willingham's screenplay takes us on a picaresque journey through all the familiar western conventions, only now we are seeing them through a funhouse mirror. Many of the episodes are comic, like the bawdy scenes involving Faye Dunaway, while others—like the staging of the infamous Washita River massacre of 1868—feel like

a reenactment of My Lai performed by cavalry and Indians (no doubt, precisely the film's point). Hoffman has rarely been better than he is here as the affectless young Jack Crabbe—a Candide of the West—while Chief Dan George is an absolute delight as the ancient wise man who philosophizes even as he prepares for his "Good Day to Die."

93) ***A Man Called Horse*** (1970)—Dorothy Johnson's wonderful short story is expanded into a potent film by director Elliot Silverstein, who keeps star Richard Harris onscreen for almost every one of its 114 minutes. Harris is an English lord who, on a trip to see the American West, is captured by the Sioux. Treated like a slave, he must subsist on scraps left over by the dogs, while enduring constant beatings from the elderly hags to whom his care has been entrusted. But Harris' pluck and intelligence slowly begin to catch the attention of the tribe's menfolk, and after he saves one of the young braves from being killed by a rival tribe, he is fully accepted. But to become an actual Sioux, he first must survive the Sun Vow initiation ceremony, one of the most grueling scenes ever presented in a western. This is a film that, like its contemporary *Little Big Man*, truly tapped into the counterculture zeitgeist. Harris appeared in the vastly inferior sequel, *Return of a Man Called Horse,* in 1976.

94) ***Monte Walsh*** (1970)—Jack Schaefer's fine novel about the impending end of the Old West is done full justice on the screen by novice director William Fraker, who made his reputation as a cinematographer (so you know this movie is going to be a visual delight—and it is.). Lee Marvin and Jack Palance play longtime cowboy partners who have to go their separate ways when the ranch they worked closes down. Palance (playing a good guy for once) settles down and gets married, but he has little time to enjoy it—he is shot to death by an unbalanced cowboy, leaving Marvin to revenge him. Jeanne Moreau, Richard Farnsworth, and Jim Davis provide able support, but once Palance is off the stage, it's all Marvin's show—and a bittersweet show it proves to be.

95) ***The Last Picture Show*** (1971)—A western, you ask? Well—sure!! Larry McMurtry's unsparing portrait of life in a very small Texas town circa 1950 is memorably brought to the screen by Peter Bogdanovich, who co-wrote the screenplay with McMurtry. Jeff Bridges is terrific as the cocky Duane, the high school hero we all loved to hate, but the true protagonist

is Timothy Bottoms, from whose disaffected point of view the story unfolds. The rich cast also includes the luminous newcomer Cybill Shepherd, Cloris Leachman (who won an Oscar), Ellen Burstyn, and—as the symbolic core of the film—Ben Johnson, who also earned an Academy Award for his performance as Sam the Lion. Just writing about this movie makes me want to watch it again.

96) ***McCabe and Mrs. Miller*** (1971)—Robert Altman was still riding high on the success of *M*A*S*H* when he elected to make this quirky but nonetheless deeply affecting western, starring Warren Beatty as McCabe, a charming drifter who lands in the frontier town of Presbyterian Church, where he soon collides with Julie Christie, the beautiful madam of the town's most prosperous enterprise. McCabe is an inveterate dreamer, so even after he begins an affair with Christie—who still requires him to ante up, like any of her other johns—he spends the bulk of his waking hours trying to expand the town, beginning with his upgrade of the bordello itself. But his improvements soon catch the attention of a mining company that decides they want in, and when the prideful McCabe refuses to sell out to

them, his fate is sealed. Surely one of Altman's three best films, enhanced by the spare, mournful tunes of Leonard Cohen.

97) ***Wild Rovers*** (1971)—Blake Edwards, of all people, directed this elegiac western about two mismatched cowpokes—William Holden and Ryan O'Neal—who decide one day to rob a bank just for the hell of it and who are then obliged to skedaddle as the vengeful Tom Skerritt sets out after them. This being a post-*Wild Bunch* picture, very bad things soon happen to our carefree heroes, even though Holden and O'Neal are shown not to have a mean bone in either of their bodies. Heavily cut by the studio before its release, the film now has been restored to its intended 136-minute form.

98) ***High Plains Drifter*** (1972)—Eastwood directs himself with much more assurance in this ambitious production than he was able in his (uncredited) maiden effort *Hang 'em High.* Here he plays a mysterious drifter who accepts the job of protecting the townspeople from a band of newly released outlaws en route to exact vengeance. But Eastwood's character—another Man With No Name, for all practical purposes—is soon revealed to be not entirely mortal, lending the tale supernatural overtones. Here we find Eastwood clearly tipping his sombrero in the direction of Leone, with numerous stylistic homages paid to his mentor along the way.

The Outlaw Josey Wales (1976), Clint's next western, did not hit the same heights, and over the next fifteen years few of the pictures he made fell into the western category. But then, in 1992, he made his masterpiece, *Unforgiven,* which won him the Academy Award for Best Director and also became the first western since *Cimarron,* way back in 1931, to be given the Oscar as Best Picture.

99) ***Jeremiah Johnson*** (1972)—Based on the excellent novel *Mountain Man* by Vardis Fisher, Sydney Pollack's visually magnificent adaptation shows the transformation of Robert Redford's Jeremiah from the greenest of would-be trappers to a hardened survivor who has become legendary even among the hostile Crow who have sworn to kill him (for violating their sacred burial ground). Redford quietly commands the role, surrounded by the spectacular wilderness settings. The picture is leavened only by occasional comic visits from a loquacious veteran trapper played by Will Geer, whose wise counsel helps keep Jeremiah alive at various critical junctures.

100) ***The Life and Times of Judge Roy Bean*** (1972)—John Huston did not film many westerns, but, aided by John Milius' blackly humorous screenplay, he made a mark with this iconoclastic biography of the infamous Hanging Judge. As imagined here, Paul Newman's scruffy Judge Bean is a far cry from the dashing figure of Butch Cassidy he cut just three years earlier. Ava Gardner plays the key role of Lily Langtry, and able support is also provided by Jacqueline Bisset and Stacey Keach. Typically, Huston also appears in a cameo role. Another excellent paean to the end of the West, for which this era of filmmaking is likely unsurpassed.

101) ***Junior Bonner*** (1972)—Why not conclude with Peckinpah's most atypical film, starring Steve McQueen as a present-day rodeo cowboy who is more than ready to cash in his chips for a job in the world of squares. But it's not going to happen, as he finds out upon returning home only to discover that his home has been sold out from underneath him by venal brother Joe Don Baker. Ida Lupino and Robert Preston make an indelible impression as their warring parents, and the presence of the indispensable Ben Johnson further signals that we have here another farewell to the Old West. Only this one is too acrid to even be termed bittersweet.

and Television
Screen Guide
May · 25¢ A HILLMAN PUBLICATION
BOB MITCHUM--
What Now?
ALSO
Esther Williams
Gary Cooper
Paulette Goddard
Bing Crosby
ROY ROGERS
and
DALE EVANS
A DOCTOR
LOOKS AT
HOLLYWOOD

CHAPTER FOUR

Shootout at the TV Corral

The early days of television were about as organized and aesthetically pleasing as a flea market. With the technology still in its rudimentary stages in the late forties, logic dictated that the safest course for television would be to produce visual equivalents of what was then working on radio, still the dominant popular medium of the day. And so, on came the quiz and game shows, the variety shows and the sit-coms. All of them were proven formulas—simple to recreate, inexpensive to produce. Milton Berle on *Texaco Star Theater* was the acknowledged King of Television in these pioneer days, winning one of the first Emmy Awards in 1949, and radio superstars like Groucho Marx (*You Bet Your Life*) and Ed Wynn were not far behind. The budget for the first *Toast of the Town* in 1948, featuring Ed Sullivan as host, was $1,375, with one thousand of that earmarked for production costs, leaving the remainder to the talent. (Today, $375 wouldn't even pay for a show's snack break, but back then it was enough to cover Martin & Lewis and several other class acts on that debut episode.)

With those limitations, recreating westerns seemed beyond the means and abilities of early television. But into that void rode Hoppy, aka Hopalong Cassidy, to save the day. Beginning with broadcasts in the New York market, Hoppy's films were aired after the war with positive results, leading to the B-pictures becoming a regular series in the 1948-1949 season (often edited down to fit time limitations). The following year, *Hopalong Cassidy* debuted on NBC as an original series, with the now fifty-year-old Boyd riding Topper, his faithful steed, in the pursuit of justice, aided by the crusty Edgar Buchanan. That one year of new episodes was

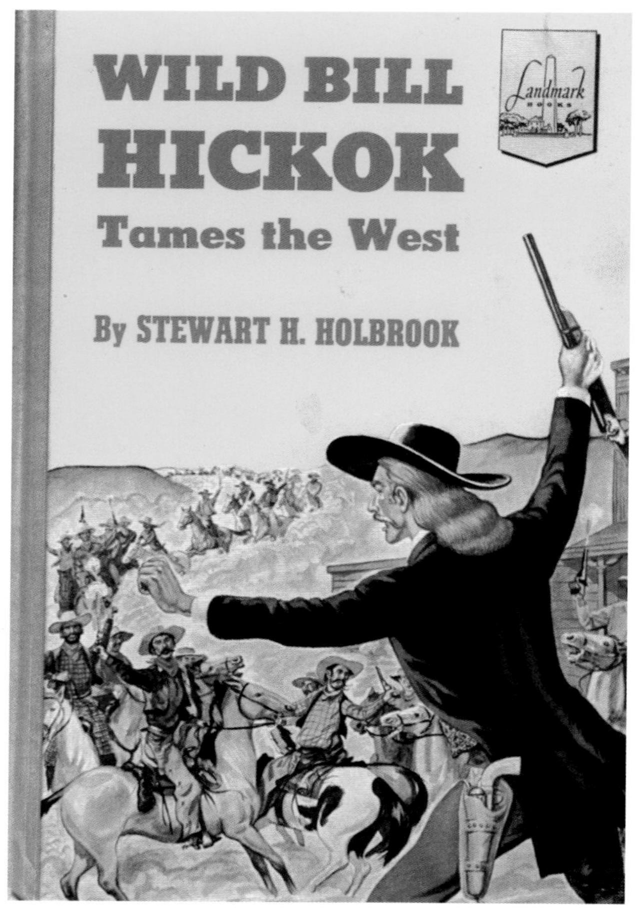

syndicated for many years afterward, making Boyd the best-paid actor per hour in perhaps all of television history.

The Lone Ranger had been the first nationally syndicated western radio show, thanks to the WJR radio station in Detroit, which created the program whole out of the fertile mind of staff writer Fran Striker. It flourished as the linchpin of the Mutual Radio network for fifteen years (also appeared as a fifteen-chapter movie serial in 1938) before it was tapped for the new television medium. Debuting in the fall of 1949, *The Lone Ranger* was played by Clayton Moore for seven of its nine seasons on the air, with John Hart replacing Moore right in the middle of the run, for the 1952 and 1953 seasons. Jay Silverheels, part Mohawk, played the loyal Tonto. But that is only half of this success story. Episodes were rerun by CBS on Saturday mornings until the end of the decade, and then it was rerun some more by the other networks, making it virtually ubiquitous.

Gene Autry was no slouch either in the genius department, parlaying his own backlog of Republic Studio Bs into a weekly half-hour series that debuted on CBS in the summer of 1950. Though, like Hoppy, he was now a bit long in the tooth to be fistfighting with hardened outlaws, Gene's charisma was such that an eight-year-old viewer was unlikely to take note of his paunch and the beginning of jowls in all the excitement—if singing a song in each episode and riding the handsome Champion hither and yon can be classified as excitement. That series ran for six seasons in prime-time, then lived on in reruns for several more.

Those series were the elite of the programs aimed primarily at children, but there was a herd of others in the early fifties, among them *Range Rider* (overseen by Gene Autry's Flying A Productions), *The Adventures of Kit Carson, The Adventures of Wild Bill Hickok, Annie Oakley* (whose star, Gail Davis, had been discovered by Gene Autry, appearing in twenty of his films and thirty episodes of his television series), and *The Cisco Kid,* all of them syndicated series sold to individual stations around the country, who could air them anytime they desired, daytime or evening. As it happened, these programs rarely appeared in prime time hours, in deference to the viewing schedules of the young audience for whom they had been crafted.

One of the more popular forms of the western during the fifties was the anthology series, which featured self-contained stories on a rotating basis, usually with different actors each week. The first to make it to television was the syndicated *Death Valley Days,* which had been a hit on radio from 1930 to 1945. It debuted in 1952, sponsored as always by "20 Mule-Team Borax," with Stanley Andrews serving as host/narrator, "The Old Ranger," until he was replaced in 1966 by Ronald Reagan, who himself was followed by Robert Taylor, Dale Robertson, and, in the final season, 1975, Merle Haggard! An amazing 558 episodes were filmed over those twenty-three years, most of them shot in location in Death Valley (just a hop, skip, and jump from Hollywood).

Dick Powell's Zane Grey Western Theater ran from 1956 to 1962, with an interesting variation: Powell served as host/narrator, as one might expect, but he also acted in a number of episodes. (The series eventually ran out of actual Zane Grey stories to adapt and had to move on to the work of other writers.)

But no adult western even existed as prime-time network series until 1955, when *Gunsmoke, The Life and Legend of Wyatt Earp,* and *Cheyenne* all debuted, each enjoying immediate (though not yet peak) success. Now it

1196
WAGONMASTER
POCKET BOOK
25¢
A novel of the American West, featuring Major Seth Adams and Flint McCullough, who are played by Ward Bond and Robert Horton in the famous NBC-TV drama WAGON TRAIN
ORIGINAL WESTERN NOT A REPRINT
ROBERT TURNER

Bat Masterson

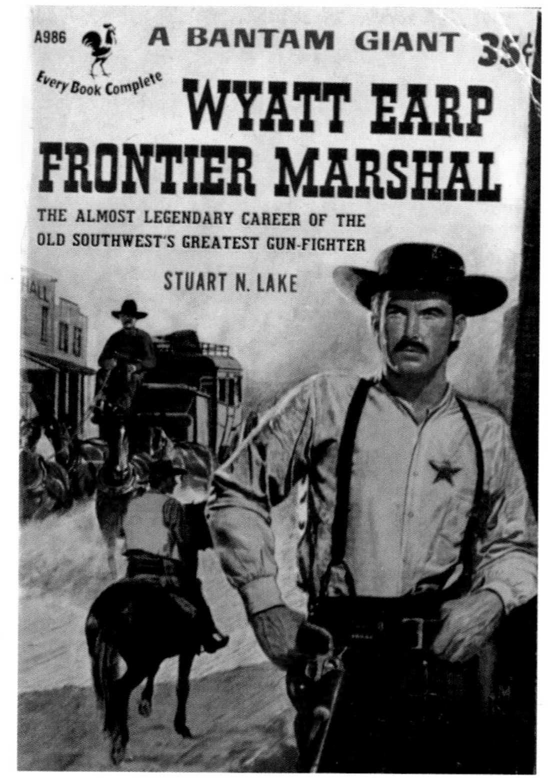
A986
A BANTAM GIANT 35¢
Every Book Complete
WYATT EARP
FRONTIER MARSHAL
THE ALMOST LEGENDARY CAREER OF THE OLD SOUTHWEST'S GREATEST GUN-FIGHTER
STUART N. LAKE

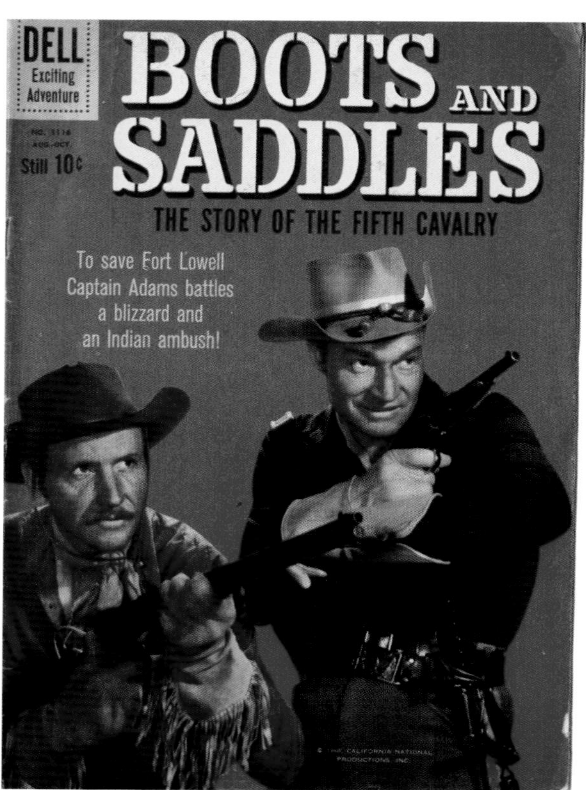
DELL
Exciting Adventure
Still 10¢
BOOTS AND SADDLES
THE STORY OF THE FIFTH CAVALRY
To save Fort Lowell Captain Adams battles a blizzard and an Indian ambush!

DELL
Western Adventure
MARCH-MAY
Still 10¢
HUGH O'BRIAN famous marshal
Wyatt Earp
Wyatt captures stage robbers and recovers their buried loot, but still must find the evidence to convict them!
© 1960, WYATT EARP ENTERPRISES, INC.
AUTHORIZED EDITION

WHY YOUR FAVORITE SHOW WENT OFF THE AIR
Local Listings • March 15-21
TV
GUIDE
15¢
AMANDA BLAKE,
JAMES ARNESS
OF 'GUNSMOKE'

became clear that there was an appetite among adults for such mature shows, allowing the TV western to finally escape from the ghetto of "the children's hour(s)," radically altering the evening TV viewing habits of Americans from coast to coast for the next ten to fifteen years. (In terms of films, of course, the adult western had been flourishing ever since John Ford's *Stagecoach* back in 1939—but then, television always has been a much more conservative medium, both because of its nigh-infinite outreach and its reliance on advertising dollars.)

Gunsmoke actually had a head start on the other debut series, already being established as a radio hit since 1952. Portly William Conrad had been persuasive as the radio voice of Marshal Matt Dillon, but he did not cut a particularly heroic figure, and so the call went out for a more imposing actor to take on the role. John Wayne famously had been the first choice of CBS but didn't want to assume the daily grind of working on a television series. Instead he nominated his pal James Arness, a giant of a man who to that point had essayed his most famous film role by playing the monster in the 1951 classic *The Thing*. Arness clicked immediately with TV viewers and twenty years later was still ensconced in Dodge City, Kansas, as Marshal Dillon, making *Gunsmoke* the longest running prime-time television drama of any genre in history.

The Life and Legend of Wyatt Earp debuted the same week as *Gunsmoke,* showing in that first episode how Earp became marshal of Ellsworth, Kansas (avenging the death of the previous marshal). Hugh O'Brian was the tight-lipped but charismatic star of the series, carrying an enormous pair of "Buntline Specials" (.45s with custom-made long barrels) to help him enforce the law. Amusingly, Earp relocated in the show's second season to Dodge City, where the (fictitious) Matt Dillon was simultaneously serving as marshal for CBS! Loosely following the arc of Earp's life, the show then moved him once again, setting him in Tombstone, Arizona, for the 1959-1960 season. And it was in Tombstone, of course, that Earp met his greatest challenge, in the form of the Clanton family. Logically enough, the final five episodes of the 1960-1961 season had Earp facing off with the Clantons, aided by Doc Holliday and his brothers, Virgil and Morgan, and culminating with the famous gunfight at O.K. Corral. And so the series concluded, as so many did not—on a high note.

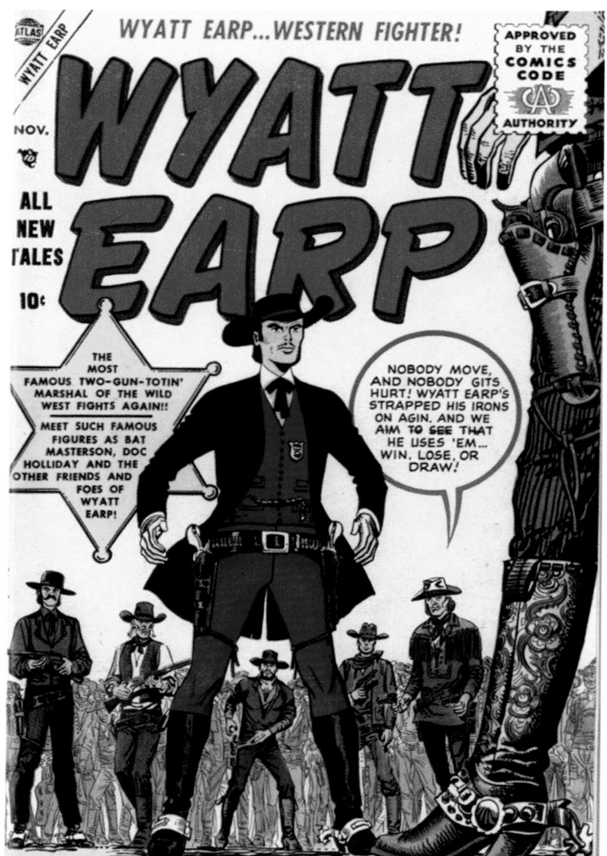

Cheyenne was perhaps the least of the three major debuts of 1955 but was revolutionary in its own way, made as it was by Warner Brothers studios with film production values. It aired on a rotating basis with other hour-long series, primarily *Sugarfoot*—but star Clint Walker (like James Arness, a towering man) fell into a dispute with Warner Brothers after the first two seasons regarding what he felt were outrageous limitations of his residuals and greedy cuts of his personal appearance deals (they claimed half). Walker decided to go on strike, sitting out the 1958 season. Incredibly, Warner continued the series under the *Cheyenne* name but with an entirely new character and actor featured—Ty Hardin playing Bronco. And when Warner gave enough concessions to Walker that he agreed to return for the 1959 season, they kept Hardin in the rotation as well, with his series now sensibly re-titled *Bronco*. Despite all the *sturm und drang, Cheyenne* stayed on the air into 1962, lasting one season beyond *Wyatt Earp*.

Considering this mere handful of westerns proffered by the networks for the 1955-1956 season, it is amazing to see how populous that prime-time

LOCAL LISTINGS • JANUARY 2-8
TV GUIDE
15¢
THE 1950'S:
DO YOU REMEMBER...?
See page 4
ADVICE TO EGGHEADS
By Gilbert Seldes
THE GROUP FROM
'GUNSMOKE'

An Original
35¢
BB
236
GUNSMOKE
—Adventures of Marshal Matt Dillon
adapted by
DON WARD
Kenneth
Boesle
CBS
BALLANTINE BOOKS

GUNSMOKE
Authorized edition featuring Matt Dillon,
western marshal of the CBS television
and radio programs.

landscape had become a mere two years later. Paging through the March 15, 1958, issue of *TV Guide* ("the Louisiana edition"), one can see dozens of westerns distributed through the week's schedule, where once only sitcoms, game shows, and cop series roamed. Even bypassing the considerable number of children's (or at least, non-adult-oriented) syndicated series that ran throughout much of Saturday and on some weekdays—including the likes of *Fury, Cisco Kid, The Lone Ranger, Hopalong Cassidy, Annie Oakley,* and *Sky King*—this representative week of that fondly recalled 1957-1958 season offered up a formidable array of six-guns and thundering hooves:

Saturday evening: *Wyatt Earp; Have Gun Will Travel; Zorro* (all programmed against each other at 8:30 P.M.); *The Californians, Gunsmoke, Zane Grey Theater; Death Valley Days.*

Sunday evening: *Maverick; G.E. Theater* (featuring Ronald Reagan himself in the original drama "The Coward of Ft. Bennett"); *26 Men.*

Monday evening: *Restless Gun; Wells Fargo*

Tuesday evening: *Union Pacific; Sugarfoot* (aired twice; no telling if the same episode was shown or a rerun along with the new episode); *Sheriff of Cochise; Wyatt Earp; Broken Arrow; The Californians; Frontier Doctor; Tombstone Territory* ("Geronimo" was the offering that week of this anthology series); *Trackdown; Colt .45.*

Wednesday evening: *Wagon Train* (aired twice); *Frontier Doctor; Trackdown*

Thursday evening: *Wild Bill Hickok; The Californians*

Friday evening: *Jim Bowie* (aired twice but present only on alternate weeks); *Boots & Saddles* (counter-programmed against itself on two different channels at 7:00 P.M.); *Zane Grey Theater; Trackdown.* (And as a footnote, let it be noted that Tex Ritter's syndicated *Ranch Party* also aired that night.)

The western explosion was, and remains, unprecedented in the history of television, but it had been percolating for some time. While in 1956 only *Gunsmoke* finished in the top fifteen shows of the year, at #8, the 1957-1958 television season saw no fewer than six westerns place among the top fifteen shows—*Gunsmoke* actually was the number one-rated program for the season, while *Tales of Wells Fargo* was #3, *Have Gun Will Travel* #4, *The Life and Legend of Wyatt Earp* #6, *The Restless Gun* #8, and *Cheyenne* #13.

Impressive—but nothing compared to the western mania that possessed American viewers the following year. For the 1958-1959 season, six of the top seven shows were westerns, a genre domination that has never since been repeated. *Gunsmoke* was again in the number one slot (it held that pinnacle for four straight years, quite an achievement), followed by *Wagon Train, Have Gun Will Travel, The Rifleman,* and (skipping the number five slot) *Maverick,* and *Tales of Wells Fargo. Wyatt Earp* was hardly a slouch at number ten, and *Zane Grey Theater, The Texan, Wanted: Dead or Alive, Cheyenne,* and *Sugarfoot* all registered between #13 and #21. So prevalent was the western that year that the Emmy Awards actually created a Best Western Series category, won by *Maverick* (an experiment that was not repeated).

The 1959-1960 season was more of the same, with western series holding down the top three slots for the year and eight others registering between #9 and #23. But none of those hit shows would prove to be quite as significant as a debut series that did not place in the top twenty-five that year—*Bonanza*. *Bonanza* was innovative in several ways. First and foremost, it was the first western to be televised in color. Hard to believe today, it's true but somewhat understandable given the relatively small number of households that owned a color TV set in 1959. (Thanks to the popularity of shows like *Bonanza,* though, those color sets would soon be flying off the shelves, relegating black & white sets to basement storage.)

Bonanza spent its first two years as a modest hit, airing on Saturday nights. But once it was shifted to a Sunday night slot in its third season, there was no holding it back. Its formula was not exactly unique, since *The Rifleman* had beaten it by a year in the Widowed-Dad-Raising-Son-Alone sweepstakes—but the stakes were tripled in *Bonanza,* with the three high-spirited Cartwright boys (Michael Landon, Pernell Roberts, and Dan

Blocker), all borne by different mothers, sometimes embodying the Ego, Superego, and Id as they were drawn into assorted misadventures, trying even the supernatural patience of dad Ben Cartwright (Lorne Greene). The grand Ponderosa spread, purportedly set in Virginia City, Nevada, was the one element of the series that failed to convince; location shooting was still years away for TV westerns. The show flourished for thirteen years, hitting the number one spot for three years running in the mid-sixties, before being unceremoniously canceled in the middle of the 1972 season.

The 1959-1960 season in many ways represented the artistic high point of the genre. Most of the earlier series were still going strong, and to their number was now added the likes of *Bat Masterson,* starring Gene Barry as the urbane lawman who was pals with Wyatt Earp; *The Deputy,* with Henry Fonda as Marshal Simon Fry, monitoring Arizona Territory; *Laramie,* with John Smith and Robert Fuller as brothers running a spread in Wyoming; *The Rebel,* with method actor Nick Adams as ex-Reb Johnny Yuma (theme song by Johnny Cash); *Shotgun Slade,* starring Scott Brady as a private eye in the Old West; and the *pièce de la résistance, Rawhide,* with Eric Fleming as trail boss Gil Favor and a young and incredibly handsome Clint Eastwood as second-in-command Rowdy Yates, which ran for seven (mostly) glorious seasons. All this, and *Bonanza* too. Life was good for kids with TV viewing privileges, no matter where they might live.

Despite the high-flying success of *Bonanza* and the continuing run of *Gunsmoke* throughout the decade, the sixties would prove to be less kind to the western than the fifties had been. While some new series like *The Virginian* (1962-1971), *The High Chaparral* (1967-1971), and *The Big Valley* (1965-1969) did become established hits, the vast majority of sixties debuts became one-season-and-out marginalia. A partial roll call of these would include *Shane* with David Carradine, *The Road West, Stoney Burke* (with a cast for the ages: Jack Lord, Bruce Dern, and Warren Oates), *Temple Houston, Whispering Smith, The Wide Country, A Man Called Shenandoah, Custer* (what network genius thought of *that* one?), *Destry, Hondo* (guys: leave these movie spin-offs alone, please!), *The Loner, The Monroes* (a sentimental favorite, largely because of the presence of a young Barbara Hershey as the doughty family leader), *The Outcasts, Empire,* and *Gunslinger* (even a theme song sung by Frankie Laine wasn't enough). *Branded,* featuring

GOLD KEY
WAGON TRAIN
STILL ONLY 12¢
WAGON TRAIN
Two exciting features
ENCOUNTER AT EAGLE CROSSING
and
THE YOUNG BRAVES
Bob Fuller
John McIntire

DELL
AUG.-OCT.
Still 10¢
NO. 1019
WAGON TRAIN
Somewhere in the wagon train lurked a traitor...
responsible for the broken treaty!

DELL
Western Adventure
JAN.-MARCH
Still 10¢
WAGON TRAIN
Two old-timers join the train and
bring a wagonload of trouble!

DELL
Western Adventure
APRIL-JUNE
Still 10¢
WAGON TRAIN
Major Adams uses an
eclipse of the sun
to save Flint
and the wagon train
from vengeful
Cheyennes!

Chuck Connors as an ex-soldier trying to prove his dismissal from the army for cowardice was unjust, was a minor hit (#14) for one season but was gone after the second. The fact that two of the biggest western hits of the decade were parodies—*F Troop* and *The Wild, Wild West*—was a tipoff that the traditional formulas were losing the interest of the viewers.

That decline became more precipitous as the seventies began. The anomaly was Michael Landon's family saga blockbuster *Little House on the Prairie,* which ran from 1974 to 1983 (an eternity for a non-comedy series), registering in the top twenty for a couple of seasons before climbing to #7 in season four and then hitting number one in the 1979-1980 season—the first western to earn the top spot since *Bonanza* thirteen years earlier. (Unless you care to argue that Walnut Grove, Minnesota, wasn't really the West. Maybe not compared to Arizona; but compared to Massachusetts, it sure was.) Landon was the Orson Welles of the small screen, producing, sometimes directing and writing, and then acting in the majority of the episodes, ensuring a quality control that enabled the series to last for ten full seasons.

But the success of *Little House* didn't translate for the majority of western programs. Indeed, few attempts were even being made by the networks to launch new westerns series at that juncture. Who remembers James Garner on his ancient motorcycle in the 1971 series *Nichols,* set in 1914 Arizona? How about Kurt Russell and Tim Matheson in the search drama *The Quest?* Or Brenda Vaccaro in *Sara,* about a feminist schoolteacher in Independence, Colorado? *Alias Smith & Jones* actually lasted for two seasons on ABC, but *The Cowboys, Dirty Sally, The Chisolms, How the West Was Won* (marking the return to TV of icon James Arness), and *The Life and Times of Grizzly Adams* each lasted for but a single season. It was fun, though, to see Richard Boone, late of *Have Gun Will Travel,* return for two seasons of *Hec Ramsey* as a frontier criminologist, and the three-year run of David Carradine's oddity *Kung Fu* was cheering to those of us who got their kicks from watching the first counter-culture western.

The eighties offered little to reverse this downward trend, flailing about with doomed attempts as James Garner returning to the scene of past glory in *Bret Maverick* (1981) and Josh Brolin and Stephen Baldwin trying to pass themselves off as twenty-something versions of Buffalo Bill Cody and Wild Bill Hickok in *The Young Riders* (1989). But the decade was not a total bust, thanks to the entirely wonderful adaptation of Larry McMurtry's epic bestseller *Lonesome Dove* that appeared in 1989, a high-water mark in the history of both the television miniseries as well as the western (of any stripe, in any medium). Robert Duvall and Tommy Lee Jones excelled as a pair of long-in-the-tooth, constantly squabbling ex-Texas Rangers who steal a herd of Mexican cattle to make one final score on a cattle drive to Montana, the yin and yang of the cowboy archetype. They were ably supported by Diane Lane as the prostitute whom you could take home to mother, Robert Urich

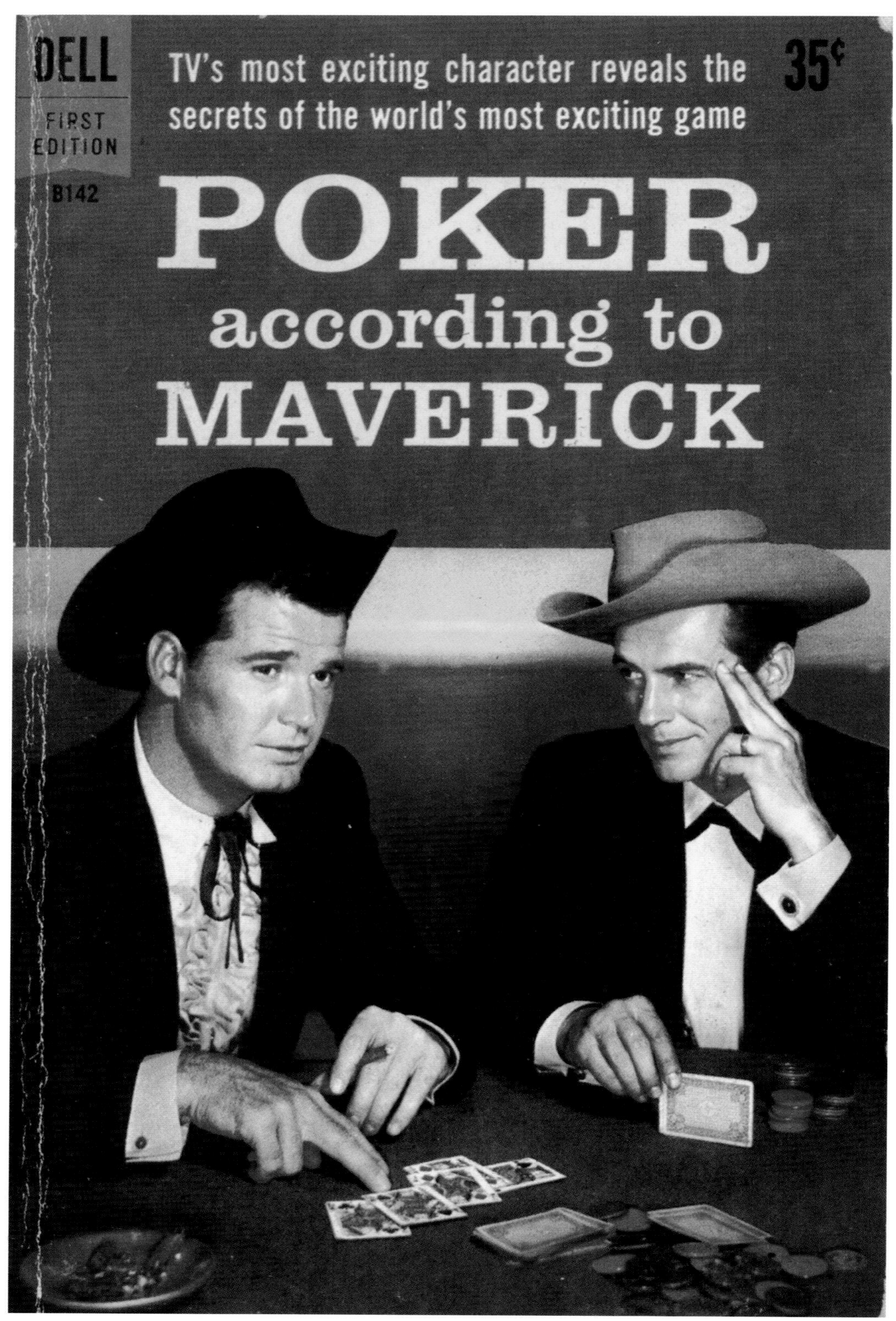
DELL
FIRST EDITION
B142
TV's most exciting character reveals the secrets of the world's most exciting game
35¢
POKER
according to
MAVERICK

as the inveterate gambler who squanders everything, Angelica Huston as the love of Duvall's life, and Frederic Forrest as the extremely frightening Indian killer Blue Duck. Too bad the subsequent McMurtry miniseries that followed over the years, *Streets of Laredo, Return to Lonesome Dove,* and *Comanche Moon,* couldn't hold a candle to it.

In the new millennium, it does appear that the miniseries is the last, best hope of the western on television. Despite the pallid job done on 2007's *Comanche Moon,* AMC's impressive *Broken Trail* in 2006 showed that it was possible to capture the epic scope of the best western films even on television, given a good enough script, top-shelf-acting, and quality directing.

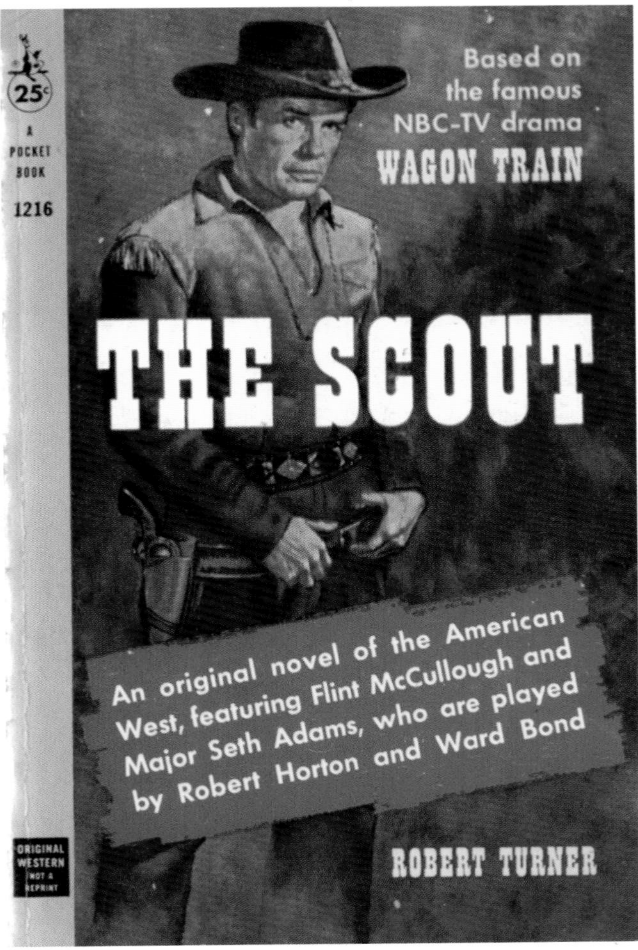

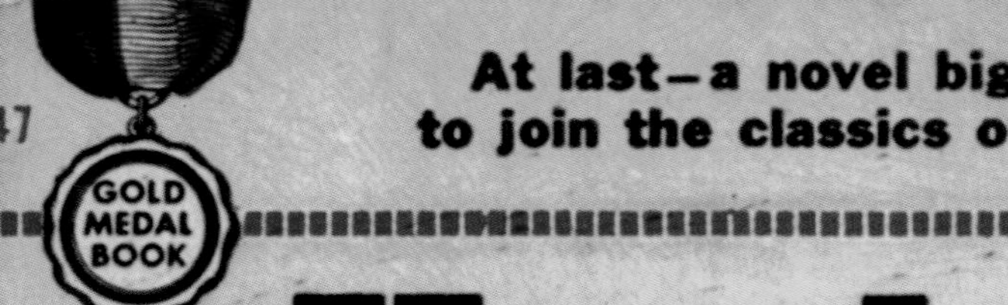

Hondo

LOUIS L'AMOUR

"Best western novel I have ever read."
—John Wayne

CHAPTER FIVE

Riders of the Purple Page: 100 Years of Great Western Lit

Whether they were honed in the crucible of the pulp magazines, seasoned in the Hollywood studio system, or simply professional wordsmiths who had a vision of the Old West and a trusty Remington (manual, if you please) to make it come alive, the following writers all helped shape the landscape of the western in the popular imagination of their time. Some are still legendary, some have seen their fame dissipate in the decades that have come and gone, and others were never particularly famous in the first place. But each made a contribution to the art of the western that we can now applaud as being significant. To their dozens and dozens of worthy colleagues who might also have been profiled here but for space considerations, my apologies.

1) **Louis L'Amour—**The godfather of them all. Perhaps not as famous a cultural figure as Zane Grey was during his lengthy reign, L'Amour nonetheless dominated the landscape of westerns for the better part of four decades. When he died in 1988, he had some eighty-six novels to his credit, a number that has since grown significantly, thanks to posthumous publications.

Born in North Dakota in 1908, L'Amour traveled all over the U.S. and then all over the world as a merchant seaman, taking whatever jobs came his way—a true roustabout. L'Amour began writing for the pulp magazines in the late thirties, using a wide array of names (Jim Mayo, Tex Burns), sometimes even his own. He wrote not only for the western pulps but also the mystery and adventure ones and demonstrated a real knack for the hard-boiled detective story. But it was the popularity of John Wayne's 1953 film *Hondo*, which adapted L'Amour's story, "The Gift of Cochise," that finally allowed him to shed his anonymity.

It would take this entire chapter, if not the entire book, to touch on all of L'Amour's accomplishments over his eighty years on earth. But here are a few: seventeen novels devoted to the Sackett clan alone. Nine Hopalong Cassidy books. Fourteen short story collections at the time of his death, and another sixteen since then. A dozen or so works adapted for the big screen, beginning with the celebrated *Hondo* and continuing with *Heller in Pink Tights* (*Heller with a Gun* when published), *Apache Territory* (*Last Stand at Papago Wells*), *Guns of the Timberland, Taggart, Shalako,* and *Catlow.* Enough TV movies to satisfy a platoon, including *The Cherokee Trail, The Sacketts, The Shadow Riders, Down the Long Hills, The Quick and the Dead, Conagher* (these last two starring the estimable Sam Elliott, who was put on the earth to act in westerns), and *Crossfire Trail.*

L'Amour was awarded the Congressional Gold Medal in 1982, and two years later became the first author ever to be given the Medal of Freedom, thanks to President Ronald Reagan. His books are estimated to have sold worldwide in the hundreds of millions. Louis L'Amour is still widely read today, and no doubt will continue to be read until the cactus itself is extinct.

2) **Zane Grey**—It's hard to believe that Grey, the pride of Zanesville, Ohio—yes, it was called that *before* Grey adopted that old family name Zane as his own—almost failed to get his career off the ground. But the fact is that his early efforts to become an author were soundly rejected by the publishing industry. His first novel, *Betty Zane*—based on the heroism of one of his own ancestors—was finally published in 1903, but even then his future as an author was unclear. Three years went by before his next novel, *Spirit of the Border,* appeared, and then a gap of two more years before Grey's first true western, *The Last of the Plainsmen,* was published; in short order it became a national bestseller.

Grey now seemed to have hit his stride, and his books began to appear at the rate of two per year (though not all were westerns; he also wrote a number of baseball novels—he had played in college at Penn and was also

2 ZANE GREY'S
TWO great outdoor romances.
Millions say ZANE GREY'S best.
RIDERS OF THE PURPLE SAGE
with GEORGE O'BRIEN
Virginia Cherrill James Kirkwood
Marguerite Churchill
Directed by IRVING CUMMINGS
and THE RAINBOW TRAIL
with GEORGE O'BRIEN
Linda Watkins · Allan Dinehart
Gaylord Pendleton · Rosalie Roy
Directed by JOHN BLYSTONE

ZANE GREY'S
The LAST TRAIL

"If you break up the Poggin gang, you'll get your pardon and chances are a thousand to one you'll be killed trying."
"Then I'll take the odds!"
ZANE GREY'S first talking picture
WILLIAM FOX presents
The Lone Star Ranger
An adventurous story of the vast cattle reaches of the LONE STAR STATE when lead bullets were more valuable than gold nuggets.
Directed by John Blystone

ORIGINALS
35¢
BB
29
INDIAN COUNTRY
DOROTHY M. JOHNSON
Outstanding stories of character and courage on the American frontier
BALLANTINE BOOKS

THE BORDER KID
by MAX BRAND
A WESTERN NOVEL
ARMED SERVICES EDITION
THIS IS THE COMPLETE BOOK—NOT A DIGEST

in the minors for a spell—and some non-fiction as well). Throughout the teens he kept them coming at a steady rate: *Riders of the Purple Sage* (probably his most famous work), *Desert Gold, The Light of Western Stars, The Lone Star Ranger, The Border Legion, The UP Trail.* And then, in the twenties: *The Mysterious Rider, Wanderer of the Wasteland, Call of the Canyon, The Thundering Herd, The Vanishing American, Nevada, Wild Horse Mesa,* and *Fighting Caravans.* A great many of these were made into silent films and then remade with sound during the thirties and forties.

Grey's popularity didn't wane during the thirties. In rapid succession came *Sunset Pass, Arizona Ames, Robber's Roost, The Hash Knife Outfit, The Code of the West, The Trail Driver, West of the Pecos, Knights of the Range,* and *Western Union.* But as the decade drew to a close, so too did Grey's time on earth. He died in 1939 at the age of sixty-seven in Altadena, California, where he had lived since 1920. But even death could not halt the flow of Zane Grey novels. All through the forties and well into the fifties new works continued to appear, though no longer at his earlier rate: *Thirty Thousand on the Hoof, Twin Sombreros, The Wilderness Trek, Rogue River Feud, The Maverick Queen, Captives of the Desert, Wyoming,* and *Black Mesa*—among many others. You could say that Grey was more prolific after his death than many authors are during their entire lives. Which is why it was possible to launch a television anthology series bearing his name in the mid-fifties; Zane Grey was not merely an author, he was a brand. Heck, he was an empire!

Grey has been the subject of numerous biographies, but his extremely unconventional lifestyle is particularly well documented in the 2005 study *Zane Grey: His Life, His Adventures, His Women* by Thomas H. Pauley.

3) **Max Brand**—Born Frederick Faust in Seattle in 1892, the man that millions of western readers have come to know and love as Max Brand grew up in California and worked as a cowhand before he attended UC Berkeley. Moving to New York City, Faust began writing for the pulps in 1919 and soon was a regular contributor to *Argosy, All-Story,* and *Western Story Magazine* among others. His first novel, *The Untamed,* was brought to the screen in 1920 for none other than Tom Mix.

It has been estimated that, at his peak, Max Brand was writing as much as two million words a year (guess he never heard of writer's block!) in a wide variety of genres (and under several pen names). In fact, Faust's most famous creation had nothing whatsoever to do with the western—Dr. Kildare, who was based on his friend Dr. George "Dixie" Fish. But he is also well remembered for his character Destry, from the novel *Destry Rides Again,* memorably portrayed onscreen in 1939 by James Stewart.

Faust moved to Florence, Italy, with his wife in 1925 and remained there for many years, returning to the U.S. in 1938 to live and work in Hollywood for Warner Bros. as a highly paid screenwriter. Incredibly, Faust enlisted during World War II at the age of fifty-one—knowing he had a heart condition—to be a war correspondent. In 1944, while on a mission with American troops in Italy, Faust was struck by shrapnel and killed.

Even after his death, many collections of his prodigious output continued to be published. It is thought his total output might have reached some thirty million words—not that anyone would have time to count it!

4) **Larry McMurtry**—When giants walked the earth, there was McMurtry. No writer has done more to keep the western alive and well—on the printed page, certainly, but also on the big screen and the small screen too. Since 1961, when his first novel, *Horseman, Pass By,* was published (to be memorably filmed as *Hud* in 1963), McMurtry has compiled a résumé of western fiction that few can match. *Leaving Cheyenne* (1963) became the film *Loving Molly,* while *The Last Picture Show* (1966) was turned into a wonderful movie five years later by Peter Bogdanovich, with a screenplay co-written with McMurtry. *Terms of Endearment* was published in 1975, although it took eight years for the multi-Oscar-winning movie to appear—but then, that contemporary drama was hardly a western.

Then there was a bit of a lull in terms of major successes, until the state-of-the-art epic *Lonesome Dove* was published in 1985. It would go on to win the Pulitzer Prize and top the national bestseller lists, but *Dove's* greatest fame may have been realized when it was mounted as a television miniseries by NBC in 1989, with the peerless Robert Duvall as the warm and wise Gus (one of McMurtry's greatest creations) and Tommy Lee Jones as the emotionally repressed Captain Woodrow F. Call, nicely supported by Robert Urich, Diane Lane, and Frederic Forrest (as the murderous Blue Duck.) Although the book was even better—no small compliment—forty million people watched this miniseries, proving yet again that the perceived demise of the western had been greatly exaggerated.

McMurtry spent the next twenty years alternating between sequels to his Big Three novels (*Texasville, The Evening Star, Streets of Laredo, Dead Man's Walk, Comanche Moon, Duane's Depressed,* and *When the Light Goes* all fall into this category) and original works like *Anything for Billy* (about Billy the Kid), *Buffalo Girls, Telegraph Days,* and the four books in the Berrybender narratives. He also wrote an impressive batch of western nonfiction, including *Crazy Horse, Sacagawea's Nickname,* and *The Colonel and Little Missie: Buffalo Bill, Annie Oakley & the Beginnings of Superstardom in America*. But for fans of McMurtry, few sights were more satisfying than seeing him ascend the stage at the 2007 Academy Awards to accept his Academy Award for co-writing the screenplay adaptation (with Diana Ossana) for the acclaimed film *Brokeback Mountain,* shod in cowboy boots, sporting jeans beneath his tux. Now, *that's* Texas.

5) **Dorothy Johnson**—Raised in Montana, journalist Dorothy Johnson's modest fiction output is belied by the impact it still has today. Her two seminal short story collections, *Indian Country* (1953) and *The Hanging Tree* (1957), elements of which first appeared in *The Saturday Evening Post,* birthed three major western movies: *The Man Who Shot Liberty Valance, A Man Called Horse* (which itself led to two sequels), and *The Hanging Tree*. She also wrote the novels *The Buffalo Woman* and *Buffalo Woman Returning* in the late seventies, and throughout her career authored a number of nonfiction works about the history of the West. Judy Alter's 1980 study *Dorothy Johnson* remains the best source on this remarkable talent.

6) **Jack Schaefer**—Best remembered as the author of the book that gave birth to the beloved 1953 film *Shane,* Schaefer is rarely given credit for the fact that his novel (published in 1949) is even better than that celebrated movie. Nor was Schaefer a one-trick pony. His other fine work includes novels and story collections such as *First Blood, The Canyon,* and *The Big Range* (all 1953), *The Pioneers* (1954), and *Monte Walsh* (1963), which was filmed in 1970 with Lee Marvin. Schaefer also wrote a number of nonfiction books about the West. A native of Ohio, his early books came out while he was liv-

ing in the East—he even attended Columbia Graduate School—but Schaefer moved to Santa Fe in 1955 and spent the rest of his life a westerner.

7) **Borden Chase**—The great 1948 Howard Hawks film *Red River* was based on Chase's *Saturday Evening Post* story and has since passed into legend, but Chase's résumé in the western genre runs deep and wide. A veteran of the detective and adventure pulp magazines, Chase authored only a handful of western novels, including *Lone Star* and *Viva Gringo!* but, more critically, he also wrote the screenplays to three of the classic Anthony Mann/James Stewart westerns, *Winchester '73, Bend of the River,* and *The Far Country.* Chase also contributed either story or screenplay to such westerns as *Lone Star* (based on his own novel, about Texas' fight for independence, starring Clark Gable), *Man Without a Star* (with Kirk Douglas), *Night Passage* (with James Stewart and Audie Murphy), and *Vera Cruz.* He also must be the only writer of westerns to have worked (many years earlier) as a sandhog building New York's Holland Tunnel, an experience he used as the basis for his first novel.

8) **Elmore Leonard**—Now famed for his quirky, hard-boiled crime bestsellers, Elmore Leonard got his start writing westerns for the pulp magazines, which paid up to two cents a word—if you were lucky. His stories "Three-Ten to Yuma" (from *Dime Western*) and "The Captives" (from *Argosy*) both made it to Hollywood in 1957, the latter filmed as *The Tall T.* Good films both, but they didn't jumpstart Elmore's career as one might have expected, and he went back to writing westerns during free time from his job in advertising. Leonard's first novel, *The Bounty Hunters,* was published in 1953, and he followed that with such full-length works as *Escape from Five Shadows, Last Stand at Saber River,* and *Hombre.* It was this last novel, adapted into a Paul Newman vehicle in 1967, that finally gave Leonard the boost he needed to write fulltime. His final western novel, *Valdez is Coming* (1970), was made into a very good film in 1973 with Burt Lancaster.

By this juncture, though, Leonard said goodbye to the western, and began writing (mostly) contemporary crime and suspense novels, many of which also made it to the big screen. Still, his body of work in the western genre—some thirty short stories and a half-dozen novels—is more than enough to establish him as worthy of a place in the pantheon. And even on

ORIGINALS
35¢
BB
22
JACK SCHAEFER
The Big Range
Ten magnificent stories
of the Western frontier
by the author of FIRST BLOOD
HOUGHTON
MIFFLIN
COMPANY
WITH
BALLANTINE BOOKS

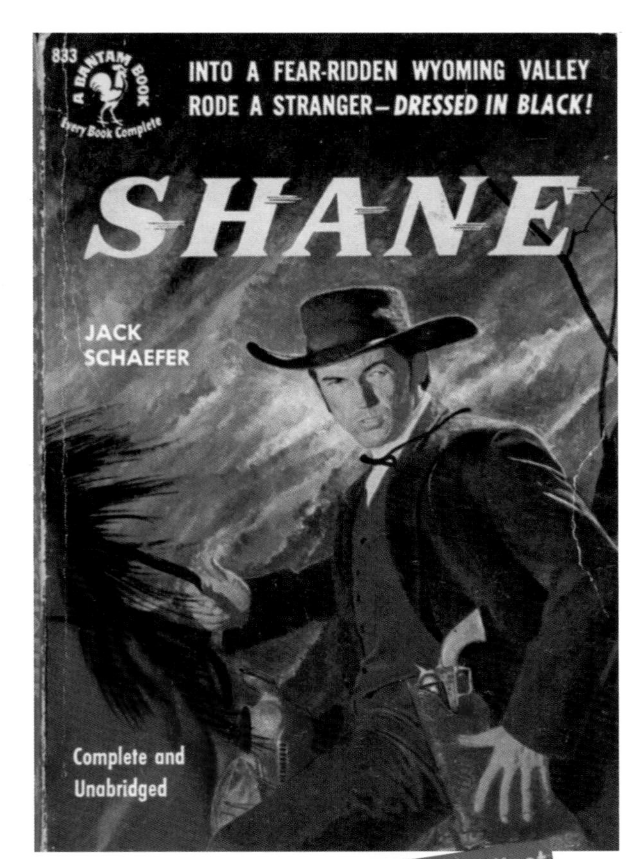
833
A BANTAM BOOK
Every Book Complete
INTO A FEAR-RIDDEN WYOMING VALLEY
RODE A STRANGER—DRESSED IN BLACK!
SHANE
JACK
SCHAEFER
Complete and
Unabridged

205
They fought to save the State of Texas
RED RIVER
(BLAZING GUNS ON THE CHISHOLM TRAIL)
borden chase
A BANTAM BOOK
Complete and Unabridged

AVON
25¢
775
A rugged and realistic story of the West
as powerful as Shane!
THE TALL T
AND OTHER WESTERN ADVENTURES
with PHOTOS from the thrilling movie starring
RANDOLPH SCOTT

the heels of all those crime bestsellers, we were reminded recently of his origins when one of Leonard's latter-day western yarns, "The Tonto Woman," (1982), was made into a short film in 2007 and nominated for an Academy Award.

9) **Elmer Kelton**—The pride of Texas, Elmer Kelton is the author of about sixty novels, covering a span of fifty years. Seven of those books won the Spur Award as best western of the year: *Buffalo Wagons* (1957); *The Day the Cowboys Quit* (1971); *The Time It Never Rained* (1973); *Eyes of the Hawk* (1981); *Slaughter* (1992); *The Far Canyon* (1994); and *Way of the Coyote* (2002). He is the recipient of lifetime achievement awards from the Texas Institute of Letters, Western Writers of America, and the Western Literature Association. The son of a working ranch foreman, Kelton professes that he never "made a hand" but still put his knowledge of ranching life and Texas history to good use in his writing.

His novels cover the years from the Texas Revolution (1836) up to the present. Best known is the classic *The Time It Never Rained,* about the 1950s drought. His hero in that one, Charlie Flagg, is older, overweight, and a bit arthritic, and he's watching his ranching world fall apart as the drought forces him to sell cattle, then sheep, and finally, to raise goats. Kelton often describes his heroes as 5'6" and nervous, as opposed to the towering John Wayne stereotype. In Charlie Flagg's story, as in his other novels, Kelton does not tie things up neatly at the end, because, he says, life isn't that way. Only one of his many novels, the wonderfully comic *The Good Old Boys,* has appeared on screen, that in a made-for-TV production starring and directed by Tommy Lee Jones. (Hollywood—take note!) His memoir, *Sandhills Boy,* was published in 2007.

10) **James Warner Bellah**—A veteran of both World Wars I and II (the latter ending with his earning the rank of colonel), James Warner Bellah was one of the stars of *The Saturday Evening Post,* perhaps the apex of short-story publishing at the mid-point of the century. Bellah's work therein (eighteen stories in all) was enthusiastically embraced by Hollywood; in fact, he was virtually co-opted by John Ford, who adapted "Massacre" as the basis for *Fort Apache,* "Command," "War Party," and "The Big Hunt" to fashion *She Wore a Yellow Ribbon,* and "Mission with No Record" as the

the man who shot
LIBERTY
VALANCE
A novelization by JAMES WARNER BELLAH of the smash Paramount motion picture starring
JAMES STEWART & JOHN WAYNE
co-starring Vera Miles * Lee Marvin * Edmond O'Brien
A JOHN FORD PRODUCTION

THE WOLF AND THE BUFFALO
An historical novel of the Black Soldier in the American West. By the author of The Time It Never Rained and The Good Old Boys.
Elmer Kelton

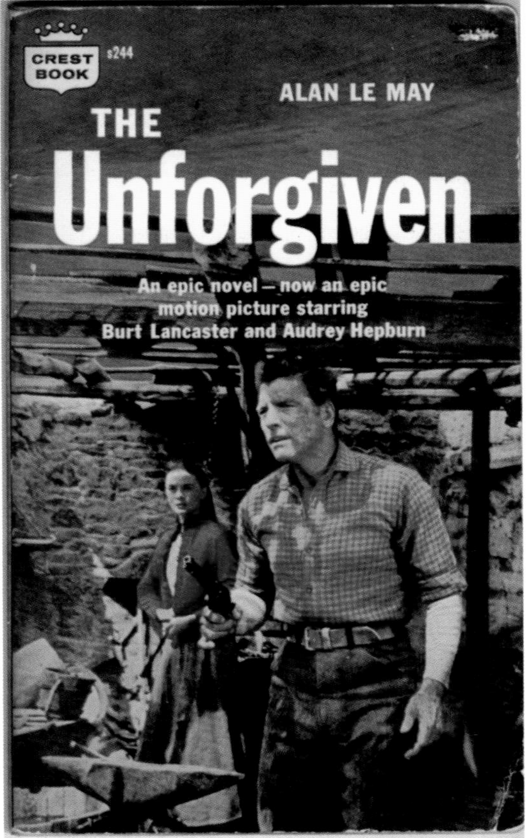
CREST BOOK
s244
ALAN LE MAY
THE Unforgiven
An epic novel — now an epic motion picture starring
Burt Lancaster and Audrey Hepburn

Hombre means man...
Paul Newman is Hombre!
She'd been loved and let down, And then she met HOMBRE
He came looking for trouble and he found it—in HOMBRE
He wanted to be a friend to a man who had none—HOMBRE
20th CENTURY-FOX PRESENTS
PAUL NEWMAN
FREDRIC MARCH | RICHARD BOONE | DIANE CILENTO
CO-STARRING CAMERON MITCHELL · BARBARA RUSH · AND MARTIN BALSAM
Directed by MARTIN RITT · Co-produced by Martin Ritt and Irving Ravetch · Screenplay by IRVING RAVETCH and HARRIET FRANK, Jr.
From the Novel by ELMORE LEONARD · Music by DAVID ROSE · Panavision®
COLOR By Deluxe
"HOMBRE"

ORIGINALS
35¢
BB
40
Yellow Hair
by CLAY FISHER
Author of War Bonnet
Custer—Hated by the Cheyenne, feared by his troops—a young man driven by reckless ambition.
HOUGHTON MIFFLIN COMPANY
Dolphin Edition
WITH BALLANTINE BOOKS

Along Came Jones—And Busted All the Records....North, South, East, West!
INTERNATIONAL PICTURES'
latest box-office sensation sets new high marks in CINCINNATI — NEW ORLEANS — WASHINGTON DENVER — BALTIMORE — DALLAS — KANSAS CITY HOUSTON — PROVIDENCE — SAN ANTONIO OKLAHOMA CITY—FT. WORTH—OMAHA—TULSA DES MOINES—CEDAR RAPIDS—SIOUX CITY . . . with the same kind of smash business rolling up in scores of openings throughout America. The story will be the same in cities and towns in the United Kingdom.
Be sure to attend the Trade Screening at the Odeon, Leicester Square, on Tuesday, October 23, at 10.35 a.m., of
GARY COOPER ★ LORETTA YOUNG
Nunnally Johnson's
"Along Came Jones"
WILLIAM DEMAREST · DAN DURYEA FRANK SULLY
A CINEMA ARTISTS CORP. Production Produced by Gary Cooper Directed by STUART HEISLER
SCREEN PLAY BY NUNNALLY JOHNSON · NOVEL BY ALAN Le MAY · AN INTERNATIONAL PICTURE · Released by RKO RADIO PICTURES, LTD.
GOOD ENTERTAINMENT IS INTERNATIONAL!

launching point for *Rio Grande*. (Those *SEP* stories had all been illustrated by Harold von Schmidt, and Ford even commissioned Schmidt to do the poster art for the films when they were released, perhaps to remind audiences of their print origins.) Though Bellah also authored nineteen novels, it was really that John Ford cavalry trilogy, along with his screenplays for Ford's subsequent *Sgt. Rutledge* and *The Man Who Shot Liberty Valance,* a Dorothy Johnson short story, which set him firmly in the pantheon.

11) **Alan Le May**—If he had written only the novels *The Searchers* and *The Unforgiven,* Alan Le May would still rank among the elite writers of westerns, so towering are those two works. The former became a legendary film—possibly the best western ever made by Hollywood—but I am here to tell you, the book is even better. (Heresy, I know.) The latter novel, also excellent, was originally published in shorter form as "Kiowa Moon" in the pages of (what else?) *The Saturday Evening Post;* but it received only serviceable treatment on the screen, largely because Burt Lancaster and Audrey Hepburn were miscast. Le May also wrote the screenplays for an array of western films, including *Cheyenne, San Antonio,* and the Cecil B. DeMille extravaganza *North West Mounted Police;* he also penned episodes of such prime western TV series as *Sugarfoot, Cheyenne,* and *Bronco.* His novel *Along Came Jones* was made into an amiable vehicle for Gary Cooper in 1945.

12) **Ernest Haycox**—One of the most prolific western authors, the Oregon born-and-raised Haycox had his first short story, "The Trap Lifters," published in 1922 and his debut novel, *Free Grass,* published in 1928. Many others would follow over the next twenty-five years, a few even appearing after his death in 1950: *Sundown Jim, The Wild Bunch* (no, not "that" *Wild Bunch*), *Bugles in the Afternoon, The Border Trumpet, Trail Town, Alder Gulch,* and *Canyon Passage.* During those years, he also published scores and scores of short stories, many in such prestigious "slicks" as *The Saturday Evening Post* and *Colliers.* His 1937 story, "Stage to Lordsburg," was filmed two years later by John Ford as *Stagecoach,* the movie generally credited with revitalizing the western genre. (To that point, most western pictures seemed to brandish a distinctly juvenile aura.) Haycox was also responsible for the stories that gave birth to such films as

Union Pacific, The Far Country, Canyon Passage, and *Abilene Town,* among others. He also penned the screenplay to the 1950 Errol Flynn picture *Montana*. Haycox died in 1950, but numerous collections of his short fiction continued to appear long after his passing.

13) **Henry Wilson Allen**—His day job was with the Tex Avery animation unit at MGM, so Allen devised the pen name of Will Henry under which to publish his first western novel in 1950, a Little Big Horn dramatization called *No Survivors.* He continued to employ the Henry name, along with the alias Clay Fisher, on what eventually stretched to fifty novels, five of which won the Spur Award as best of the year. Among the highlights: *Yellow Hair,* another novel about Custer (a veritable cottage industry unto itself), with the neat twist of having the story related from the point-of-view of Indian scout J. Kelso; *The Texas Rangers; MacKenna's*

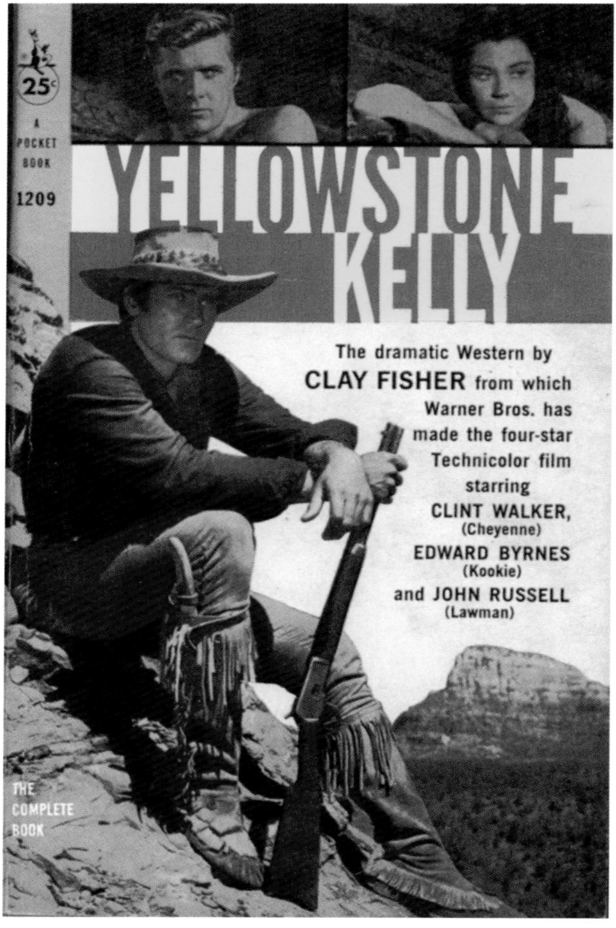

Gold (made into a movie in 1969); *The Last Warpath; Chiricahua; I, Tom Horn; Yellowstone Kelly;* and *Pillars of the Sky.*

14) **Loren D. Estleman**—His body of work the past thirty years has been mighty impressive—fine western novels like *The Stranglers, The Hider, Aces and Eights* (winner of the Spur Award for 1981), *This Old Bill, Mister St. John, Bloody Season* (about the gunfight at the O.K. Corral), *Gun Man,* and *Sudden Country.* He also won a Spur Award for his 1986 collection *The Best Western Stories of Loren D. Estleman.* While the past fifteen years have seen Estleman focus more on his crime fiction, he did edit a collection called *American West: Twenty New Stories* in 2001 for the Western Writers of America.

15) **James Welch**—Born in 1940 in Browning, Montana, to a father who was from the Blackfeet tribe and a mother who hailed from the Gros Ventre, James Welch was educated at schools on the Blackfeet and Fort Belknap reservations in Montana and then attended and graduated from the University of Montana. He was not a prolific writer, but what he did produce was uniformly excellent. His 1986 novel *Fools Crow* is considered his finest work, but he also penned *Winter in the Blood, The Death of Jim Loney, The Indian Lawyer,* and *The Heartsong of Charging Elk,* along with three volumes of poetry about native American life and the nonfiction work *Killing Custer: The Battle of Little Big Horn and the Fate of the Plains Indians,* which was connected to a PBS special that utilized Welch. He passed away in 2003 at his home in Missoula, far too young.

16) **Cormac McCarthy**—Recognized universally as a major literary writer for nearly three decades now, McCarthy used the West as the setting for three of his greatest works: *Blood Meridian, Or, The Evening Redness in the West* (1985); *All the Pretty Horses* (1992; the first of the Border Trilogy that continues with the somewhat less transcendent *The Crossing* and *Cities of the Plain*); and *No Country for Old Men* (2005), each widely separated from the others in time but not in distance, as each is set in the territory ranging from just above the Mexican border to just beyond it.

Blood Meridian is a picaresque horror story featuring a teenage protagonist who runs afoul of a many-faceted villain, Judge Holden, who is as frightening—and deadly—as Hannibal Lecter on his worst day. *All the*

Critic Allen Barra Selects the Top 12 Western Novels of the Past 45 Years

Used with permission of Mr. Barra, author of Inventing Wyatt Earp; *from his 2005 Salon.com article "The new true West."*

[M. Barson's comments are in brackets]

1) ***Little Big Man*** by Thomas Berger (1964). [A favorite of everyone from Marlon Brando to Janis Joplin to Pauline Kael to Ralph Ellison, Barra points out. He also admires the 1999 sequel *The Return of Little Big Man*.]

2) ***Lonesome Dove*** by Larry McMurtry (1986). [Winner of the Pulitzer Prize for Fiction was turned into a great television miniseries in 1989; but the book is greater still.]

And, listed in chronological order of publication:

3) ***True Grit*** by Charles Portis (1968). [The 1969 film relied heavily on Portis' tangy dialogue.]

4) ***The Collected Works of Billy the Kid*** by Michael Ondaatje [*Note: Poetry]

5) ***Desperados*** by Ron Hansen (1979). [About the Dalton Gang.]

6) ***The Assassination of Jesse James by the Coward Robert Ford*** by Ron Hansen (1983). [It took 24 years to bring it to the screen, and a good job it was.]

7) ***Deadwood*** by Pete Dexter (1986). [Jumping-off point for the much-admired HBO series.]

8) ***Mamaw*** by Susan Dodd (1988). [Barra calls this fictional biography of the mother of James and Frank James "superb."]

9) ***The Ancient Child*** by N. Scott Momaday (1989). [The legends of Billy the Kid and a Kiowa boy cross paths.]

10) ***Ghost Town*** by Robert Coover (1998).

11) ***Liar's Moon*** by Philip Kimball (1999).

12) ***Bucking the Tiger*** by Bruce Olds (2001). [Doc Holliday, reimagined.]

Pretty Horses is a romantic coming-of-age story that ultimately yields to tragedy; it won the National Book Award and was filmed, with mixed results, in 2000, with Matt Damon in the role of teenage protagonist John Grady Cole. Set in 1980, *No Country for Old Men* has more of the nightmare quality of *Blood,* with the monstrous professional hitman Anton Chigurh dominating every moment of the tale, whether "onscreen" or not. The Coen Brothers' film version was the big winner of the Academy Awards for 2007, with Cormac McCarthy sitting in the audience as the film won Best Picture, the Coens won for both Best Direction and Best Adapted Screenplay, and Javier Bardem won Best Supporting Actor for his indelible portrait of the mad-as-a-hatter but infinitely lethal Chigurh. All of which just goes to prove, the western is still alive and well, if presented with enough imagination and conviction.

BING CROSBY'S OUTSTANDING HIT

I'm An Old Cowhand

(FROM THE RIO GRANDE)

Words and Music by
JOHNNY MERCER

AS SUNG BY
BING CROSBY
in his latest Paramount Picture
"RHYTHM ON THE RANGE"
musical direction by BORIS MORROS

Leo Feist inc.
1629 BROADWAY · NEW YORK · N. Y

CHAPTER SIX

Songs of the Open Range

There isn't anything more personal than one's memory of a favorite song, and for a great many of us kids growing up in the 1950s and '60s, so many pleasant memories were forged by the appearance every week or so of a great new western ditty (and I'm sure some of those weeks had two or three). If it wasn't the theme song to a popular TV show or new movie, then it was a Top 40 tune, several dozen repetitions of which guaranteed a permanent spot in the memory bank (or so I have found, anyway, half a century later). These songs of the open range could tell about a gun-toting confrontation, about driving a herd of recalcitrant cattle on horseback, or maybe just offer a meditation on the pleasure of sleeping under a wide-open sky. Or even—as a necessary evil, we kids understood—an occasional tune centered on love and romance. (As if even the prettiest woman was going to be any help in getting a herd of bawling cattle from Texas to Kansas.)

Here, then, is a highly subjective guide to five groundbreaking, watershed achievements in the history of western music, viewed from a national perspective and not merely a regional one. In other words, music that could reach the ears of kids living in New England, Oregon, and Florida, and not just those fortunate enough to have been born within an hour's drive of Lubbock, Texas.

1) **The Collected Works of Bing Crosby.** Yes, I said: Bing Crosby. No one did more to popularize western music in the 1930s and '40s than the old Bingster himself, a lifelong fan of the West who famously spent much of his downtime on his ranch in the San Fernando Valley. Bing had first come to the attention of pop music fans as a vocalist for Bix Beiderbecke and the Paul Whiteman Orchestra in the late twenties, and soon was appearing in early soundies in featured musical numbers—one of the first recording artists to make that transition to the silver screen.

BRITISH LION PRESENTS
ROY ROGERS in
YELLOW ROSE OF TEXAS
DALE EVANS
BOB NOLAN
and the SONS of the PIONEERS
A REPUBLIC PICTURE
TRADE SHOW SEPTEMBER 19TH STUDIO ONE 11 A.M.
LAMBDA

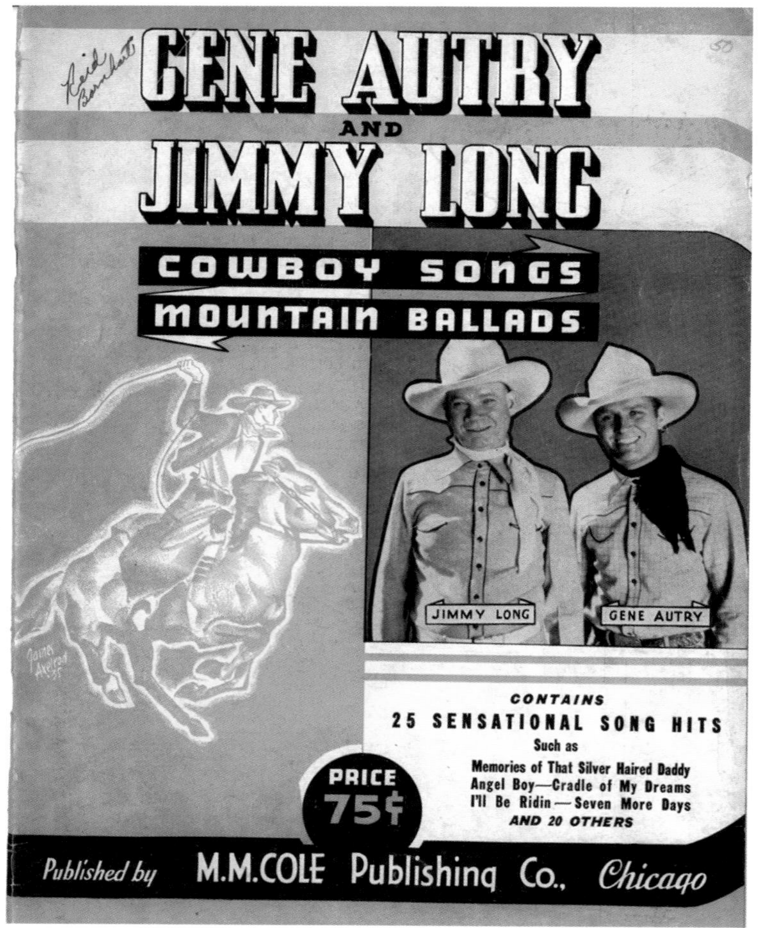
GENE AUTRY AND JIMMY LONG
COWBOY SONGS
MOUNTAIN BALLADS
JIMMY LONG
GENE AUTRY
CONTAINS
25 SENSATIONAL SONG HITS
Such as
Memories of That Silver Haired Daddy
Angel Boy—Cradle of My Dreams
I'll Be Ridin—Seven More Days
AND 20 OTHERS
PRICE 75¢
Published by M.M.COLE Publishing Co., Chicago

Bing went on to become one of the top screen stars of the thirties, but he never stopped making hit records either. And so Bing was happy to hijack his vast audience in the direction of a musical genre they otherwise might have ignored. One of his first western hits was his (rather plummy) version of "Home on the Range" in 1933, which established the song as a contemporary classic. "The Last Roundup," recorded at the same session, was showcased in the film *Ziegfeld Follies of 1934,* and "After Sundown" was another 1933 chart success. "Take Me Back to My Boots and Saddles" was a hit in 1935, leading into one of Bing's biggest years for western music, 1936, when his popular film *Rhythm on the Range* provided the perfect setting for Bing—in character as a cowboy—to sing "I'm an Old Cowhand (from the Rio Grande)" to Martha Raye and a wayward steer (thank you, songwriter Johnny Mercer and backing vocalists The Sons of the Pioneers). Also hits that year were the cowboy quartet "Twilight on the Trail," "Empty Saddles in the Old Corral," "We'll Rest at the End of the Trail" and "A Round-up Lullaby."

"Silver on the Sage" and "When the Bloom is on the Sage" were recorded in 1938, followed by "El Rancho Grande (My Ranch)," "(Drifting Along with the) Tumbling Tumbleweeds," "The Singing Hills," "Along the Santa Fe Trail" (from the 1940 movie with Errol Flynn), and "San Antonio Rose" (one of Bob Wills' many classic compositions, with which he and the Texas Playboys also had a major hit). Bing covered two popular Gene Autry tunes in 1941, "Ridin' Down the Canyon" and "Goodbye, Little Darlin', Goodbye," and also recorded the standard "Clementine" that year. "Deep in the Heart of Texas" was a huge smash in 1942, with Woody Herman's band backing. Bing's final wave of western hits came in 1943 and 1944 in the form of "Pistol Packin' Mama" (with the Andrews Sisters, a million-seller), "San Fernando Valley," and Cole Porter's wonderful "Don't Fence Me In" (yet another million-seller).

Bing would go on to have scores of other huge hits on the pop charts well into the fifties but moved away from cowboy tunes in those subsequent years, more's the pity. And never let it be forgotten that, for an audience of millions, Bing was one of the first to demonstrate that loving western music could be "cool."

Some Sunday Morning
Lyric by TED KOEHLER Music by M. K. JEROME and RAY HEINDORF
From WARNER BROS. PICTURE
"SAN ANTONIO"
Starring
ERROL FLYNN
and
ALEXIS SMITH
SOME SUNDAY MORNING
SOMEWHERE IN MONTEREY
PRINTED IN U.S.A.
HARMS INC.
NEW YORK

OLE BUTTERMILK SKY
Lyrics and Music by HOAGY CARMICHAEL and JACK BROOKS
WALTER WANGER presents
DANA ANDREWS BRIAN DONLEVY SUSAN HAYWARD
"Canyon Passage"
IN TECHNICOLOR
and introducing
PATRICIA ROC with HOAGY CARMICHAEL WARD BOND ANDY DEVINE STANLEY RIDGES
BURKE AND VAN HEUSEN, INC.
1619 BROADWAY • NEW YORK 19, N.Y.

stereo
UNITED ARTISTS
LEROY HOLMES
and His Orchestra
"FOR A FEW DOLLARS MORE"
and other
MOTION
PICTURE
THEMES

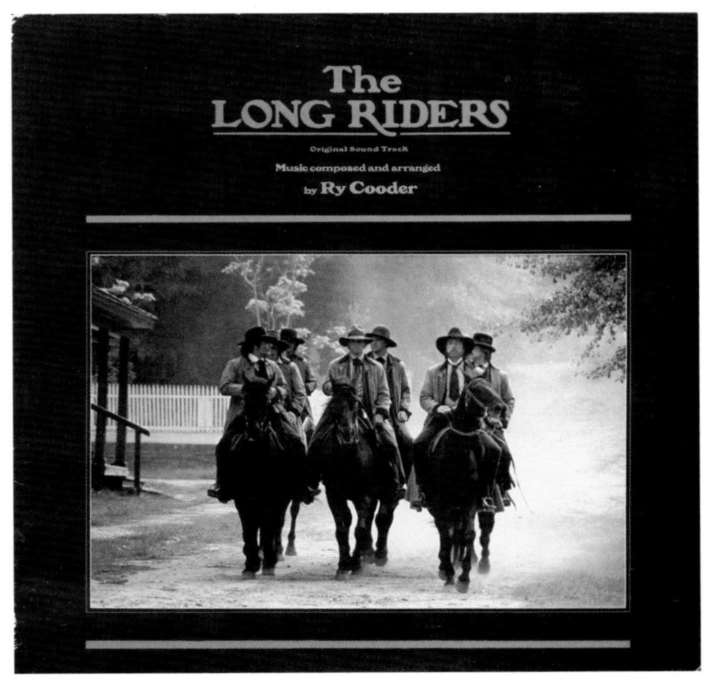

2) **Movie and Television Theme Songs**—It goes without saying that those most massive of mass media, TV and movies, were the most successful at permeating the bedrock of American popular culture. Movie theme songs had been embraced on the pop charts since the advent of sound pictures, so it only follows that a number of them derive from western pictures. Probably the most memorable of all was "High Noon (Do Not Forsake Me)," from the 1952 *High Noon*. It starred Gary Cooper as the retiring marshal who must stand alone against a vengeful gunman named Frank Miller, just released from the state prison to which Coop sent him and now traveling via train with a few cronies to gun down Coop. And this all plays out on Coop's wedding day, as he prepares to marry a much, much younger Grace Kelly, cast as a Quaker whose pacifist philosophy is about to prove singularly unhelpful to the targeted Coop. Written by Dimitri Tiomkin and Ned Washington, the Oscar-winning theme song was sung for the movie by cowboy star Tex Ritter. "For I must face a man who hates me/Or lie a coward/A craven coward/Or lie a coward in my grave" were part of the compelling lyrics. But "High Noon" was covered by the peerless Frankie Laine, whose trademark brio quickly made the song his own.

Laine went on to launch something of a cottage industry of western movie theme songs, recording the signature tunes "Gunfight at the O.K.

Corral" (1957), "The Hanging Tree" (1959), and "The 3:10 to Yuma" (1957) for their eponymous films. Years later, Frankie was drafted to belt out the hilarious—but nonetheless stirring—theme song to Mel Brooks' classic deconstruction of the western movie, *Blazing Saddles* (1974), which ranks with the very best of his (Laine's) estimable work and won an Oscar nomination. In fact, Frankie was called on to perform the song on the 1975 Academy Awards broadcast (his third such appearance for them).

Frankie Laine is also associated with what may be the very best television theme song ever recorded, the pulse-pounding "Rawhide," written by that unsurpassable Tiomkin-Washington team. If ever the cowboy ethos was better summed up in three-minutes of two-fisted gumption, I'd like to know what it might be: "Keep them dogie's movin'/Though they're disapprovin'/Keep then dogie's movin'/Rawhide!/Through all kinds of weather/Hell-bent for leather/ Soon we'll be livin' high and wide." Then, in a more contemplative mood, the song concludes with "Rawhide's estimatin'/My true love will be waitin'/Waitin' at the end of my ride." (Of course, the show itself offered up no true loves, the better to keep the series rollin', rollin', rollin' through six-plus seasons—until it did finally hit the end of its glorious ride.)

DL 34057
Country Music Time
DECCA RECORDS
JIMMIE DAVIS
BILL MONROE
WEBB PIERCE
TOMMY JACKSON
MONTANA SLIM
REX ALLEN
RED FOLEY
RED SOVINE
BILLY GRAMMER
ROY DRUSKY
BILL ANDERSON
ERNEST TUBB

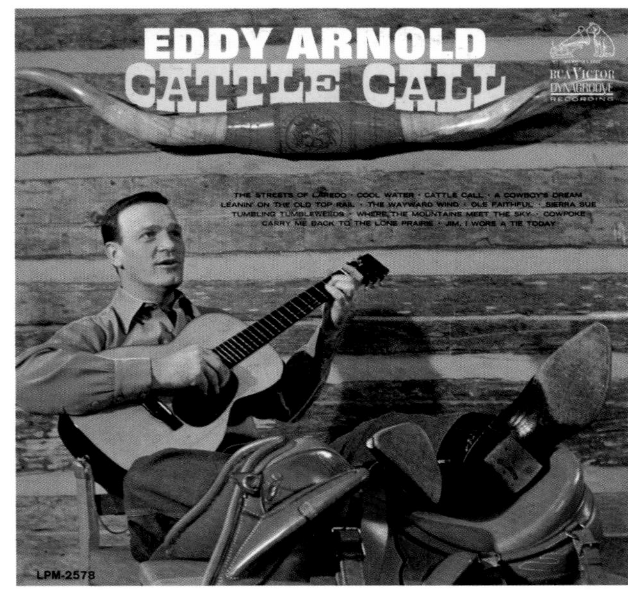
EDDY ARNOLD
CATTLE CALL
RCA VICTOR DYNAGROOVE RECORDING
THE STREETS OF LAREDO · COOL WATER · CATTLE CALL · A COWBOY'S DREAM
LEANIN' ON THE OLD TOP RAIL · THE WAYWARD WIND · OLE FAITHFUL · SIERRA SUE
TUMBLING TUMBLEWEEDS · WHERE THE MOUNTAINS MEET THE SKY · COWPOKE ·
CARRY ME BACK TO THE LONE PRAIRIE · JIM, I WORE A TIE TODAY
LPM-2578

CAL 527
RCA CAMDEN
LONG PLAY 33⅓ RPM
Montana Slim
WILF CARTER
I'm Hittin' the Trail
I'm Thinking Tonight of My Blue Eyes
It Makes No Difference Now
The Prisoner's Song
Red River Valley Blues
Rye Whiskey
Sittin' by the Old Corral

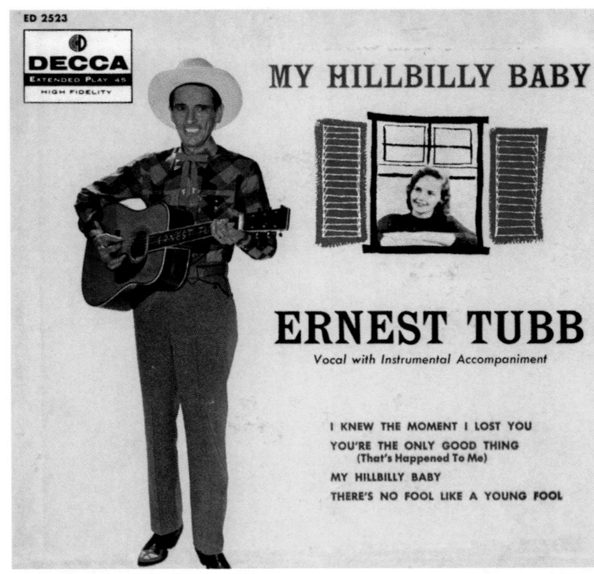
ED 2523
DECCA
EXTENDED PLAY 45
HIGH FIDELITY
MY HILLBILLY BABY
ERNEST TUBB
Vocal with Instrumental Accompaniment
I KNEW THE MOMENT I LOST YOU
YOU'RE THE ONLY GOOD THING (That's Happened To Me)
MY HILLBILLY BABY
THERE'S NO FOOL LIKE A YOUNG FOOL

STEREO
COLUMBIA
MORE GREATEST HITS
MARTY ROBBINS
EL PASO
DON'T WORRY
BALLAD OF THE ALAMO
LIKE ALL THE OTHER TIMES
IS THERE ANY CHANCE
RIDE, COWBOY RIDE
A TIME AND A PLACE FOR EVERYTHING
STREETS OF LAREDO
SADDLE TRAMP
I TOLD MY HEART
RED RIVER VALLEY
BIG IRON

KX 11
THE ORIGINAL: GENE AUTRY SINGS RUDOLPH THE RED-NOSED REINDEER
& other CHRISTMAS favorites
RUDOLPH, THE RED-NOSED REINDEER
HERE COMES SANTA CLAUS
UP ON THE HOUSE TOP
SLEIGH BELLS
NINE LITTLE REINDEER
O LITTLE TOWN OF BETHLEHEM
SILENT NIGHT
JOY TO THE WORLD
JINGLE BELLS
WHAT CHILD IS THIS
AWAY IN A MANGER
WE WISH YOU A MERRY CHRISTMAS

MORE HANK SNOW SOUVENIRS

LET ME GO LOVER • THE GAL WHO INVENTED KISSIN' • THE NEXT VOICE YOU HEAR • ONE MORE RIDE • STOLEN MOMENTS • A FADED PETAL FROM A BEAUTIFUL BOUQUET • MILLER'S CAVE • THE WRECK OF THE OLD '97 TANGLED MIND • THE GOLD RUSH IS OVER • DOWN THE TRAIL OF ACHIN' HEARTS • THE CHANGE OF THE TIDE

LPM-2812

There were many other excellent theme songs for western TV shows over the years. A few particular favorites: Johnny Cash's "The Ballad of Johnny Yuma" for the Nick Adams series *The Rebel;* the theme to *Maverick,* with its evocative lyric "Natchez to New Orleans/Livin' on Jacks and Queens/Luck is the lady that I love the best"; and the instrumental, wholly stirring theme to *Bonanza,* composed by Jay Livingston and Ray Evans. (If only the show itself had always delivered that much energy!)

3) **Frankie Laine**—As noted in the preceding item, Frankie Laine (born Francesco Paolo LoVecchio) was the king of the western theme song. But his body of work is not limited to that territory alone, and so he rates a second salute for the rest of his terrific songbook. His affinity for songs that evoked the Old West was uncanny, whether he was singing about the rigors of a "Mule Train," the wanderlust infecting the narrator of "Cry of the Wild Goose," the calculated attitude about love intoned by the swaggering hero of "Moonlight Gambler," or the elaborate history recounted in "Bowie Knife." Most of these memorable tunes, along with Frankie's vivid movie and TV theme songs, can be found on his LPs *Hell-Bent for Leather* (a nod to a phrase in the theme to *Rawhide*—on which he once guest-starred) and *Deuces Wild* (as you might guess, dominated by songs with a gambling theme). He also covered such western chestnuts as "Wagon Wheels," "Along the Navajo Trail," "Tumbling Tumbleweeds," and "Riders in the Sky," among many others. Once you heard Frankie's version of a song, it was hard to return to the original brand.

One of his final hits was the grand but despairing "Lord, You Gave Me a Mountain," penned for him by Marty Robbins, who must have realized (correctly) that it would take a voice as grand as the Tetons themselves to do it full justice. Frankie Laine died in 2007, but those songs of his will live on for lovers of western music for another 2,007 years, minimum.

4) **Gunfighter Ballads and Trail Songs**—There are few more iconic images than the one of Marty Robbins on the cover of his 1959 album *Gunfighter Ballads and Trail Songs.* There he is, clad all in black, halfway through drawing his six-gun, with a very odd hat (also black, of course) perched on top of his head. Quite a stretch, one might think, for the singer who had among his earlier hits a confection called "A White Sportcoat and a Pink Carnation"—but the cowboy ethos had long since permeated the

Arizona-raised Robbins, and so, for him, making this album was a true labor of love.

Possibly the first western concept album and surely the first devoted to gunslingers, *Gunfighter Ballads* was released at the very height of the western boom on TV and in the movies, so the positive reaction it earned should have come as no surprise. The album soon reached #6 on *Billboard's* top LPs chart, where it would remain for two-thirds of the year 1960. What propelled the album's success was its breakout single, "El Paso," an epic saga of illicit love that ends fatally for its young cowboy narrator. At nearly five minutes in length, the ballad originally had been deemed too lengthy even to release for Top 40 radio. But a month's worth of increasing demand from disc jockeys around the country forced Columbia Records' hand, and the song was issued as a single in December. On January 4, 1960, the song ascended to the number one spot on the charts, making it the first official chart-topper of the sixties. The remainder of the LP was pretty impressive too, with cuts including "Big Iron," "They're Hanging Me Tonight," the classic "Cool Water," "Billy the Kid," and "Running Gun." Marty's gunslinger tunes are still a pleasure to listen to today.

A number of other outlaw-concept LPs would follow over the years. Texas-born Waylon Jennings jump-started his career by donning the mantle of "The Outlaw" as his official epithet. His signature tunes included the 1978 hit "Mama, Don't Let Your Babies Grow Up to Be Cowboys" and "Luckenbach, Texas"—focal points on the hugely influential LP *Wanted: The Outlaws,*" on which Waylon appeared with cohorts Willie Nelson, Jessi Colter (his wife), and Tompal Glaser. Of course, by this point, the outlaw element was more about an ethos and a style than it was ventilating some varmint with a six-shooter (though Waylon always looked like he'd be game for that too, given half a chance).

Another particularly good piece of work, though not nearly as wide a popular success, was Tom Rush's 1974 LP *Ladies Love Outlaws,* which along with the great title tune (also covered by Waylon) featured the haunting "Indian Woman from Wichita" and "Desperadoes Waiting for a Train," along with "Black Magic Gun." Famously from Merrimac County, New Hampshire, Tom Rush nonetheless had the chops for western music that was probably the envy of many a Texas-born lad. (In fact, Rush *sounds* like Sam Elliott *looks* in so many of his fine western films.)

5) **Bitter Tears**—Look what Johnny Cash recorded while everyone was sitting around listening to the Beatles and the Dave Clark Five in the spring of 1964! Already a major star on the pop music scene thanks to his enormous crossover hit "Ring of Fire" in 1962, country-western stalwart Johnny Cash was famously proud of his part-Cherokee heritage. So it made sense that he would opt to do a concept album one day that focused on the history, past and present, of the American Indian. And that album turned out to be *Bitter Tears: Ballads of the American Indian*. Appearing on the LP jacket with a rawhide band tied across his brow, shielding his eyes from the sun, Cash looks a hundred percent in character. Most of the songs, which are told uniformly from an Indian point of view, were written by Cash with the help of Peter La Farge.

The LP actually did spawn one hit single, "The Ballad of Ira Hayes," about the tragic Native American Marine who helped raise the flag at Iwo Jima, briefly shared in the celebrity spotlight with the other soldiers who joined in that task, and then skidded into alcoholism, homelessness, and, eventually, death at an early age. Downbeat as that tragic tale was, it was practically a laughfest next to some of the other cuts on the album. "As Long as the Grass Shall Grow" details the broken promises made to the Seneca tribe when their land was taken from them to build the Kinzua Dam just a few years earlier, while "Apache Tears" and "The Vanishing Race" (the latter co-written with Johnny Horton) are self explanatory. But the LP does offer one light moment—a wholly mocking ditty called "Custer," which makes mincemeat of white efforts to glorify that benighted casualty of Little Big Horn.

The commercial effect of the album, released in October 1964, on a musical landscape still reeling from the British invasion, was minute. But today, forty-odd years later, *Bitter Tears* stands as one of Johnny Cash's most formidable, and (I suspect) proudest, achievements.

CHAPTER SEVEN

All in Color for a Dime: The Great Western Comic Book Classics

Considering how prevalent western movies had been since the 1920s, it's a bit surprising that they didn't have more of a presence in the comics—not in the newspaper funnies and not in comic books—until well into the forties. But by the dawn of the fifties, western comics were dominating the newsstands, a trend that only tapered off once the dormant superhero category began to revive itself in the latter part of the decade. But even then, western comics limped into

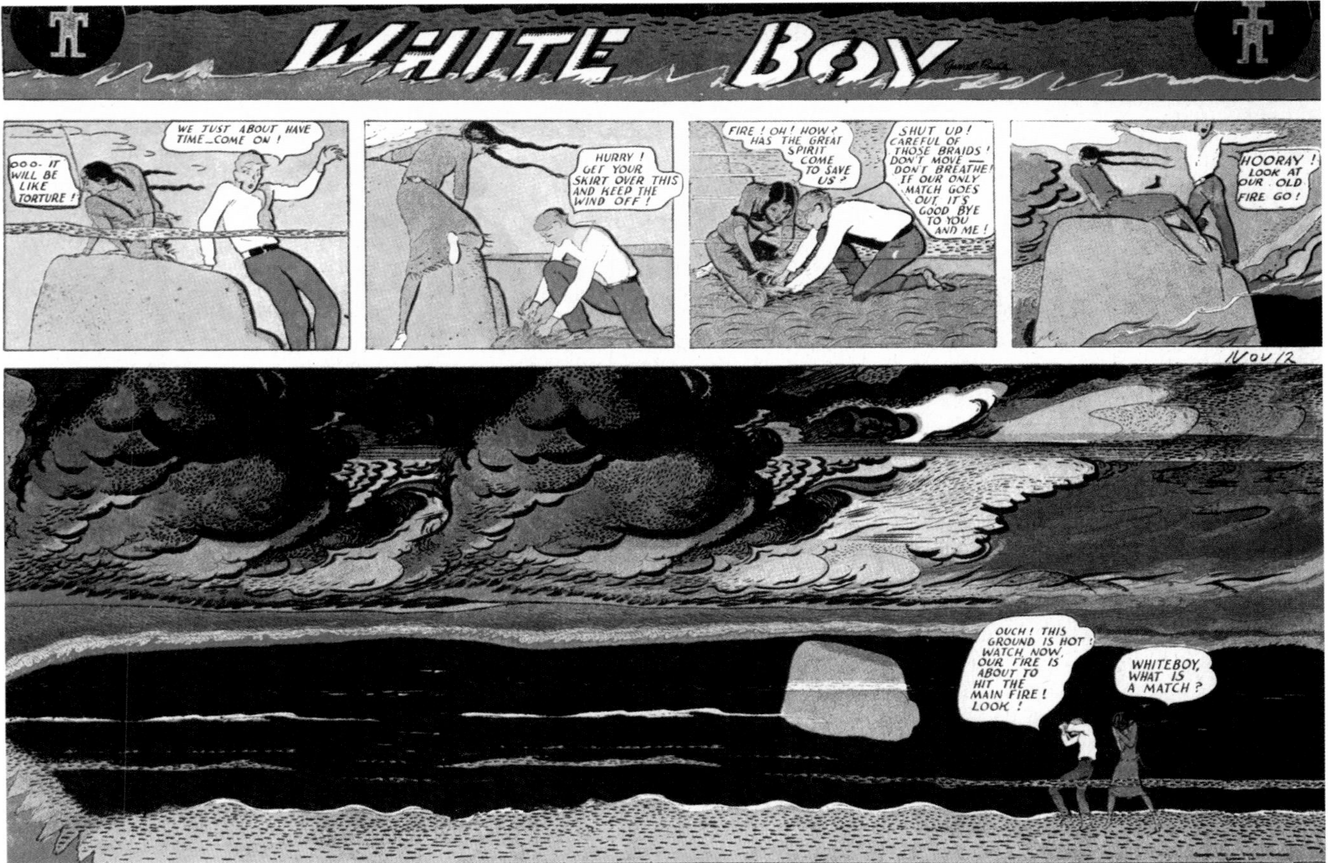

the sixties as something of a presence in the comic book spectrum. Here, then, is an impressionistic sketch of what I would argue are the key western comics—either strips or comic books, based on their popularity, impact, or innovation. And if a soupçon of nostalgia should enter into the equation, we hope it won't be considered a hanging offense.

One of the first original western newspaper strips was Garrett Price's *White Boy,* which debuted as a Sunday page in 1933. Inventively drawn (Price would become a cartoonist for the *New Yorker*) with a terrific use of color, it failed to find much of an audience. Price retooled it after a year or so into *Skull Valley,* featuring some of the same characters but a different setting. But that overhaul didn't change the popularity of the strip either, and it was canceled in 1936.

Fred Harman's *Red Ryder* was notably more successful, debuting in the Sunday funnies in the late thirties and lasting through most of the fifties. In fact, the strip was so popular that not only was it collected into its own monthly comic book but it even became the source for a number of B-movies starring Don "Red" Barry, Wild Bill Elliot, and Allen "Rocky" Lane at various points. Red Ryder's sidekick was an Indian boy named Little Beaver, who became pretty popular in his own right—he not only had his own comic book for a time but was played in the movies by Robert ("Baretta") Blake. During WWII, there was even a Red Ryder Victory Patrol connected to a fan club that could order all kinds of Red Ryder premiums—maps, decoders, and the like.

The mid to late forties was the golden age of the personality western comic; every star worth his weight in hardtack starred in his own comic book, immediately identifiable by their lovingly posed photographic covers (the contents were usually pretty underwhelming, sad to say.). The roll call included *John Wayne Adventure Comics* (trumpeted on the masthead as "The Greatest Cowboy Star of them All"), *The Lone Ranger* (a bit later the character would become a hit on ABC-TV; these comics reprinted material from the long-running newspaper comic strip), *Roy Rogers Comics, Gene Autry Comics, Tom Mix Western* (launched in 1948, though he had been dead since 1940), *Hopalong Cassidy, Johnny Mack Brown, Tim Holt Western Adventures, Rocky Lane Western, Rod Cameron Western, Tex Ritter Western*

REDSKIN
THRILLING INDIAN STORIES
SEPT.
10¢
LN

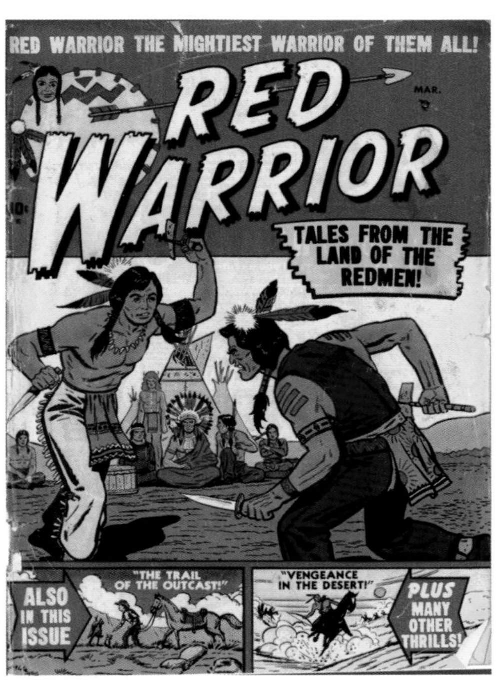
RED WARRIOR THE MIGHTIEST WARRIOR OF THEM ALL!
RED WARRIOR
MAR.
TALES FROM THE LAND OF THE REDMEN!
ALSO IN THIS ISSUE
"THE TRAIL OF THE OUTCAST!"
"VENGEANCE IN THE DESERT!"
PLUS MANY OTHER THRILLS!

THE FIGHTING CHEYENNE WARRIOR!
RED HAWK
No. 11
10¢

WESTERN ACTION AND THRILLS!
TWO-GUN KID
FEB.
NO. 6
MARVEL COMIC
10¢
WE'RE SAFE NOW! THE KID CAN NEVER JUMP THAT... UH OH! GRAB YER HARDWARE!

APPROVED BY THE COMICS CODE AUTHORITY
TWO-GUN KID
IND.
MARVEL COMICS GROUP 9d
72
BLAZING ACTION!! THRILLING DRAMA!!
"TWO-GUNS AGAINST GERONIMO!"

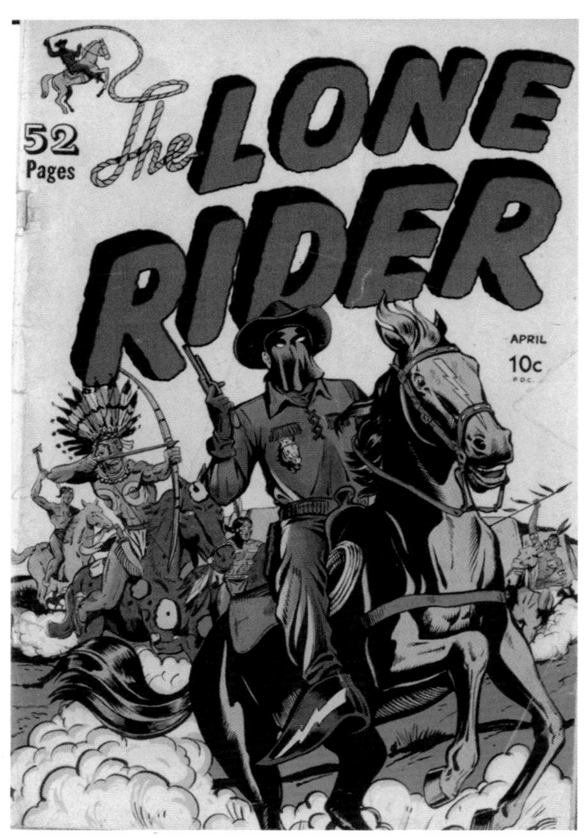
The LONE RIDER
52 Pages
APRIL
10c

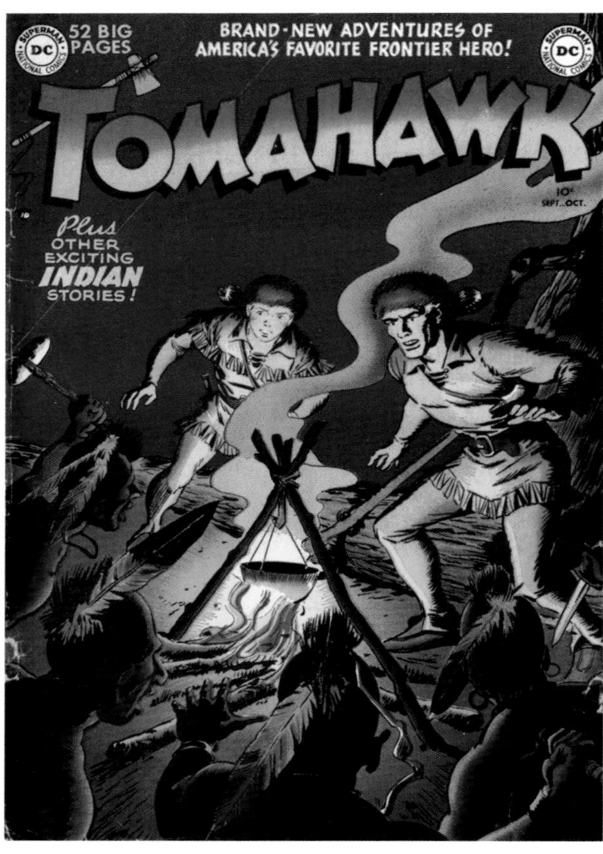
DC
52 BIG PAGES
BRAND-NEW ADVENTURES OF AMERICA'S FAVORITE FRONTIER HERO!
TOMAHAWK
10¢
SEPT.-OCT.
Plus OTHER EXCITING INDIAN STORIES!

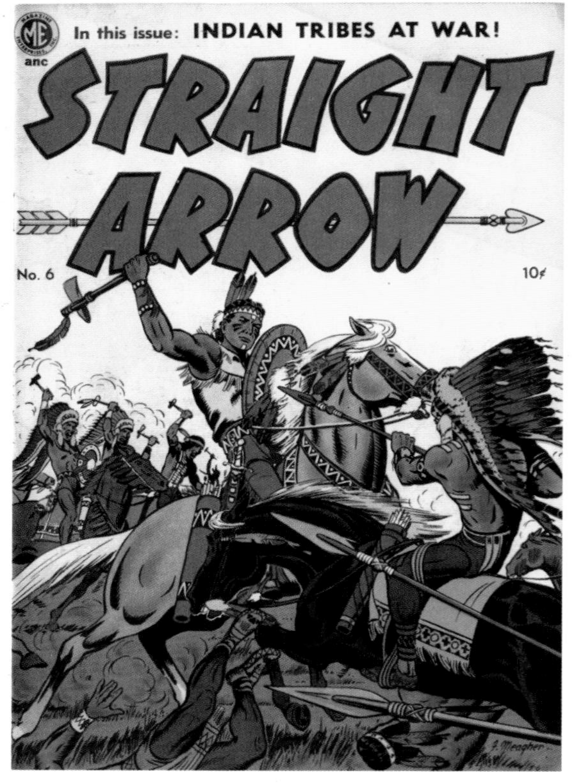
ME
In this issue: INDIAN TRIBES AT WAR!
STRAIGHT ARROW
No. 6
10¢

ME
SEE your favorite radio hero!!!
STRAIGHT ARROW
No. 2
10¢

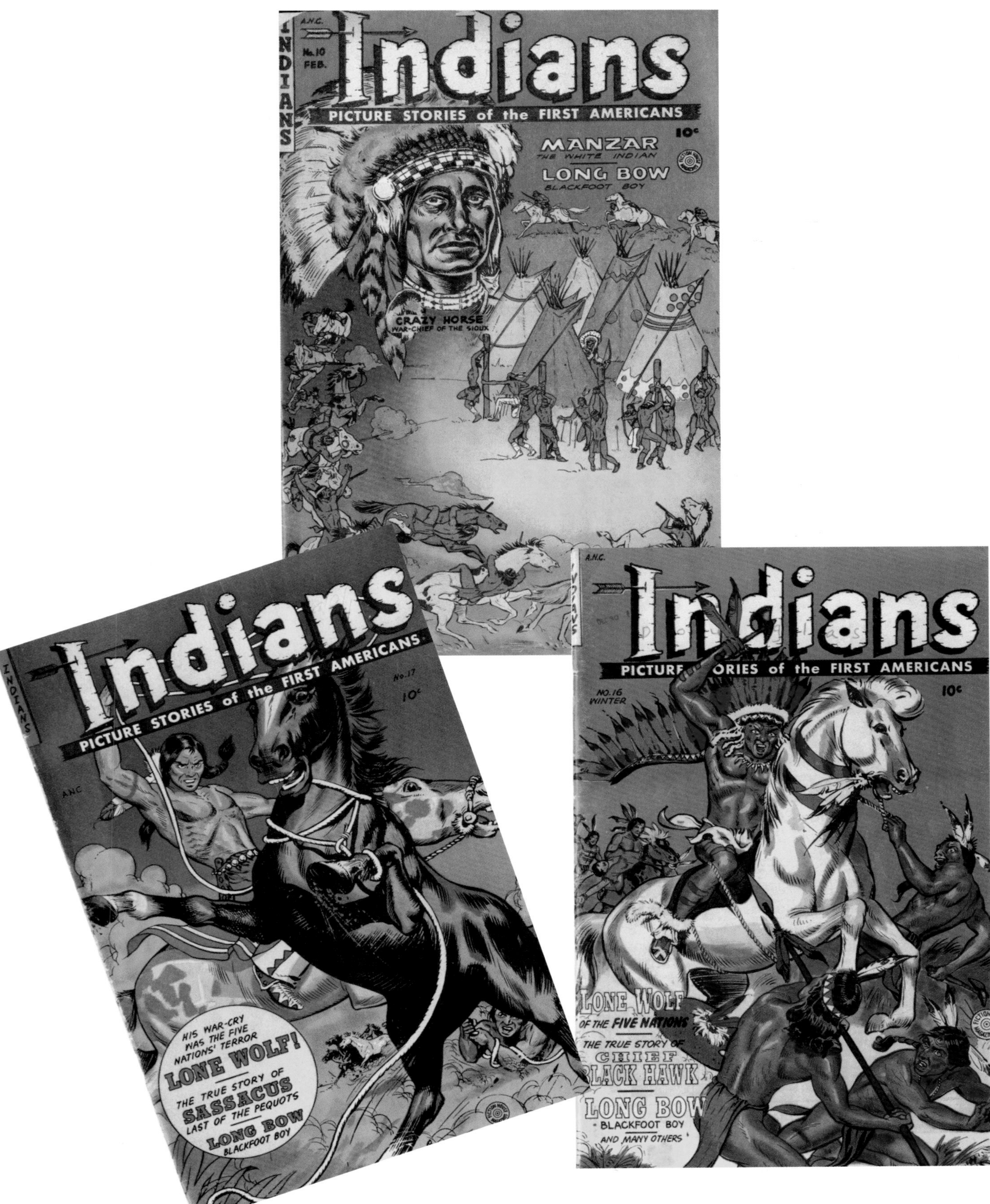
A.N.C.
No. 10
FEB.
Indians
PICTURE STORIES of the FIRST AMERICANS
10¢
MANZAR
THE WHITE INDIAN
LONG BOW
BLACKFOOT BOY
CRAZY HORSE
WAR-CHIEF OF THE SIOUX
Indians
PICTURE STORIES of the FIRST AMERICANS
No. 17
10¢
HIS WAR-CRY
WAS THE FIVE
NATIONS' TERROR
LONE WOLF!
THE TRUE STORY OF
SASSACUS
LAST OF THE PEQUOTS
LONG BOW
BLACKFOOT BOY
A.N.C.
Indians
PICTURE STORIES of the FIRST AMERICANS
NO. 16
WINTER
10¢
LONE WOLF
OF THE FIVE NATIONS
THE TRUE STORY OF
CHIEF
BLACK HAWK
LONG BOW
BLACKFOOT BOY
AND MANY OTHERS

(co-starring his horse White Flash and dog Fury), and so on and on. It got to the point where there was even a comic book starring Gene Autry's famous stallion—*Gene Autry's Champion*—along with *Roy Rogers' Trigger.* Some of the titles featuring the major stars ran straight into the sixties.

Not every western comic book was built around the exploits of movie cowboys, though. Even cheaper than making a licensing deal was just inventing your own cowboy characters. And that is exactly what the hordes of comic book publishers did in those boom days of the late 1940s. Atlas Comics (the forerunner to Marvel) came up with *Rawhide Kid, Two-Gun Kid,* and *Kid Colt* (Outlaw) as their big three, while the ME company offered *Ghost Rider, Bobby Benson, The Durango Kid,* and others. There was a pretty good knock-off of the Lone Ranger called *The Lone Rider* that lasted for four years. Avon Periodicals found its own niche with fanciful takes on various historical characters, in the form of *Wild Bill Hickok, Jesse James,* and *Kit Carson* comics, and Toby Press had *Billy the Kid Adventure Magazine.* DC Comics struck pay dirt with its early frontier series *Tomahawk,* which started as a back-up strip in *Star Spangled Comics* in 1947, but which earned its own book in 1950 and lasted into the early seventies, a real rarity among western comics.

As the fifties began, a new trend developed that was considerably more interesting than these conventional cowboy comics. Suddenly comics that featured Indian protagonists—sometimes heroic, sometimes not—began to sprout up like prairie dogs on the Kansas plains. (There *were* prairie dogs out there, right?) Perhaps the very best of the group was *Prize Comics Western,* converted into western content in 1948 after a long run (since 1940) as a superhero comic book. Initially the comic was nothing out of the ordinary, with covers sometimes depicting cowboy stars of the day, like Randolph Scott and George O'Brien, tying into whatever new B-movie they then had in release. But the January 1951 issue (#85) introduced an exciting new character called American Eagle, a noble Crow brave around whom all the stories were centered, revolving equally between conflicts with hostile Indian tribes (the Sioux and Arapahoe were often cast in this role) and conflicts with venal, corrupt White Men (in issue #95, "Renegade guns in Blackfeet hands threaten to set the frontier afire"). Lovingly drawn by

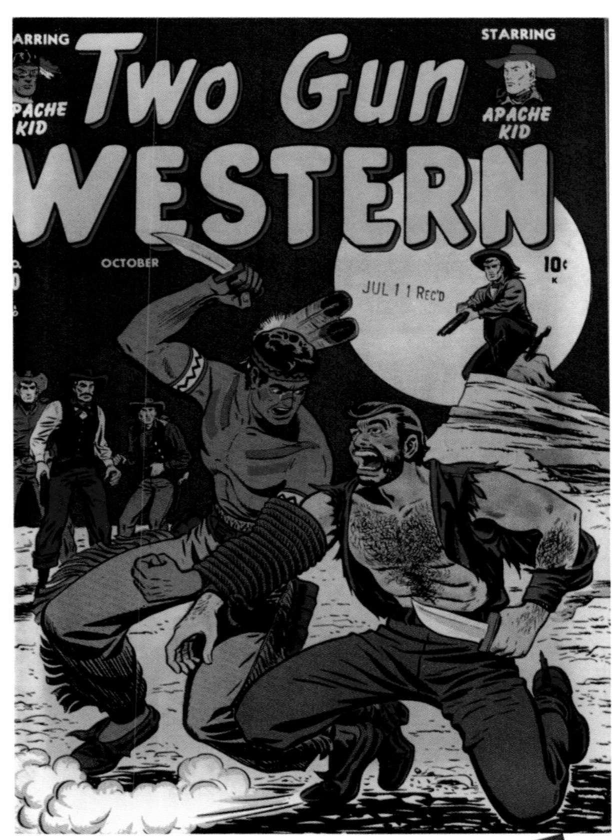
STARRING
APACHE KID
Two Gun
WESTERN
OCTOBER
10¢
JUL 1 1 REC'D

WILD WESTERN STORIES!
KID COLT
OUTLAW
NOV.
No. 7
MARVEL COMIC
10¢
"BETWEEN TWO FIRES!"

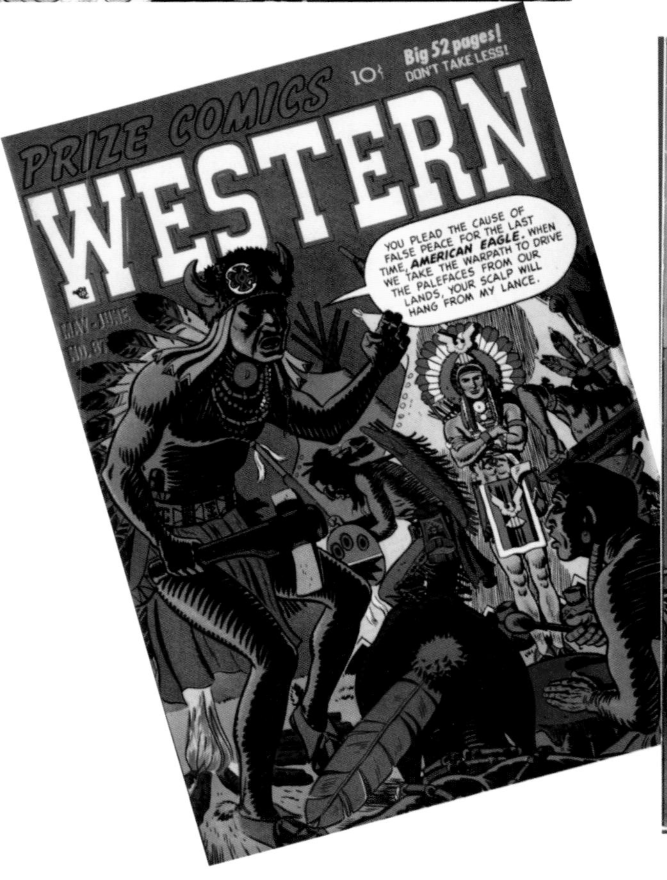
Big 52 pages!
DON'T TAKE LESS!
10¢
PRIZE COMICS
WESTERN
YOU PLEAD THE CAUSE OF FALSE PEACE FOR THE LAST TIME, AMERICAN EAGLE. WHEN WE TAKE THE WARPATH TO DRIVE THE PALEFACES FROM OUR LANDS, YOUR SCALP WILL HANG FROM MY LANCE.

THRILLING ADVENTURES of the WILD WEST'S GREATEST HERO — BUFFALO BILL
BUFFALO BILL
OK
BUFFALO
BILL
10¢
No. 5 APRIL
BUFFALO BILL on the DYNAMITE TRAIL
GHOST DANCE of DEATH

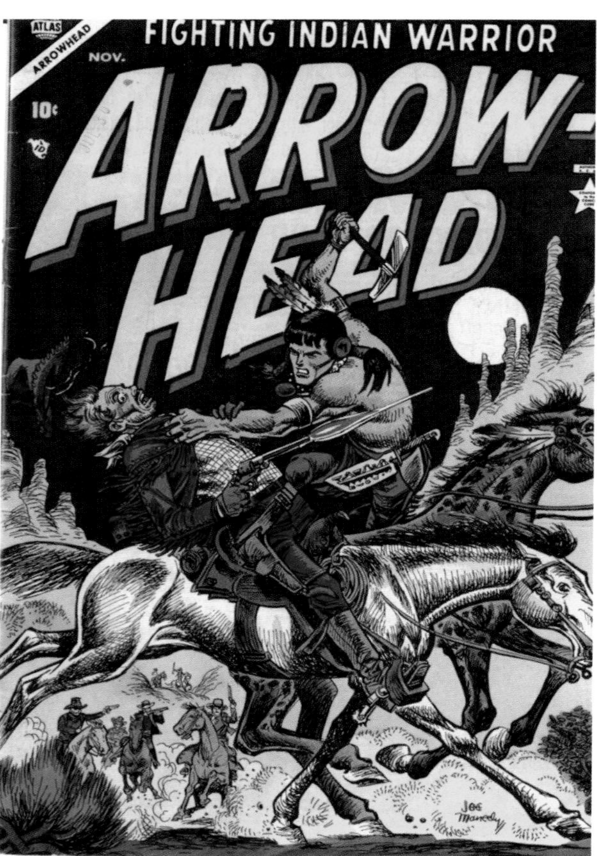

John Severin, often with the aid of frequent EC comics partner Will Elder, *American Eagle* ran as the lead feature (often with two or three stories per issue) in *Prize Western* through 1955, totaling more than thirty issues. When it comes to comic books with Native Americans stars, *American Eagle* has never been topped.

Preceding *American Eagle* by a year into the comics was *Straight Arrow*, another very good series. Its Indian protagonist actually had a secret identity—in "real" life he was Steve Adams, owner of the Broken Bow cattle spread. Based on the popular Mutual Radio series, the comic book debuted at the start of 1950 and ran until 1956, a healthy run of fifty-five issues. Fred Meagher handled the bulk of the art and had many chances to show his stuff in the course of stories involving lost civilizations, mythical treasures, and even dinosaurs. Also of interest was the back-up feature about an Indian boy, Red Hawk, nicely drawn by Bob Powell. *Straight Arrow* was enough of a hit to warrant fan club perks, including nifty premiums underwritten by the radio show's sponsor, Shredded Wheat—a favorite is the

AN AVON PUBLICATION
GERONIMO
INDIAN FIGHTER
No. 1
10¢
THE MASSACRE AT SAN PEDRO PASS

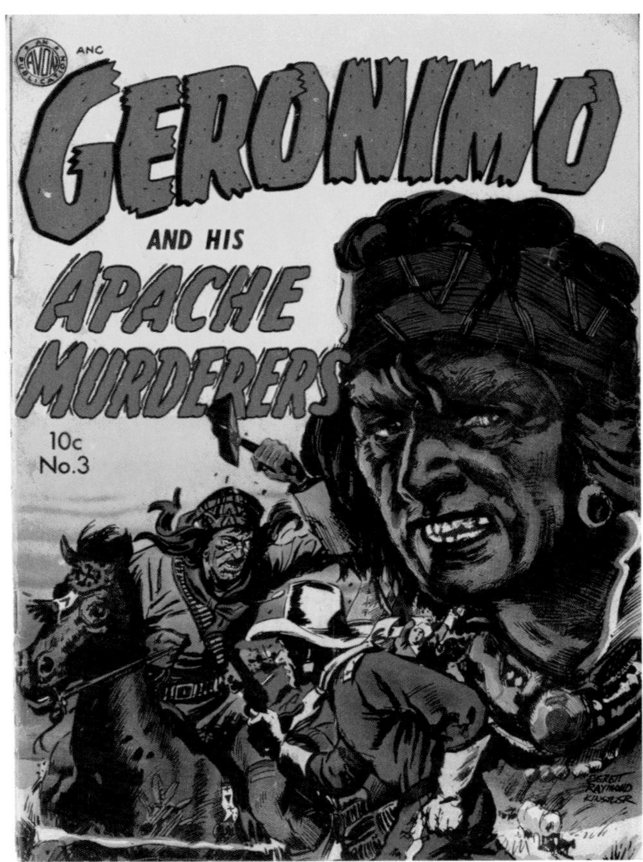
AVON
ANC
GERONIMO
AND HIS
APACHE MURDERERS
10c
No.3

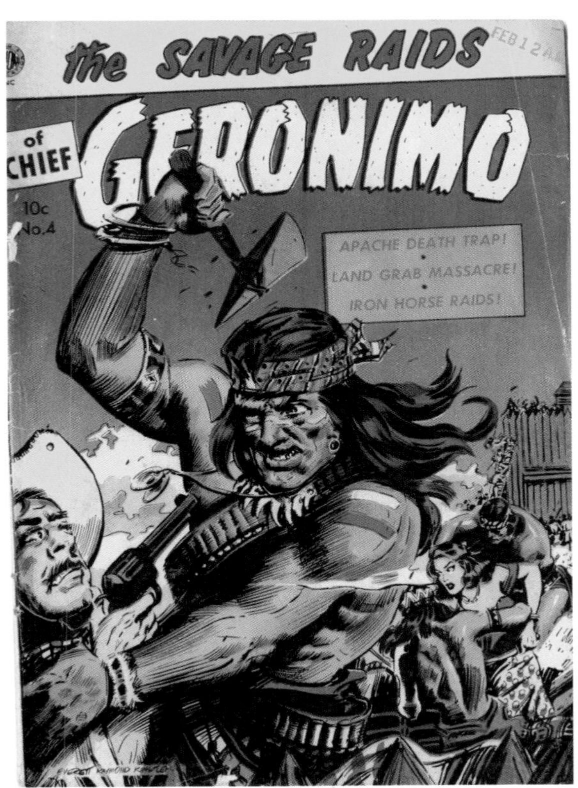
the SAVAGE RAIDS
of CHIEF GERONIMO
10c
No.4
APACHE DEATH TRAP!
LAND GRAB MASSACRE!
IRON HORSE RAIDS!

AVON
ANC
INDIAN CHIEF
GERONIMO
ON THE
WARPATH!
10¢
No. 2
'THE MURDEROUS BATTLE AT KISKAYAH!'

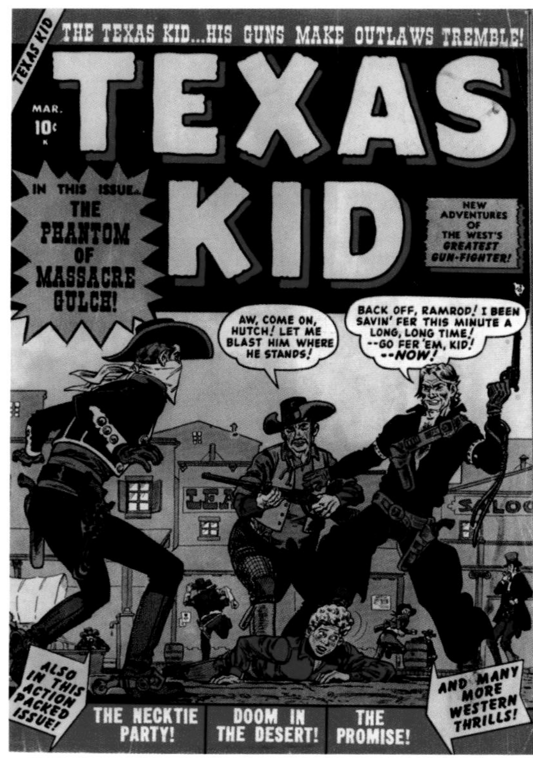

Straight Arrow "Injun-uity Manual" found inside every box of Shredded Wheat, according to an ad in one of the comics. ("Teaches you all the Indian wisdom and skills," the ad promised prospective customers of that breakfast cereal.)

Another key title, though shorter-lived, was *Indians,* published by pulp giant Fiction House. Bearing the legend "Picture Stories of the First Americans," the first of *Indians'* seventeen issues appeared in 1950, featuring three different strips with Native American characters: Manzar the White Indian, Long Bow, Indian Boy, and Orphan of the Storm; a character named Starlight was introduced in the second issue. Loaded with Indian lore, including informative features on famous Native Americans like Sacajawea, the comic was popular enough to spin off Long Bow into his own book for a few years. Dell's *(White Eagle) Indian Chief* also had a healthy run, from 1950 to 1959. The strip "Pow-Wow Smith, Indian Lawman," though, only rated a backup feature in DC's *Western Comics* for forty-odd issues.

During the first half of the fifties, many other comics featuring Native American protagonists emerged—this was truly the golden age for that genre-within-a-genre. Among the most distinct was Atlas's *Arrowhead,* featuring the ill-tempered title character, a renegade Pawnee warrior cast in the Geronimo mold; despite fine art by Joe Sinnott, the title ran for a mere four issues. Even more interesting was Avon's series of one-shot biographies of several legendary Indian warriors; the phrasing of their titles tips off their point of view before a word has been read: *Geronimo and His Apache Murderers; The Savage Raids of Chief Geronimo; Geronimo, Indian Fighter (and His Horde of Redskin Devils); Indian Chief Geronimo on the Warpath;* and *The Blackhawk Indian Tomahawk War* all were issued in 1950 or 1951. Slightly less incendiary Avon specials were *White Chief of the Pawnee Indians* and *Fighting Indians of the Wild West* (offering bios of Crazy Horse, Victorio, Black Hawk, and Geronimo). And then there was Dell's entertaining *Turok, Son of Stone,* about two Indian braves who fall into a lost prehistoric valley, complete with dinosaurs, and must use all their wiles to survive. (It still exists today as a video game, of all things.)

In the late forties, the EC comics line hadn't yet established its now-legendary line of genre (horror, crime, and science-fiction) triumphs. But they did take a crack at the western category with *Saddle Justice* and *Gunfighter* in 1948 and a year later with *Saddle Romances* (love comics meet the western). Other than providing some nice early work by such legends-in-the-making as Graham Ingels, Wally Wood, Al Feldstein, and Johnny Craig, the stories weren't particularly special. But that changed with the advent of *Two-Fisted Tales* in 1950, which started as a general adventure anthology but altered its format primarily to war stories once the Korean conflict started; in 1951 the companion comic, *Frontline Combat,* began publication. While the majority of the stories centered on Korea, most issues of both *Two-Fisted* and *Frontline* took time to also essay period pieces, some set in the Old West. Among the best of EC's western tales: "Oregon Trail," "Stampede," "Alamo," "Warpath," "Colt Single Action Army Revolver," and "Custer's Last Stand." A personal favorite is *Warrior,* which examined a turning point in the life of Washakie, the warrior chief of the Shoshoni, whose leadership of his people persuaded the U.S. government to establish the beautiful Wind River Reservation in Wyoming for them. But the EC line was mortally wounded by the advent of the anti-violence Comics Code

DELL
A MOVIE CLASSIC
NO. 687 10¢
the INDIAN FIGHTER
A Bryna-United Artists Production in CinemaScope Printed by Technicolor

2ND BIG CONTEST—ENTER NOW!
DELL 15¢
LAWMAN
JOHN RUSSELL
PETER BROWN
Trade for super values at the
DELL TRADING POST SEE INSIDE

DELL Western Adventure
JUNE
15¢
NO. 1181
Walt Disney's
TEXAS JOHN SLAUGHTER
John Slaughter stands between a brave youth and Geronimo's revenge!

GOLD KEY
DANIEL BOONE
15¢
FESS PARKER
10135-810
OCTOBER
DANIEL BOONE
Daniel befriends
a schoolmaster
whose scalp is
worth a British bounty!

SUPERMAN
DC
NATIONAL COMICS
SHOWCASE PRESENTS
12¢
AUG. NO. 76
APPROVED BY THE COMICS CODE AUTHORITY
BAT LASH
WILL HE SAVE THE WEST-OR RUIN IT?
WANTED
REWA

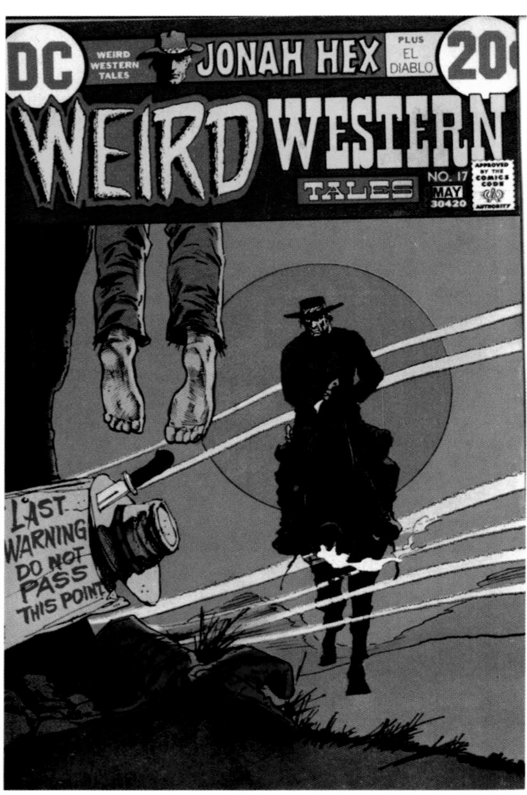

in 1955 and never was able to regain its footing, even though there was little in any of its pre-code western yarns that wouldn't have passed muster under this new regime.

Dell Comics' movie and TV tie-ins were a godsend to kids living in the fifties, since there wasn't much chance any of us could really keep up with more than a fraction of the cascade of western movies being released—it was a seemingly endless stream, every week, month after month. Nor could even the luckiest kid hope to follow all of the western series then appearing on television, night after night, for hours on end.

One of the only defenses against being swept away by this tidal wave of western shows was to follow them via Dell Comics' authorized tie-in editions. Though a few other comic publishers occasionally adapted a movie or TV show, the Dell Comics empire—like a latter-day Caesar—came, saw, and conquered 98 percent of those western programs. One caveat: It rarely paid to actually read Dell's tie-in stories—the artwork usually ranged from mediocre to abysmal (unless artists Alex Toth and Everett Raymond Kinstler were on the case) and the writing leaned toward the perfunctory.

Leaving what to savor, you ask? Why, the wonderful photo covers. Having a full-color close up of the stars of *Wagon Train, Sugarfoot,* or *Bat Masterson* whenever you felt the need to study it was one of the true pleasures for a ten-year-old, and it only cost a dime (or, a bit later, fifteen cents) to make it your personal property. (A cheap thrill, yes—but hey, these were the pre-video days, kids!)

Dell had already enjoyed success publishing comics centered on cowboy (and cowgirl) personalities like Johnny Mack Brown, Gene Autry, "Queen of the West" Dale Evans, Rex Allen, and Wild Bill Elliot, so it was a simple evolutionary step for them to commission adaptations for the top TV series of the mid-fifties: *Davy Crockett; Steve Donovan, Western Marshal; Buffalo Bill, Jr.; Gunsmoke; Texas Rangers; Brave Eagle; Cheyenne; Broken Arrow; Wyatt Earp; Tales of Wells Fargo; Frontier Doctor; Maverick; Jim Bowie; Colt .45; Have Gun Will Travel*—all were adapted by Dell, in multiple issues spread out over months and even years, if the TV show became a hit. And many of the key western films of that period also were given the Dell photo-cover treatment: *Drum Beat; The Searchers; The True Story of Jesse James; Light in the Forest; The Left-Handed Gun; The Big Country, Rio Bravo,* and *The Horse Soldiers* among them. Nice souvenirs for kids who couldn't attend movie screenings five times a week, indeed!

Sad to say, those glory days of the western comic book petered out as the superhero boom ultimately dominated the sixties—most of the other once-ubiquitous categories, like war comics, were also steamrolled in the superhero wake. Mimicking the rollback described elsewhere in this volume in both the film and (especially) television industries, by the seventies the comic book business had pretty much relegated the western to a closet in the attic. One exception was DC Comics' 1970 revival of its *All Star Western* title, which combined reprints of the old Pow-Wow Smith stories with a striking new one, El Diablo, a Zorro knockoff beautifully drawn by Gray Morrow.

That strip made little impact, predictably, but in the tenth issue, a new character debuted—Jonah Hex, a disfigured Civil War vet who has become a hired gun; his Reb uniform accompanied a horribly disfigured face and omnipresent cheroot (lifted directly from Clint Eastwood's Man with No Name playbook). Jonah and his dark, quasi-supernatural plotlines quickly caught on, and he was awarded headliner status when the book changed its title to *Weird Western Tales* in 1972. But after a few years Jonah, too, was sent to boot hill, bringing down the curtain on one of the proudest chapters in the history of the comic book industry—when westerns rode the range!

CHAPTER EIGHT

Boots & Saddles: A Gallery of Cool Western Duds

For That Real WESTERN Touch!

HARD WEARING SANFORIZED TWILL

Texas Blackie Shirts & Pants

PRICED WITHIN REACH OF EVERY HOME

$6.95

SUIT SIZES 2 to 12

★ STYLED BY ESSKAY OF TEXAS ★

Johnnie Walker knows that there are thousands of children who have wanted a suit of these real western Black Embroidered Shirt and Pants because they are made just like the ones worn by western cowboys.

69 HANOVER ST. LA 3-5498 BOSTON 13, MASS.

OPEN EVERY EVENING UNTIL 9:00—DEC 1 UNTIL XMAS

Mail and Phone Orders Add 25c for P. P. and Handling Charges (Except C.O.D.'s)

Here's the Sportsman's Safety Code for
DAISY
AIR RIFLE OWNERS
LITTLE BEAVER, DO YOU SAVVY THE 10 RULES IN TH' SPORTMAN'S SAFETY CODE?
YOU BETCHUM, RED RYDER! YOU LISTEN--- ME REPEAT-UM!
FRED HARMAN
①" ME WILL NEVER POINT-UM GUN AT ANYTHING ME NOT INTEND TO SHOOT-UM. ② ME WILL NEVER LOAD-UM GUN WHEN MUZZLE IS POINTED AT ANYBODY. ③ ME WILL NEVER COCK-UM GUN OR PULL-UM TRIGGER JUST FOR FUN. ④ ME WILL NEVER SHOOT-UM AT OBJECT WHICH MAKE BULLET BOUNCE-UM OFF. ⑤ ME WILL NEVER HANDLE GUN WITHOUT FIRST TAKE-UM PEEK TO BE SURE GUN IS EMPTY. ⑥ ME WILL NEVER CARRY MY GUN WHILE IT IS COCKED OR OFF SAFETY, YOU BETCHUM. ⑦ ME WILL NEVER SHOOT-UM AT SONG-BIRD, ILLEGAL GAME OR LIVE TREE, ME THINK-UM. ⑧ ME WILL NEVER SHOOT-UM AT ANYTHING BEFORE MAKE-UM SURE ME NOT INJURE SOMETHING IF ME MISS-UM TARGET. ⑨ ME WILL ALWAYS BE PLENTY CAREFUL WHEN CLIMBING THROUGH FENCE BY POINT-UM GUN MUZZLE THROUGH FENCE FIRST. ⑩ ME WILL ALWAYS CLEAN AND OIL-UM MY GUN PRONTO AFTER USING IT."
Learn and follow the Sportsman's SAFETY Code—explained here in Little Beaver's language—printed in *complete* form inside the famous Daisy Handkook! If you do not obey the Code or otherwise abuse the privilege of Daisy ownership—your parents or police *should take your Daisy away from you.* Show this message to your folks. Tell them you'll shoot *safely* with a Daisy—the *fun* gun MILLIONS of American DADS shot safely when *they* were boys!
DAISY HANDBOOK READY!
TELLS HOW TO SHOOT SAFE
DAISY HANDBOOK 10¢
128-page Handbook features Red Ryder, Buck Rogers comic strips, atomic bombs, jet power, jokes, trick shots, safety rules, complete Daisy Air Rifle Catalog, etc Limited supply. Rush name, address, dime (10c), unused 3c stamp we'll mail Handbook postpaid.
MODEL No. 111 $4.25
1000 SHOT
RED RYDER
COWBOY CARBINE
Famous Western saddle carbine features Lightning-Loader, Carbine Ring, Leather Thong, Carbine Bands, Double-Notch Sight, Pistol-Grip Stock.
No. 25—DAISY PUMP GUN $5.95
No. 155—DAISY 1000-SHOT REPEATER $3.25
Don't order air rifles direct from the factory. Prices subject to change without notice.
Duty Added in Canada
USE
SHOOT SAFE BUDDY!
DAISY MANUFACTURING COMPANY, 811 UNION STREET, DEPT. 7, PLYMOUTH, MICHIGAN, U. S. A.
Published in the interests of Parents, Present and Future Air Rifle Owners, and the General Public

MERRY CHRISTMAS, PARTNER!
THANKS, RED RYDER! THIS NEW HANDBOOK HELPED ME GET MY DAISY!
Bill is holding his new No. 111, 1000-Shot RED RYDER CARBINE —Daisy's cowboy carbine.
LICENSED BY STEPHEN SLESINGER N. Y.
DAISY AIR RIFLE CATALOG
RED RYDER
TRY THIS, BOYS!
• Daisy's completely new HANDBOOK No. 2 has already helped many boys convince their folks they should own a beautiful new Daisy! Send for your Handbook now! Show Catalog Section to the person most likely to get you a Daisy! Enjoy the 128 HANDBOOK picture pages featuring comics, jokes, science, hobbies, cowboy lore, camping-fishing tips, etc. Rush only one thin dime (10¢) plus unused 3¢ stamp—we'll send HANDBOOK No. 2 (with Catalog) postpaid. Supply limited. Hurry!
SEE THEM BIG IN COLOR CATALOG!
NO. 118—TARGETEER AIR PISTOL SET
NO. 81—AIR RIFLE ACTION RANGE
TARGETEER
NO. 25—DAISY PUMP GUN
NO. 155—1000 SHOT REPEATER
MAIL COUPON!
DAISY MANUFACTURING CO.
1319 Union St., PLYMOUTH, MICHIGAN, U.S.A.
Send postpaid.......copies of HANDBOOK NO. 2 (CATALOG bound in). I enclose one thin dime (10¢) plus unused 3¢ Stamp for EACH copy ordered. (A TIP: Thousands of boys are ordering an extra copy for the Girl Friend.)
Name
St. & No.
City
State
BARGAIN SPECIAL: I enclose 25¢ in coin. Rush postpaid Handbook No. 2 AND big, 8-color "BOY'S BILL OF RIGHTS" Picture for my room!
LATEST AIR RIFLE CATALOG Comes Bound Inside This HANDBOOK No. 2
NO. 2
DAISY HANDBOOK
10¢
THE AMERICAN BOYS' FUN AND FACT DIGEST
128 PAGES • POCKET SIZE
Do not order Air Rifles, Range or Pistol from factory. Ask your Dealer.
Daisy Bulls Eye
BULLS EYE
is the Best Shot for
DAISY
AIR RIFLES
DAISY MANUFACTURING CO. • 1319 UNION ST. • PLYMOUTH, MICH.

An Ideal Gift for the LITTLE COWGIRL

VEST and FRINGED SKIRT

Authentic • Genuine • Exclusive

The Most Attractive Washable Sanforized Cavalry Twill Outfit for the Little Girl

Sizes 2 to 14 $4.95

- GREEN AND MAIZE
- BROWN AND MAIZE
- RED AND WHITE
- BLACK AND WHITE

69 HANOVER ST. LA 3-5498 **BOSTON 13, MASS.**

OPEN EVERY EVENING UNTIL 9:00—DEC. 1 UNTIL XMAS
Mail and Phone Orders Add 25c for P. P. and Handling Charges
(Except C.O.D.'s)

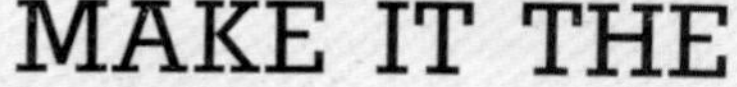

GREATEST GIFT

WITH OF THEIR LIVES!

Frye's Rancher BOOTS

FOR BOYS AND GIRLS
NO IMITATION BOOTS . . . THIS IS THE REAL McCOY, FRYE'S — ONE OF AMERICA'S OLDEST AND MOST FAMOUS MAKER OF WESTERN BOOTS SINCE 1863.

- New V-Front Stove Pipe Leg
- Leather Lined Leg
- Colored Welt Side Seam
- Real Cowboy Last
- Pegged Cottage Shank
- Genuine Oak Bend Sole

$11.75

COLORS:
Black, White Trim
Basque Red, White Trim
Basque Green and Yellow

PAIR SIZES 11 to 3

Johnnie Walker's
RIDING APPAREL
SADDLERY

69 HANOVER STREET
LA 3-5498
BOSTON 13, MASS.

OPEN EVERY EVENING UNTIL 9:00—DEC. 1 UNTIL XMAS
Mail and Phone Orders Add 25c for P. P. and Handling Charges
(Except C.O.D.'s)

23

There Will Be Many Happy Children Christmas Day Who Will Receive These Real Western

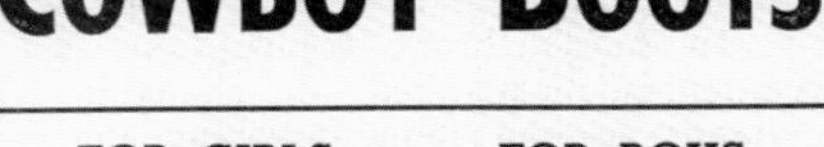

$6.95 Pair

FOR GIRLS — Sizes 8½ to 12
FOR BOYS — 12½ to 3
Youth's Sizes 3½ to 6 — $9.95 Pair

Johnnie Walker's knows that there are thousands of children who have wanted a pair of these real Western cowboy boots because they are just like the ones worn by the Western cowboy stars, with all the fine quality and details found only in authentic cowboy boots.

COLORS: • BLACK AND WHITE • BROWN AND GREEN • BROWN AND RED • BROWN AND BROWN

The Perfect Gift for Every Boy and Girl on Your Xmas List

RIDING APPAREL
SADDLERY

69 HANOVER ST. LA3-5498 **BOSTON 13, MASS.**

OPEN EVERY EVENING
UNTIL 9:00—DEC. 1
UNTIL XMAS

Mail and Phone Orders Add 25c for P. P. and Handling Charges

16

Roy Rogers
KING OF THE COWBOYS
AUTHENTIC WESTERN STYLES
AT POPULAR PRICES
NOW AT YOUR FAVORITE RETAIL STORE
OFFICIAL ROY ROGERS BELT BY HICKOK ... THE ONLY AUTHORIZED VERSION OF THE HAND-TOOLED BELT ROY WEARS IN THE MOVIES.
Manufactured by HICKOK MANUFACTURING COMPANY
ROY ROGERS COWBOY SUIT BY SACKMAN
COMPLETE OUTFIT STYLED JUST LIKE ROY'S. INEXPENSIVE, BUT STURDY, SAVES WEAR AND TEAR ON YOUR REGULAR CLOTHES.
Manufactured by SACKMAN BROTHERS
ROY ROGERS SWEATSHIRTS BY NORWICH .. THESE SWEATSHIRTS WILL MAKE YOU THROW OUT YOUR CHEST. BLUE, TAN, YELLOW OR WHITE.
ROY ROGERS
Manufactured by NORWICH KNITTING COMPANY
ROY ROGERS WESTERN JACKETS BY FOSTER .... YIPPEE! THIS WESTERN STYLE CORDUROY JACKET IS A DANDY! REAL SUEDE FRINGE TRIMMINGS AND ZIPPER FRONT.
Manufactured by IRVIN FOSTER SPORTSWEAR COMPANY
ROHR COMPANY, P. O. Box 3001, Hollywood, Calif.
Please enroll me as a member of the Roy Rogers Riders club and send me my membership card and lucky pocket coin.
NAME
ADDRESS
CITY
STATE
Print name and address plainly—enclose 10¢ in coin (no stamps). Your membership card and coin will be delivered in about 3 weeks.
ROY ROGERS STARS IN REPUBLIC PICTURES
WANT TO JOIN THE ROY ROGERS RIDERS?
Hi Pard! This is the club for red-blooded American boys and girls. Mail the coupon today with 10¢ in coin (no stamps) for your membership card and the Roy Rogers Lucky Pocket Coin.
ROY ROGERS RIDERS
LUCKY PIECE
HURRY—MAIL THE COUPON TODAY
COPYRIGHT 1948, BY ROHR COMPANY
LISTEN TO THE ROY ROGERS RADIO SHOW SPONSORED BY QUAKER OATS EVERY SUNDAY EVENING

Send Secret Messages With The
LONE RANGER
SILVER BULLET BALL PEN SET
An Everlast Product
WEAR IT ON YOUR BELT—WRITE YOUR OWN SECRET CODES!
TRY IT OUT FOR 10 DAYS FREE!
HEY kids, here's your chance to get the Lone Ranger's own Silver Bullet Pen Set! Three smooth-writing pens—each one shaped just like the silver bullets the Lone Ranger has in his gun belt! Each pen writes a different color—BLUE, RED, GREEN—and each one writes up to three years! But that isn't all! Besides these three secret code pens, you get a snappy-looking genuine leather belt cartridge holster. Attach it to your belt and you always have the Lone Ranger pens ready to use, wherever you are. What's more, this leather holder is beautifully embossed with pictures of the Lone Ranger himself, Silver and Tonto! And best of all, you get all three pens, plus the holder, for only $1.00 on this 10-day home approval offer!
Only $1.00 Per Set
Write BLUE to send Secret Codes
Write RED when in danger—
Write GREEN to send a message
THE LONE RANGER
SILVER
TONTO
Lone Ranger's Own Pen
Danger Signal Pen
Tonto's Own Pen
Genuine Leather Holder
SEND NO MONEY
Send no money to get this official Lone Ranger Silver Bullet Ball Pen Set. Just mail coupon. When the postman brings your Lone Ranger set to your door, pay him only $1.00 plus postage and delivery. If, at the end of 10 days, you don't agree that this is the greatest bargain you've ever seen, return the pens and holder—and your money will be cheerfully refunded. But hurry! Be first in your neighborhood to get this wonderful pen set! Mail coupon—NOW.
FUN INDUSTRIES, 45 E. 17 ST., N. Y. 3, N. Y.
FUN INDUSTRIES, Dept. PJK-18
45 E. 17 St., New York 3, N. Y.
Rush me—Lone Ranger Silver Bullet Ball Pen Sets complete with leather holders. On arrival I will pay postman only $1.00 each plus postage and delivery. If I am not satisfied for any reason at all, I'll return them within 10 days, and you will refund my money.
Name
Address
City Zone State
NOTE: Send cash, check, or money order with this coupon, and we pay postage. Same refund guarantee.

See a Rodeo for exciting entertainment and . . . wear the cowboy pants preferred by millions coast-to-coast

Lee RIDERS

Lee Riders, Snug-Fitting in True Western Style

Lee 11-oz. Cowboy Pant Denim
Ladies' and Boys' Sizes 8-oz. Denim

U-shaped Saddle Crotch for Comfort

SANFORIZED for permanent Fit—Buy Your Correct Size

Lee

None Genuine Without This Branded Cowhide Label

GUARANTEED: A new pair free or your money back if Lee Riders do not look better, fit better and wear longer than any you've ever worn!

COMPLETE SIZE RANGES FOR MEN, LADIES AND BOYS

THE H. D. LEE COMPANY

San Francisco, Cal.—Kansas City, Mo.—Minneapolis, Minn.—South Bend, Ind.—Trenton, N. J.—Boaz, Ala.—Dallas, Texas

Round up the family for fun!
ACME COWBOY BOOTS
• Suntanned Texans or wind-blown Vermonters—you're just a step from adventure whenever you put on your Acme Cowboy Boots. They've an astonishing (and incurable) habit of kicking up their heels like a frisky colt. Things you've never done before you'll do in Acme Boots —and it'll all be *fun!*
For all the family
Sizes for men, women, boys and girls from $7.95 to $18.95
© Acme Boot Co., Clarksville, Tenn.
TESTED IN THE STIRRUP WHERE IT REALLY COUNTS
ACME—WORLD'S LARGEST MAKERS OF COWBOY BOOTS

BLAZING ACTION OUT OF THE
RIP-ROARING
WEST!
The
LONE RIDER
AND HIS HORSE LIGHTNIN'
JAMBOREE GALORE!
Thrills-Suspense-Action. Ride with THE LONE RIDER. Watch him as he outrides, outshoots and outsmarts the dangerous PANTHER outlaws and brings justice to the West. Thrill to the thunder of the hoofbeats of the wonder horse LIGHTNIN! See how they run down clues, meet danger, escape in a hair-raising episode. The man who could do the impossible, with his six gun shooter as he rides the gunpowder trails of the rip-roaring West!
New Sensational TELEVIEWER
ONLY 39¢
plus 11¢ for two extra films
needs no screen ... no batteries ... no electricity nothing else to buy a whole movie outfit in itself!
TELEVIEWER
Pat. U. S. Pat. Off.
Ask for the Televiewer & many famous comic characters AT YOUR FAVORITE 5c & 10c or chain TOY store If your dealer doesn't have it yet ... order direct.
THE LONE RIDER
Box 352, New York 3, N. Y.
EXTRA EXCITING FILM!
Be the first in your neighborhood to receive the TELEVIEWER together with this exciting complete episode of THE LONE RIDER and the PANTHER outlaws. This NEW TELEVIEWER is the finest viewer in the world. Durable beautiful colored plastic, superfine lens, compact, easy to carry, together with 66 pictures in three 16mm films. Each film a complete exciting story. Packed full of thrill, action and adventure. Nothing to get out of order, lasts a lifetime. Original, exclusive, no other like it.
☐ Enclosed 50¢ in coin. Rush TELEVIEWER together with the film THE LONE RIDER, "TROUBLE IN TEXAS" and two other films.
☐ Enclosed $1.00 for two Lone Rider TELEVIEWERS and extra films.
☐ Enclosed $1.00 for TELEVIEWER and 10 (ten) other films.
Name
Address
City Zone State
Print Clearly.
No COD
HURRY MAIL TODAY

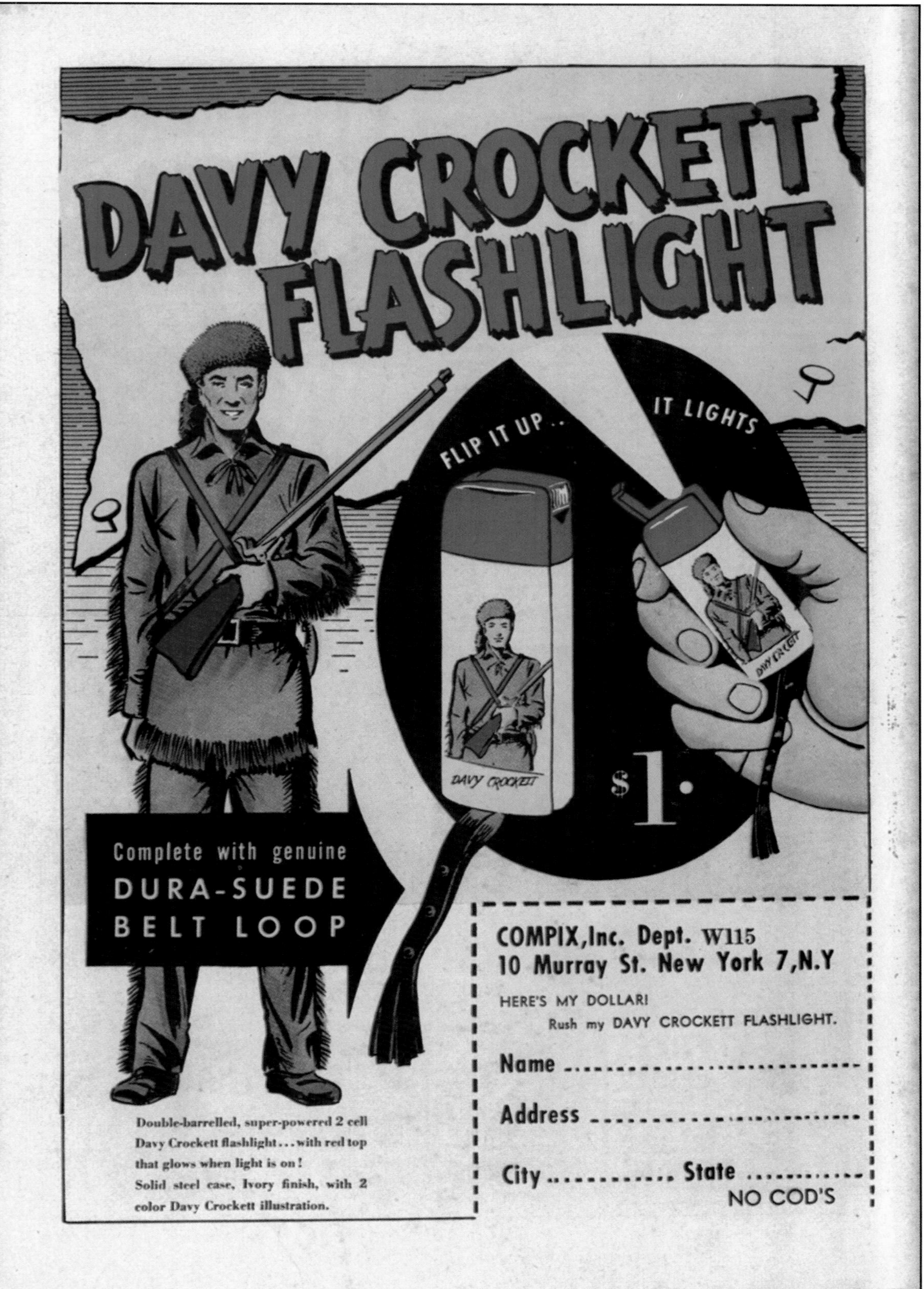
DAVY CROCKETT FLASHLIGHT
FLIP IT UP..
IT LIGHTS
DAVY CROCKETT
$1.
Complete with genuine
DURA-SUEDE
BELT LOOP
COMPIX,Inc. Dept. W115
10 Murray St. New York 7,N.Y
HERE'S MY DOLLAR!
Rush my DAVY CROCKETT FLASHLIGHT.
Name
Address
City
State
NO COD'S
Double-barrelled, super-powered 2 cell Davy Crockett flashlight . . . with red top that glows when light is on!
Solid steel case, Ivory finish, with 2 color Davy Crockett illustration.

Assemble it Yourself--Takes Only 12 Minutes--Save Paying up to $5 & $10
Complete 15 Piece "TEXAS RANGER" COWBOY OUTFIT
All for $1.98
Never Before-Never Again
A VALUE LIKE THIS!
These are ACTUAL PHOTOGRAPHS of ENTIRE COWBOY and COWGIRL OUTFIT
Just as Each Will Look on Your Own Boy or Girl
YOU GET THIS AT NO EXTRA COST!
FAMOUS CLICKER "Repeating" SIX SHOOTER GUN
Clicks noisily as it shoots
Looks Real!
Provides Plenty of Action
HERE'S WHAT EACH OUTFIT CONTAINS!
• Western-style Ranger EYE MASK.
• Wide, roomy NECKERCHIEF.
• Pair of Western-type ARM CUFFS.
• Texas Ranger VEST complete with Ranger SHERIFF'S BADGE and decorated fringes.
• Two beautifully-styled, full width Texas Ranger CHAPS with 2 realistic-looking Six Shooter GUNS, designed right on the material, simulating those used by all the best Cowboy Marksmen. (Cowgirl Outfit has two-piece Ranger Skirt instead of Chaps.)
• 2 Attractive GUN HOLSTERS.
• 144 inches of Cowboy-type ROPE.
• 2 Handsome COWBOY BOOT TOPS
INCLUDED AT NO EXTRA COST—the Sheriff's Model "Clicker" Repeating Gun shown above.
BACK VIEW
You would expect to pay $5 to $10 for a good Cowboy Outfit anywhere in America today. Now, on this 12 minute easy to assemble offer, you get this COMPLETE 15-Pc. COWBOY OUTFIT FOR THE SENSATIONAL LOW PRICE OF ONLY $1.98 or TWO OUTFITS FOR ONLY $3.79.
Satisfaction Guaranteed or Money Back
"Hi There, Pardner!"—Here's that complete 15-piece Texas Ranger Cowboy Outfit you've always wanted . . . at a price so low it's virtually a giveaway. You get everything you need—not just a suit or skirt—but the entire outfit as pictured—like those you've admired on your favorite cowboy heroes. You simply put outfit together according to easy to follow directions. Takes only about 12 minutes to separate and assemble the entire 15-piece outfit. You then have a Cowboy Outfit you couldn't duplicate for 2 or 3 times our low price. The material will literally "wear like iron." It's a fine quality water-resistant white vinyl plastic, beautifully trimmed in brown and white—the color combination now so popular with all boys and girls. You don't even have to wash it to keep this material clean. Just wipe with damp cloth and it stays like new each day. Here is an outfit to thrill every young buckaroo from ages 2 to 12. But hurry. This sensational offer may be withdrawn at any time. Mail the order coupon today to avoid missing out on this great value.
SEND NO MONEY! Rush This Order Coupon!
ILLINOIS MERCHANDISE MART, Dept. 1901
1227 LOYOLA AVE., CHICAGO 26, ILLINOIS
Gentlemen: Please send the complete 15-piece Texas Ranger Cowboy Outfit as checked below C.O.D. plus postage on your 10-day money back guarantee offer.
☐ Cowboy Outfit @ $1.98 ☐ Cowgirl Outfit @ $1.98
☐ 2 Cowboy Outfits @ $3.79 ☐ 2 Cowgirl Outfits @ $3.79
☐ 1 Cowboy and 1 Cowgirl Outfit @ $3.79
Please state age of youngster getting Outfit
NAME
ADDRESS
TOWN STATE
☐ Enclosed is full amount plus two dimes for postage for each outfit. Ship my order as checked above all shipping charges prepaid to my door.

EXCITING NEWS FOR EVERY LIVE-WIRE BOY AND GIRL!
STRAIGHT ARROW
"INJUN-UITY" MANUAL
TEACHES YOU ALL THE INDIAN WISDOM AND SKILLS—
YOU BECOME THE INDIAN EXPERT OF YOUR NEIGHBORHOOD!
GET YOURS!
THREE cards in every package of NABISCO SHREDDED WHEAT! 36 cards in set! Lots of "how-to-do-it" pictures!
LOOK! Here are only a FEW of the Indian skills you can learn:
How to signal for help! • How to keep from getting lost in the woods! • Danger signals! • How to build an Indian grill, raft, bow and arrow! • Good horsemanship! • Secrets of archery! Animal tracks! • How to teach your pet tricks! Many, many others!
See the inside front and back covers of this book for examples of the Injun-uity Cards!
The breakfast full of POWER from Niagara Falls
START BUILDING YOUR COMPLETE MANUAL—NOW!
Every package of NABISCO SHREDDED WHEAT contains 3 of these information-packed cards. So eat this 100% whole wheat body-building cereal for breakfast every day! Tastes plenty good, too! And listen to Straight Arrow's thrilling radio adventures. Look in your paper for time and station.
NABISCO SHREDDED WHEAT
BAKED BY NABISCO • NATIONAL BISCUIT COMPANY

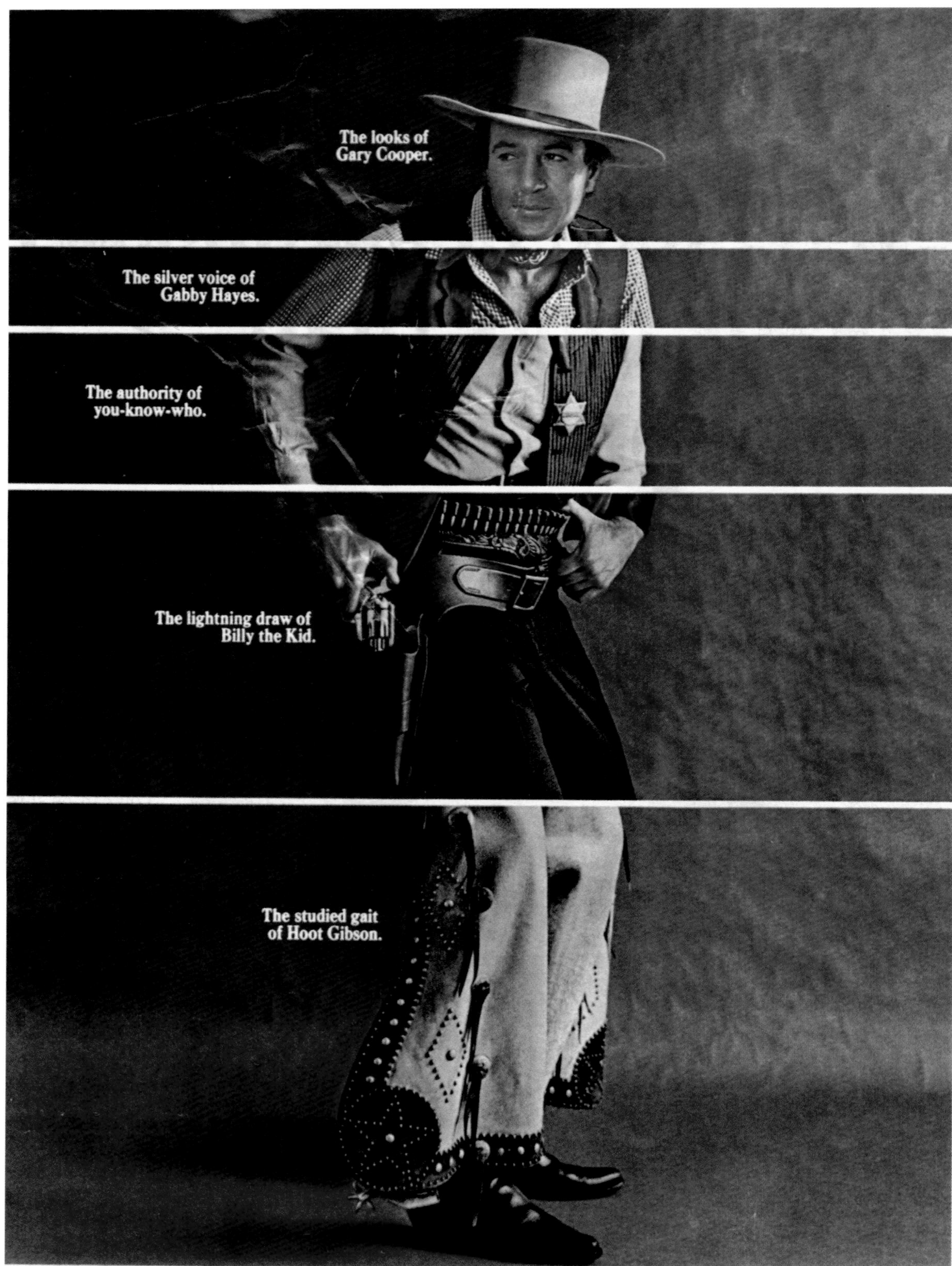
The looks of
Gary Cooper.
The silver voice of
Gabby Hayes.
The authority of
you-know-who.
The lightning draw of
Billy the Kid.
The studied gait
of Hoot Gibson.

Mothers! What a Gift!

DeLuxe "RODEO KING" Suit
SIMULATED FACET CUT COLORED STONES
JEWELED
LUXURIOUSLY FINE WASHABLE CAVALRY TWILL
So Rich, So Elegant, Yet So Moderately Priced
IT DOES SOMETHING TO THE BOY !
• Zipper Fly Front
• Gabardine Two-Tone Shirt
• Sanforized — Color Fast
• Multi-Colored Embroidery
• Pearlized Snaps
• CUT TO FIT
[STYLED BY H BAR C]
$11.95
SHIRT and PANTS SUIT
SIZES 2 to 14
Colors: Brown–Black–Green
When ordering by Mail please include 25c for mailing and handling charges (except C.O.D.'s). Open every evening till 9:00 P.M., Dec. 1 until Xmas.
Johnnie Walker's
RIDING APPAREL
SADDLERY
69 HANOVER ST. LA 3-5498 BOSTON 13, MASS.

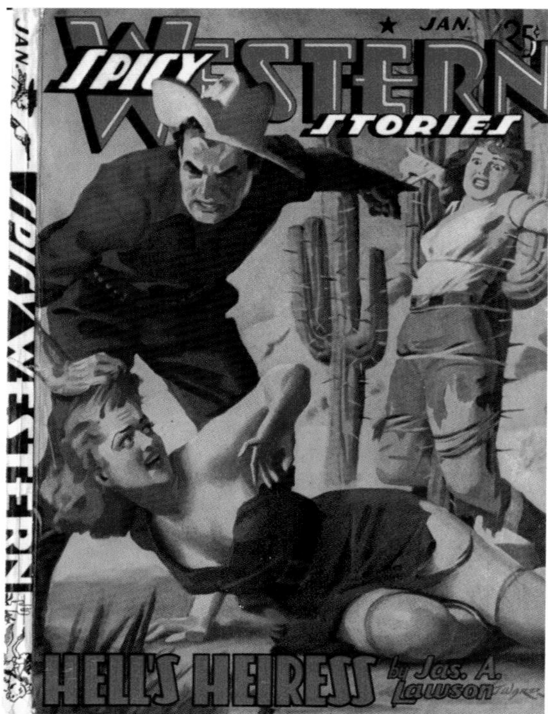
JAN.
25¢
SPICY WESTERN STORIES
HELL'S HEIRESS by Jas. A. Lawson
JAN.
SPICY WESTERN

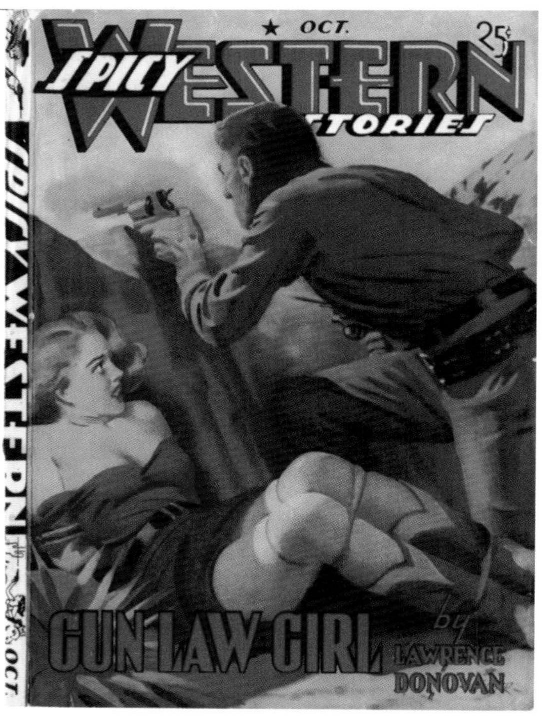
OCT.
25¢
SPICY WESTERN STORIES
GUN LAW GIRL by LAWRENCE DONOVAN
SPICY WESTERN
OCT.

COMIC SECTION in this Issue
JULY 25¢
SIX-GUN WESTERN
SIX-GUN SMITH
BAR-K-KATE
32 More Pages!
BULLETS MAKE NEWS!
by E. Hoffmann Price
Bigger and Better than Ever

March
25¢
SPICY WESTERN STORIES
RIDER from HELL
by Stuart Adams
Mar.
SPICY WESTERN STORIES
25¢

WORKS CONSULTED

The following reference works were consulted during the writing of True West. *Primary source materials illustrated in the book are not included here.*

Barra, Allen. *Inventing Wyatt Earp.* New York: Carroll & Graf, 1998.

Blackbeard, Bill, and Martin Williams. *The Smithsonian Collection of Newspaper Comics.* New York: Harry N. Abrams and the Smithsonian Institution Press, Washington, D.C., 1977.

Bronson, Fred. *The Billboard Book of Number One Hits.* New York: Billboard Publications, Inc., 1988.

Brooks, Tim, and Earle Marsh. *The Complete Directory of Prime Time Network TV Shows: 1946-Present,* 5th edition. New York: Ballantine, 1992.

Carnes, Mark C., general editor. *Past Imperfect: History According to the Movies.* New York: Henry Holt, 1995.

Collins, Ace. *The Stories Behind Country Music's All-Time Greatest 100 Songs.* New York: Boulevard Books, 1996.

Fraser, George MacDonald. *The Hollywood History of the World.* London: The Harvill Press, 1996 (revised and updated edition).

Hardy, Phil. *The Western: The Overlook Film Encyclopedia.* Woodstock, New York: The Overlook Press, 1994.

Maltin, Leonard, editor. *Leonard Maltin's Movie Encyclopedia.* New York: Dutton Books, 1994.

Munn, Michael. *John Wayne: The Man Behind the Myth.* New York: New American Library, 2003, 2005.

Overstreet, Robert M. *The Overstreet Comic Book Price Guide, 29th Edition.* New York: Avon Books, 1999.

Roquemore, Joseph. *History Goes to the Movies: A Viewer's Guide to the Best (and some of the Worst) Historical Films Ever Made.* New York: Doubleday, 1999.

Rose, Brian, editor. *TV Genres.* Westport, CT: Greenwood Press, 1985.

Thompson, David. *The New Biographical Dictionary of Film,* 4th edition. New York: Knopf, 2002.

Whitburn, Joel. *Joel Whitburn Presents BILLBOARD #1's, 1950-1991.* Menomonee Falls, Wisconsin: Record Research Inc. 1991.

The
ALL-AMERICAN
ACTION FAVORITES
OF 1939
GENE AUTRY
ROY ROGERS
WILLIAM BOYD
BUCK JONES
The
ALL-AMERICAN
ACTION FAVORITES
OF 1939
CHARLES STARRETT
BOB LIVINGSTON
TEX RITTER
JOHNNY MACK BROWN
SMILEY BURNETTE
RAY CORRIGAN

ACKNOWLEDGMENTS

I would like to thank each of the following good folk for helping me realize the completion of *True West*—a labor of love that has either taken me four years to complete, or fifty-six years, depending on whether one is willing to credit the "research and development" I conducted in front of my TV set back in 1957, '58, '59, etc.

A heartfelt thank you goes to each of the following:

Allen Barra, a true scholar of this noble genre (as well as about fifteen others), who generously let me adapt one of his fine articles about western fiction.

Steven Heller, master of all things graphic, and several things not.

Eric Rachlis of Getty Images, who helped get me copies of several films not currently in commercial release.

Brian Rose of Fordham University, whose counsel in the area of western films was invaluable.

Michael Sterling, native of the wild western section of Minneapolis, who generously lent me several items from his collection.

Loren Baxter and his intrepid staff at the Center for Instructional Services at TCU for their professionalism in scanning the hundreds of objects in this collection.

Judy Alter of TCU, who helped concoct this project and stuck with it through a long, long period in limbo. I hope you feel it was worth waiting for, Judy!

And first and foremost, my wife Jean, who had to live with those teetering piles of pulps, comics, paperbacks, movie posters, and other detritus involving westerns for far too long. I promise I will remove them from the dining room table the very first chance I get, Hon.

—Michael Barson, *April 2008*

HE HURLED THE LANCE THAT SMASHED CUSTER
THAT HISTORIC DAY AT LITTLE BIG HORN!
CHIEF CRAZY HORSE
The saga of the greatest of all the Sioux warriors ...the story of his love ...the glory of his strength ...the legend of his deeds!
IN CINEMASCOPE
PRINT BY TECHNICOLOR
A Universal-International Picture starring
VICTOR MATURE · SUZAN BALL · JOHN LUND
with KEITH LARSEN · ROBERT WARWICK
and introducing RAY DANTON

W. R. FRANK presents
"SITTING BULL"
in
CINEMASCOPE
AND MAGNIFICENT NEW EASTMAN COLOR
STARRING
DALE ROBERTSON · MARY MURPHY · J. CARROL NAISH
with JOHN LITEL · IRON EYES CODY (Indian TV Star) · DOUGLAS KENNEDY
a W. R. FRANK and TELE-VOZ DE MEXICO PRODUCTION · Directed by Sidney Salkow
Screenplay by Jack DeWitt and Sidney Salkow · Released thru United Artists

273
WILLIAM FOX
PRESENTS
BUCK
JONES
in
The 20th Century
Brand
26 Productions in 1920-1921
Fox Entertainments

True West

Composed in ITC Galliard
with Kaufman display
Design and production by
Barbara Mathews Whitehead
Printed in China by Everbest
through Four Colour Imports,Ltd.
Louisville, Kentucky
2008

True West:
An Illustrated Guide to the Heyday of the Western
ISBN 978-0-87565-379-2
Paper. $29.95
Printed in China